1974

INTERNAL EVIDENCE
AND ELIZABETHAN
DRAMATIC AUTHORSHIP

INTERNAL EVIDENCE
AND ELIZABETHAN
DRAMATIC AUTHORSHIP

An Essay in Literary
History and Method

S. SCHOENBAUM

Northwestern University Press

EVANSTON   1966

FOR
MARILYN

PREFACE

In this book I return to a subject that has occupied me in one way or another for many years—since, indeed, my student days when I first wrestled with the formidable problem of the authorship of *The Revenger's Tragedy*. Almost half my youthful book on Middleton's tragedies, published in 1955, was given over to an attempt to evaluate the dramatist's claim to several doubtful plays and his share in *The Changeling*. But not until I set about revising Alfred Harbage's *Annals of English Drama* in 1957, and turned to the attribution columns, did I realize how central a concern authorship is for the historian of the stage and how insecure are the foundations on which so many assignments rest. A by-product of my labors on the *Annals* was my 1960 English Institute paper, "Internal Evidence and the Attribution of Elizabethan Plays," published in the *Bulletin of the New York Public Library* in February, 1961. The friendly reception given that essay, which provides the basis of my third section, has encouraged me to undertake the present study. The first two parts of this book deal in roughly chronological fashion with the origins and curious history of inquiries into Elizabethan dramatic authorship. The third is concerned largely with methodology. In it I also return, hopefully for the last time, to the *cause célèbre* of *The Revenger's Tragedy*.

I like to think that a compendious survey of backgrounds and principles will hold interest not only for the specialist confronted with a specific attribution problem, but also for the student concerned in a general way with methods of literary research. The discussion, although limited to Elizabethan plays, should have application to other periods and genres, and perhaps also to related but different problems, such as dates and sources. The compact presentation I have sought carries penalties of which I am only too well aware. Some contributions by previous writers I have had to treat briefly or allusively, although in another context they might profitably have received fuller consideration. I have had to ignore entirely other studies which in a more comprehensive volume would have received mention, whether honorable or dishonorable. These deficiencies I have endeavored to remedy at least in part by amplitude of documentation, and I have asked that notes be placed at the foot of the page rather than gathered together at the back, where they are more easily ignored. The extensive bibliography should serve as a useful finding list for those wishing to pursue the subject further. I should perhaps forewarn readers that they will find no mention, in either the text or bibliography, of the Baconians or similar sects—an omission for which I find myself unable to apologize.

Although I have tried not to emulate the manner of Cortez, I am conscious of having more than once passed severe judgment on my predecessors. Some cautionary examples are provided by authorities justly esteemed for their contributions to more than one branch of Elizabethan dramatic scholarship. Several scholars with whom I take issue are personal acquaintances. I have not relished this aspect of my task, but it seemed to me essential to maintain an austere standard for a species of inquiry which has in the past so often tolerated rationalized impressionism masquerading as impartial science. Where my own previous work has violated the principles to which my quest has inevitably led, I have not exempted it from censure.

From an author's point of view this necessity must be reckoned a disadvantage. There have been others. Criticism by its very nature lies away from the creative center. When, as in this case, the criticism is concerned less with plays than with specialized commentaries on plays, it is removed still further from the primary sources of inspiration. For my survey of the great mass of past work I have had to take into account hundreds of books and articles occupying many thousands of pages. Much of this material (candor requires me to confess) is rubbish. Who in his right mind, one may ask, would willingly read three thousand obstinately wrong-headed pages of J. M. Robertson? Yet the historian's task—or an aspect of his task—is to reevaluate previous efforts, however dreary some of them may be, so that others will be spared the same enervating confrontation. If I have to this limited extent succeeded, I will have accomplished one of my purposes.

The nature of the subject, at times unavoidably technical, has imposed a style that I fear the reader may find dry and inelegant. I must especially apologize for the uncouth but useful term *canonical* in such constructions as *canonical* (i.e., authorship) *investigation*. I can at least say that I have resisted the temptation to employ the barbarism *canonicity*.

I have modernized the spelling, capitalization, and punctuation of the titles of Elizabethan plays when they appear in the text. In quotations I have normalized the long *s*. Because a great many journals are cited in the footnotes, I have so far consulted the reader's convenience as to supply readily understandable abbreviations in preference to the symbols prescribed by current convention; thus I refer to *Papers of the Bibl. Soc. of Amer.* rather than to *PBSA*.

In writing this book I have incurred a number of debts, which it is a pleasure to be able to recall here. I am grateful to the John Simon Guggenheim Memorial Foundation for a fellowship for the 1956–57 academic year, during which I began some of the investigations here brought to completion. By granting me a leave of absence for the spring term of 1965, Northwestern University much facilitated my work. To Mr. Robert P. Armstrong, the Director of the Northwestern University Press, I am indebted for warm encouragement throughout the actual process of composition. Mr. David Erdman has kindly permitted me to reprint portions of my essay in the New York Public Library *Bulletin,* which he edits.

I have benefited from the hospitality of four great institutions. At the Newberry Library, Mr. Lawrence W. Towner, the Director, volunteered the use of his personal study so that I might have maximum space and privacy when they were most needed; upon such sacrifices the university presses throw incense. To the British Museum I am, as so often in the past, obliged for many courtesies. Mr. Joseph W. Scott, the accomplished librarian of University College London, gave me full access to the excellent facilities there. I owe a very special debt to the University of London Library where, a mere stranger, I was furnished with a carrel and given every assistance by a capable staff. I must make particular mention of Miss Mavis Oswald, Miss M. B. C. Canney, Miss Doris Dormer, Miss Angela Whitelegge, Mrs. Joan Kovats, and Mr. Alan H. Wesencraft.

My typist, Mrs. Dorothy Hartnell-Beavis, coped bravely and most effectively with the always harrowing pressures of a deadline. Two friends, Professor W. A. Armstrong of the University of Hull, and Professor Arthur Brown of University College London, took time away from their own busy schedules to read the final typescript; to both I am grateful for valuable suggestions, although they are of course in no way responsible for whatever faults this book has.

S. S.
London
July 24, 1965

CONTENTS

INTRODUCTION

THOSE WHO STUDY PLAYS want to know who wrote them. The editor needs to decide which works to include in his edition. The critic who has as his concern not only the individual play but also the dramatist and his *œuvre* must proceed from assumptions about the authentic canon. To the theatrical historian the facts of attribution are second in importance only to those of chronology, without which stage history could not be written. For the Elizabethan drama—and I use the term *Elizabethan* loosely but conveniently to cover the long period from the accession of Elizabeth I until the closing of the theaters in 1642—the simple facts of authorship are far from simple to come by. Too many documentary records have vanished irretrievably, and such external evidence as exists is often fragmentary, contradictory, or erroneous.[1] Inevitably scholars have had recourse to internal data, chiefly the evidence of style. The thrust of inquiry has moved in two separate but related directions: first, to determine the authorship of anonymous, misattributed, or doubtful plays; and secondly, to establish the shares of the several authors in collaborations where some at least of the participants are known, as in the voluminous Beaumont and Fletcher corpus.

1. See below, Part Three, pp. 151–159.

The quest has produced a specialist literature of intimidating quantity and scope. A list of the poets and critics, scholars and antiquarians, who have contributed in some way to the subject would boast such names as Johnson, Capell, Malone, R. W. Chambers, and E. K. Chambers; Pope, Coleridge, Tennyson, Browning, and Eliot. But if such a catalogue would possess qualities of Homeric grandeur, it would be mock-heroic as well and include more than its share of cranks and fantastics. Yet, despite an eventful and significant history, this movement in scholarship has found no chronicler to trace it back to its beginnings in the late seventeenth century, and thus to provide the substantial advantages of a historical perspective. Nor, until quite recently, has much effort gone into meeting E. K. Chambers' eminently reasonable plea of forty years ago. "The problem," he said in his now famous British Academy lecture on the disintegration of Shakespeare, "seems to me one which calls for exploration upon a general and disinterested method, rather than along the casual lines of advance opened up by the pursuit of an author for this or that suspected or anonymous play." [2]

That the need exists for a historical perspective and impartial methodology, the present state—and status— of attribution study makes evident. For the better part of a century, enthusiasts have devised and applied tests of authorship. They have ransacked scenes for parallel passages. They have pointed to peculiarities of diction and phraseology. They have counted nouns, adjectives,

---

2. "The Disintegration of Shakespeare," read on May 12, 1924; reprinted in *Aspects of Shakespeare* (Oxford, 1933), p. 36. The specific problem to which Chambers refers is "the quest for alien hands, with the clues of vocabulary and phraseology"; but a broader application does not violate the spirit of his remark. Chambers had made a similar plea as early as 1907; see below, Part Two, pp. 115-116.

and interjections, rhymes, end-stopped lines, redundant syllables, and double and triple endings. They have strained their ears to catch the elusive notes of the "indefinite music" permeating the verse. The overall result of so much energetic but uncoordinated effort—some of it brilliant but misguided, some misguided but not brilliant, some lunatic, some (not enough) persuasive—has been predictable chaos.

In recent years the situation has perhaps improved, but not much. In his *Philip Massinger* (1957), T. A. Dunn attributes the dramatist's eclipse to the fact that ". . . he is deeply involved in the tangled undergrowth of collaboration which surrounds the Beaumont-Fletcher *corpus.*" [3] Dunn excludes from his undertaking—a general work on the playwright—all questions of collaboration and attribution, the consideration of which "would have confused the reader and obscured the object of . . . study, Massinger himself." [4] Dunn's forbearance derives, one fears, not so much from self-discipline as from despair in the face of a monstrous accretion of scholarship and pseudo-scholarship. Such accretions, like so many hoardings, clutter the landscape of Elizabethan theatrical history.

The example of the University Wit, George Peele, is instructive. In the section devoted to anonymous plays in volume four of *The Elizabethan Stage,* Chambers reports the following titles as having been at one time or another ascribed in whole or in part to Peele: *Alphonsus, Emperor of Germany; Clyomon and Clamydes; George a Greene; The Life and Death of Jack Straw; The Troublesome Reign of King John; A Knack to Know a Knave; King Leir; Locrine; Mucedorus; The*

3. Preface, p. v.
4. *Ibid.,* p. vi.

*True Tragedy of Richard III; Soliman and Perseda;
The Taming of a Shrew;* and *The Wisdom of Doctor
Dodypoll.* The list does not include plays from the Shakespeare canon—*Titus Andronicus,* for example, or the
Henry VI trilogy—in which Peele is often thought to
have had a hand; nor does it contain works assigned to
him after 1923, the publication date of *The Elizabethan
Stage.* Peele died at the age of forty. During his short
lifetime he wrote five extant plays of unquestioned authenticity—*The Arraignment of Paris, David and Bethsabe, The Battle of Alcazar, The Old Wives Tale,* and
Edward I—as well as three which have perished: a
translation of Euripides' *Iphigenia, The Hunting of
Cupid,*[5] and *The Turkish Mahomet and Hiren the Fair
Greek.* He also turned out several courtly and civic entertainments and a certain amount of nondramatic work.
We can, then, conclude only that Peele must have been
exceedingly industrious if he produced a fraction of the
plays which his admirers and detractors have pressed
upon him. From what we know of his character, the hero
of the *Merry Conceited Jests of George Peele* was not
notably industrious. Peele's case is hardly unique. Many
of the plays hopefully assigned to him, and additional
titles which are not, are given by other conjecturists to
Robert Greene, who wrote more and died younger.

The special pleading of some enthusiasts and the indifference to method of others, as well as the seemingly
endless debate over the authorship of a handful of
plays, have inevitably resulted in widespread mistrust of
the validity of any hypothesis founded on internal evidence. "The case . . . for Fletcher's participation in the

5. Fragments of *The Hunting of Cupid,* amounting in all to about one
hundred lines, survive in the Drummond MSS. and elsewhere; see *The
Life and Minor Works of George Peele,* ed. David H. Horne (New
Haven, 1952), pp. 153–154, 204–208.

writing of *Henry VIII* seems to be a strong one," remarks R. A. Foakes, *"even though* the evidence is all internal." [6] G. E. Bentley is frankly exasperated:

> After working painfully through the attributions of an anonymous play like *The Revenger's Tragedy* to Webster and to Tourneur and to Middleton and to Marston, the disgusted historian is tempted to lay down this principle: Any play first published in a contemporary quarto with no author's name on the title page and continuing without definite ascription of authorship for twenty-five years or more should be treated as anonymous world without end Amen. [7]

Yet the editor ignores at his peril questions about the homogeneity of *Henry VIII* raised, on stylistic and linguistic grounds, since the last century. Bentley himself is too responsible a historian to subscribe to his own tempting formula: such a principle, he is quick to note, would not only deprive Marlowe of *Tamburlaine* but also Beaumont and Fletcher of *The Woman Hater;* and the logical corollary of the principle—that every title-page ascription unchallenged for twenty-five years must be accepted—would thrust *The Thracian Wonder* upon Webster and *The London Prodigal* upon Shakespeare. [8]

Despite the prevailing skepticism, a number of attributions dependent upon internal evidence have gained general acceptance, even in such rigorously conservative summations as Bentley's *Jacobean and Caroline Stage.* On the basis of such evidence, Shakespeare's hand is now universally recognized to be present in *Sir Thomas More.* No one today questions Chapman's responsibility for *Sir*

---

6. William Shakespeare, *Henry VIII*, ed. R. A. Foakes ([New] Arden Shakespeare [London, 1957]), Introduction, pp. xix–xx. Italics supplied.

7. "Authenticity and Attribution in the Jacobean and Caroline Drama," *English Institute Annual 1942* (New York, 1943), p. 102.

8. *Ibid.*

Giles Goosecap. As a result of very recent work, future students of Massinger will be unable to exclude the collaborate plays from assessments of the dramatist's achievement. Internal evidence is a limited but essential instrument of literary scholarship; our task is to recognize the nature of the limitations and to profit from the benefits it is able to confer when properly employed. I hope in the following pages to make some contribution towards these ends.

I

Mischief
on Gower
Street

» I «

THE MOVEMENT that is the subject of this study had its inception at 8:00 P.M. on Friday the thirteenth of March, 1874, on Gower Street in London. On that occasion a small company of enthusiasts gathered at University College for the first meeting of the New Shakspere Society. Before the session began, the indefatigable F. J. Furnivall, who had founded the Society during the previous autumn and now presided as Director, placed on the table the proofs of three papers by the Rev. F. G. Fleay, "On Metrical Tests as Applied to Dramatic Poetry." Fleay had been first drawn to the rhyme test as an instrument for fixing the chronological succession of Shakespeare's plays. But his inquiries, as Furnivall explained, soon led him to other verse tests by means of which he had

been able also to detect the spurious passages in Shakspere's plays; to point out often the writers of them; to distinguish the works of Beaumont from those of Fletcher; to show in what plays Beaumont or Massinger helpt Fletcher, and so on, as you will see in Mr Fleay's second Paper, a Paper in which, as I believe, he has conferrd a truly great benefit on the literary public of England, and on the students of our Middle Literature in particular.[1]

1. Notices of Meetings, *Transactions of the New Shakspere Society,* Ser. I, Part 1 (London, 1874; reprinted 1903), p. vii.

That evening Fleay's first installment, on the Shakespeare chronology, was read by the Rev. Dr. E. A. Abbott. Furnivall distributed copies of the second paper—on Beaumont, Fletcher, and Massinger—and urged each member to read one of the plays analyzed by Fleay, examine the conclusions regarding authorship, and report his opinion of Fleay's judgment at the next meeting.

Throughout 1874 attribution problems dominated the Society's programs and discussions. The atmosphere during those fortnightly gatherings was heady with the sense of exploration and discovery. The Society's First Report, published in July, 1875, notes with pride that the organization "has forc't on the notice of the English public that most powerful and useful instrument in Shakspere criticism, 'Metrical Tests'; it has made known to this generation the genuine and spurious parts of *Henry VIII, The Two Noble Kinsmen, Pericles,* and perhaps *The Shrew* and *Timon.* . . ." [2] Henceforth the tests would become "an indispensable part of Shakspere criticism here, as they have long been in Germany, though there their value in helping to distinguish spurious work from genuine had been quite overlookt." [3] Prophecy was at once fulfilled, and other tests of style were shortly enlisted to further the Society's laudable end. From the first, as we have seen, these investigators did not limit themselves to the Shakespeare canon, but examined also the plays of Fletcher and company; soon they would subject other dramatists, as well as a host of anonymous plays, to their energetic scrutiny.

Thus began a vast outpouring of imaginative speculation inspired by intuition, fortified by learning, and sustained by industry; speculation from which theatrical

2. *Ibid.,* p. 6.
3. *Ibid.,* p. 3.

4

history and dramatic criticism have not yet fully recovered. Yet all movements in thought, however novel,
have antecedents, and ours (as Fleay and his followers
readily granted) is no exception. The aims as well as
some of the methods of the New Shakspere Society—but
not its sweeping and systematic program—were anticipated in England two centuries previously in the first tentative efforts to disintegrate the Shakespeare canon.

» II «

BEFORE TURNING to these early disintegrators, we must
take note of Gerard Langbaine's famous compilation,
*An Account of the English Dramatick Poets. Or, Some
Observations and Remarks on the Lives and Writings,
of All Those That Have Publish'd Either Comedies,
Tragedies, Tragi-Comedies, Pastorals, Masques, Interludes, Farces, or Opera's in the English Tongue* (1691).[4]
No doubt Isaac Disraeli exaggerated somewhat when he
remarked, in *The Calamities of Authors*, that Langbaine
"read poetry only to detect plagiarism," but he *did* take
far greater interest in uncovering sources than in identifying authors. In his attributions Langbaine was guided
mainly by external information: catalogues, traditions,
and the title-pages of the old plays, of which he amassed
an enormous collection. He accepted the Shakespeare
apocrypha *en bloc* as authentic because the plays were
included in the Third Folio; his *Account* elsewhere provides sufficient additional evidence of Langbaine's gross

4. The evolution of the *Account* is too complicated to be described
here, but it may be noted that the compilation grew out of Langbaine's
earlier catalogue, first printed in an unauthorized edition entitled *Momus
Triumphans: or, The Plagiaries of the English Stage* (1687), and reprinted with corrections as *A New Catalogue of English Plays* (1688).
The *New Catalogue* merely lists authors and titles, with footnotes on
the sources of plays.

deficiencies of sensibility. But there is more to the story.

For Langbaine carried attribution study a step further than the previous cataloguers—Rogers and Ley, Archer, Kirkman—upon whose groundwork he built. They merely list titles and authors. Langbaine comments, and his observations contain the earliest extant toyings with stylistic impressionism in connection with problems of Elizabethan dramatic authorship. In assigning (for example) *Two Wise Men and All the Rest Fools* to Chapman, he has obvious misgivings: Chapman would certainly have known the rules better than to construct a play with seven acts. Perhaps an ignorant printer had perpetrated a faulty division, "tho' [Langbaine writes] I am led only by Tradition to believe this Play to be his; since 'tis published without any mention of the Author, or the Place where 'twas printed." [5] He gives both parts of *Tamburlaine* to Marlowe on the testimony of Heywood's prologue to the 1633 quarto of *The Jew of Malta*. Still, "Had I not Mr. *Heywood's* Word for it . . . I should not believe this Play to be his; it being true, what an ingenious Author said, That *whoever was the Author, he might ev'n keep it to himself, secure from Plagiary.*" [6] Langbaine, however, resists making the obvious expansion of the initials "B. J." on the title-page of *Guy, Earl of Warwick:* ". . . the Gentleman that shew'd it [the play] me, told me it was writ by *Ben Johnson;* tho' by that little I read, I guess'd it to be writ by a Pen far inferiour to that Great Master in *Poetry.*" [7] His most interesting comment with regard to attribution concerns *The Fair Maid of the Exchange,* which he dis-

5. *Account,* pp. 64–65.
6. *Ibid.,* pp. 344–345. The ingenious author is Charles Saunders, whose profound observation appeared in the preface to his *Tamerlane the Great* (1681).
7. *Ibid.,* p. 519.

cusses in his section on Heywood: ". . . in my opinion it is not worth reviving. Nay further, I question notwithstanding Mr. *Kirkman* has ascrib'd it to our Author, whether it be his, since his Name is not prefixt, neither does the Stile, or Oeconomy resemble the rest of his Labours." [8] The remark is unusual not only for the overt recourse to stylistic criteria, but also because Langbaine elsewhere usually defers to the authority of Kirkman, with whom he apparently had some personal association. Heywood's claim to *The Fair Maid* remains controversial.

The *Account* passed at once into the mainstream of theatrical history. Oldys, Percy, Haslewood, Steevens, Malone, and others annotated their copies; Halliwell-Phillipps used his as the foundation for his *Dictionary of Old English Plays* (1860), which was in turn revised by W. Carew Hazlitt as *A Manual for the Collector and Amateur of Old English Plays* (1892). Long since superseded, Langbaine's *Account* is still consulted directly or indirectly. It and the compiler deserve more attentive study than they have received.

» III «

SO FAR AS WE KNOW, the earliest attack on the authenticity of a play included by Heminges and Condell in the First Folio was made in 1687 by Edward Ravenscroft in an *Address* prefixed to his *Titus Andronicus, or The Rape of Lavinia,* which had been acted almost a decade earlier:

I think it a greater theft to Rob the dead of their Praise then the Living of their Money. That I may not appear Guilty of such a Crime, 'tis necessary I should acquaint you, that there is a Play

8. *Ibid.,* p. 263.

7

in M^r. *Shakespears* Volume under the name of *Titus Andronicus,*
from whence I drew part of this. I have been told by some anciently
conversant with the Stage, that it was not Originally his, but
brought by a private Authour to be Acted, and he only gave some
Master-touches to one or two of the Principal Parts or Characters;
this I am apt to believe, because 'tis the most incorrect and indi-
gested piece in all his Works; It seems rather a heap of Rubbish
then a Structure.[9]

Despite the defensiveness of tone and vagueness about
the sources of his information, Ravenscroft's account is
not without surface plausibility. He was close enough
in time to Shakespeare's age to be in touch with an authentic theatrical tradition; as Chambers observes, William
Beeston, whose father had belonged to the Chamber-
lain's men in 1598, lived on until 1682.[10] But Ravenscroft
had been attacked as a plagiarist some years before by
Thomas Shadwell in his preface to *The Sullen Lovers.*
More damaging, Ravenscroft had offered his adaptation
of *Titus* with a prologue in which he sought shelter from
critical censure by invoking Shakespeare's name:

> To day the Poet does not fear your Rage,
> Shakespear *by him reviv'd now treads the Stage;*
> *Under his sacred Lawrels he sits down*
> *Safe, from the blast of any Cricks Frown.*
> *Like other Poets, he'll not proudly scorn*
> *To own, that he but winnow'd* Shakespear's *Corn;*
> *So far he was from robbing him of's Treasure,*
> *That he did add his own, to make full measure.*[11]

Ravenscroft's inconsistency was detected by Langbaine,
who cited the damaging passage in his *Account* with the
dry comment: "I will here furnish him with part of his

9. Reproduced in E. K. Chambers, *William Shakespeare: A Study of
Facts and Problems* (Oxford, 1930), II, 254–255.
10. Chambers, "Disintegration of Shakespeare," p. 25.
11. Chambers, *William Shakespeare*, II, 255.

Prologue, which he has lost; and if he desire it, send him the whole." [12]

In his 1709 *Life,* Nicholas Rowe cast doubt on the substantial Shakespearean authorship of *Pericles,* which had indeed been excluded by the Folio compilers.[13] But this isolated speculation, as well as Ravenscroft's special pleading, is trifling in comparison with the large-scale attack on the integrity of the First Folio launched by Alexander Pope in his 1725 edition of *The Works of Shakespear.* Disturbed by the presence in the text of "trifling and bombast passages," "mean conceits and ribaldries," and "low scenes of Mobs, Plebeians and Clowns," Pope attributed these "many low and vicious parts and passages" to the actors who had—he supposed —conveyed them into the playhouse manuscripts which provided the Folio copy. Pope rejects the "wretched" apocryphal pieces (including *Pericles*) on grounds that they are lacking in "all the distinguishing marks of his [Shakespeare's] style, and his manner of thinking and writing," and he goes on to apply his strictures to the Folio plays as well:

> . . . I should conjecture of some of the others, (particularly *Love's Labour Lost, The Winter's Tale,* and *Titus Andronicus*) that only some characters, single scenes, or perhaps a few particular passages, were of his hand. It is very probable what occasion'd some Plays to be supposed *Shakespear*'s was only this; that they were pieces produced by unknown authors, or fitted up for the Theatre while it was under his administration: and no owner claiming them, they were adjudged to him, as they give Strays to the Lord of the Manor. . . .

> If we give into this opinion, how many low and vicious parts and passages might no longer reflect upon this great Genius, but appear unworthily charged upon him? And even in those which are

12. *Account,* p. 465; Chambers, *William Shakespeare,* II, 255.
13. Chambers, *William Shakespeare,* II, 265–266.

really his, how many faults may have been unjusty [*sic*] laid to his account from arbitrary Additions, Expunctions, Transpositions of scenes and lines, confusion of Characters and Persons, wrong application of Speeches, corruptions of innumerable Passages by the Ignorance, and wrong Corrections of 'em again by the Impertinence, of his first Editors? From one or other of these considerations, I am verily perswaded, that the greatest and the grossest part of what are thought his errors would vanish, and leave his character in a light very different from that disadvantageous one, in which it now appears to us.[14]

Pope has thus early furnished a quintessential statement of the disintegrator's position. Certain passages, scenes, even whole works, fall short of the critic's own standards of correctness or elegance, and are therefore deemed unworthy of the Master. They are then expunged in accordance with a rationalization which purportedly accounts for the inconvenient appearance of those passages, scenes, or works in the received text. The standard of taste applied is that of the critic's own age, and hence anachronistic and unreliable as a measuring instrument; the factual basis for his rationalization is incomplete or mistaken or both. Pope, in this case, misunderstood both the nature of the playhouse copy and the qualifications of the first editors.[15]

He went about his self-appointed task of expurgation with gusto. "Some suspected passages [Pope forewarns readers] which are excessively bad, (and which seem Interpolations by being so inserted that one can intirely omit them without any chasm, or deficience in the con-

14. *The Works of Shakespear,* ed. Alexander Pope (London, 1725), I, Preface, pp. xx, xxi.

15. For a modern estimate of Heminges and Condell, and an explanation of the sources for Pope's misconceptions, see Peter Alexander, *Shakespeare's Life and Art* (London, 1939), pp. 27–42; also, by the same author, "Conjectural History, or Shakespeare's *Henry VIII,*" *Essays and Studies,* XVI (1930), 94–99.

text) are degraded to the bottom of the page. . . ." [16]
No fewer than nineteen plays suffered these "degrada-
tions." Among the over 1,500 un-Shakespearean lines
relegated to the status of footnotes are Julius Caesar's
extended simile of the Northern Star (III, i, 61–65) and
the closing lines of Mark Antony's apostrophe to the
fallen emperor ("O world, thou wast the forest to this
hart . . ." [III, i, 207–210]). Similarly rejected are
the "Sleep that knits up the ravell'd sleeve of care" in
Macbeth (II, ii, 37) and the tremendous image of the
multitudinous seas incarnadined by the assassin's bloody
hand (II, i, 61–63). The critic who is himself a poet
has often been regarded as speaking with special authority on the identity of the poet's voice. Yet, as Pope's
example shows, even a poet of genius may go sadly astray.
Browning and Eliot were to prove no less vulnerable in
their pronouncements on authorship.

The editors who followed Pope were by and large
not poets but scholars—"literal" critics who busied themselves with "curious learning"—and they were quick to
fasten upon their predecessor's deficiencies. In his *Shakespeare Restored* (1726) Lewis Theobald provided *A
Specimen of the Many Errors As Well Committed, as
Unamended, by Mr Pope in His Late Edition,* and for
his pains Pope pilloried him in *The Dunciad.* Yet Pope's
Shakespeare was profoundly influential.[17] Even Theobald
was intimidated: he apparently considered including
Pericles in his own edition—he sent Warburton a copy
of the play, asking him to read it over "wth. a strict
Eye" [18]—but in the end omitted it and contented himself

---

16. *Shakespear,* ed. Pope, I, p. xxii.
17. On the reception of Pope's edition, see Thomas R. Lounsbury, *The
First Editors of Shakespeare (Pope and Theobald)* (London, 1906);
also Richard Foster Jones, *Lewis Theobald* (New York, 1919).
18. The letter is printed by Jones, p. 272.

with the footnote remark that "This absurd Old Play . . . was not entirely of our Author's penning; but he has honour'd it with a Number of Master-Touches, so peculiar to himself, that a knowing Reader may with Ease and Certainty distinguish the Traces of his Pencil." [19]

The literal critics by no means set themselves against the disintegration of the Shakespeare canon, and in fact could take support from the powerful precedent of the classicists. Chief among these was the formidable Richard Bentley, "the new light of learning." In his later career (as James Harris observed) "the rage of *Conjecture* seems to have seized him, as that of *Jealousy* did *Medea;* a rage, which she confest herself unable to resist, altho' she knew the mischiefs, it would prompt her to perpetrate." [20] But Bentley's fame rests securely on his early *Dissertation upon the Epistles of Phalaris* (2nd ed.; 1699). The genuineness of these 148 letters, attributed to the legendary tyrant of Agrigentum, had long been questioned, but Sir William Temple defended them on impressionistic grounds in his *Essay on Ancient and Modern*

19. *The Works of Shakespeare,* ed. Theobald (London, 1733[34]), II, 490n. George Lillo expressed a similar view five years later in the Prologue to his *Marina,* an adaptation of Acts IV and V of *Pericles:*

> *Though some mean scenes, injurious to his fame,*
> *Have long usurp'd the honour of his name;*
> *To glean and clear from chaff his least remains,*
> *Is just to him, and richly worth our pains.*
> *We dare not charge the whole unequal play*
> *Of* Pericles *on him; yet let us say,*
> *As gold though mix'd with baser matter shines,*
> *So do his bright inimitable lines.* [sic]
> *Throughout those rude wild scenes distinguish'd stand,*
> *And shew he touch'd them with no sparing hand.*
> (*The Works of Mr. George Lillo; with Some Account of His Life* [London, 1775], II, 61)

20. *Philological Inquiries* (London, 1781), Part I, p. 37; quoted by Jones, *Lewis Theobald,* p. 50.

Learning (1692). Temple's enthusiasm gave the *Epistles* a new lease of life. They were edited in 1695 by Charles Boyle, who did not, however, insist upon their authenticity. Boyle's edition set in motion a controversy which, however fascinating, cannot be chronicled in detail here.[21] Suffice it to say that the debate produced in the *Dissertation* its one lasting monument. Bentley demonstrates, with overwhelming erudition and remorseless logic, that the *Epistles* were not the correspondence of a sixth-century B.C. Sicilian despot, but rather the exercises of a sophist or rhetorician of the second century A.D. Bentley's instrument is internal evidence: he shows that the letters refer to places not yet in existence and events that had not yet taken place, that they imitate writers as yet unborn and are composed in a dialect not yet spoken. The "Immortal Dissertation" is the product of strict and sustained reasoning; Bentley had abandoned tradition in favor of a systematically ordered set of deductions inferred from historical fact.

Bentley's conclusions reinforced the skeptical tendencies in the scholarship of his day. He was followed—to cite but one example—by Jeremiah Markland, who in his edition of Statius (1728) calls into question passages of the *Aeneid* which do not satisfy his own standards of Virgilian grandeur or consistency.[22] Doubts concerning classical texts provided students of Shakespeare with convenient analogies to support their own arguments. Thus, in rejecting Shakespeare's claim to *Pericles* Richard Farmer remarks, in his *Essay on the Learning of Shakespeare* (1767), that "*Aulus Gellius* informs us, that some

21. For a compendious survey of the argument, see R. C. Jebb, *Bentley* (London, 1889), pp. 40–63.
22. See Jones, *Lewis Theobald*, pp. 42–43.

Plays are ascribed absolutely to *Plautus,* which he only *retouched* and *polished;* and this is undoubtedly the case with our Author likewise." [23]

Theobald, the first of the scholar-critics to concern us directly, finds Shakespeare's hand in *The Two Noble Kinsmen.* He sides with the "better Judges" who reject *Titus Andronicus:* it is too early to be Shakespeare's, although (Theobald owns) "he afterwards introduc'd it a-new on the Scene, with the Addition of his own masterly Touches." [24] But Theobald's special contribution to the inquiry was to raise doubts about the *Henry VI* trilogy, and thus to initiate a debate the reverberations of which may still be heard. After noting that historical events are shuffled backwards and forwards in the three parts, he goes on to remark:

. . . tho there are several Master-Strokes in these three Plays, which incontestibly betray the Workmanship of *Shakespeare;* yet I am almost doubtful, whether they were entirely of his Writing. And unless they were wrote by him very early, I shou'd rather imagine them to have been brought to him as a Director of the *Stage;* and so to have receiv'd some finishing Beauties at his hand, An accurate Observer will easily see, the *Diction* of them is more *obsolete,* and the *Numbers* more *mean* and *prosaical,* than in the Generality of his genuine Compositions.[25]

The words *unless they were wrote by him very early* are revealing, for they show that uncertainty regarding the chronology—an uncertainty which Theobald and the other editors unavoidably share—may have been to a large extent responsible for doubts concerning authenticity.

23. *Essay* (3rd ed.; London, 1789), p. 25.
24. *Shakespeare,* V, 307n–308n.
25. *Ibid.,* IV, 110n. In 1919 as responsible a scholar as Jones could still say that "Little fault can be found with these opinions" (*Theobald,* p. 187).

In his justly maligned Oxford edition of *The Works*
of Shakespear (1744) Sir Thomas Hanmer added *The*
Two Gentlemen of Verona to the list of disputed pieces.
Shakespeare's hand in the play, he casually asserted, was
limited to *"enlivining it with some speeches and lines*
thrown in here and there, which are easily distinguish'd,
as being of a different stamp from the rest." [26] Regretful
that Pope had not cast out "spurious" passages with a
freer hand, Hanmer remedied the negligence with his
own excisions,

the most considerable of which is that wretched piece of ribaldry
in King Henry V. *put into the mouths of the* French *Princess and*
an old Gentlewoman, improper enough as it is all in French *and*
not intelligible to an English *audience, and yet that perhaps is*
the best thing that can be said of it.[27]

Hanmer, a gentleman editing for gentlemen, objected
particularly to the ribaldry. In the demands of actors
and audiences he found a convenient explanation for its
presence:

There can be no doubt but a great deal more of that low stuff
which disgraces the works of this great Author, was foisted in
by the Players after his death, to please the vulgar audiences by
which they subsisted: and though some of the poor witticisms
and conceits must be supposed to have fallen from his pen, yet as
he hath put them generally into the mouths of low and ignorant
people, so it is to be remember'd that he wrote for the Stage, rude
and unpolished as it then was; and the vicious taste of the age
must stand condemned for them. . . .[28]

In his 1747 edition Warburton treated Hanmer with
a scorn to which his own good parts little entitled him.

26. *Shakespear,* ed. Hanmer, I, 143n.
27. *Ibid.,* Preface, I, iii.
28. *Ibid.,* I, iii–iv.

Warburton himself made no original contribution to canonical argument: the judgments, based upon stylistic impressionism, of the earlier commentators, especially Pope, were already showing signs of hardening into an orthodoxy. Warburton rejects, at the same time that he reprints, *The Taming of the Shrew* and *The Comedy of Errors,* the three parts of *Henry VI,* and *Titus Andronicus.* "The most that can be said of them is, that he [Shakespeare] has, here and there, corrected the dialogue, and now and then added a Scene." [29] With Theobald (at whom he sneers) he finds that "the whole first Act of *Fletcher's Two Noble Kinsmen* was wrote by *Shakespear,* but in his worst manner." [30] It is perhaps unnecessary to add that Warburton provides no basis in fact or reason for his oracular pronouncements.

The efforts of Pope, Theobald, Hanmer, and Warburton are overshadowed in importance and influence by Dr. Johnson's celebrated edition of 1765. On disputed plays, Johnson is noteworthy for his statements of principle, which are conspicuously absent from previous discussion. Yet he does not always bow to the clear implications of his own decrees. Thus, while acknowledging that "it is very difficult to decide whether short pieces be genuine or spurious," he nevertheless places the prologue and epilogue to *Henry VIII* in the doubtful category.[31] When he turns to *Henry VI,* however, Johnsonian good sense triumphs. In restoring the plays to Shakespeare, he gets to the root of the fallacy from which so much needless controversy, before and since, has sprung:

29. "A Table of the Several Editions of Shakespear's Plays," *The Works of Shakespear,* ed. Alexander Pope and William Warburton (London, 1747), I, sig. e1ʳ.
30. *Ibid.*
31. *The Plays of William Shakespeare* (London, 1765), V, 492; *Johnson on Shakespeare,* ed. Walter Raleigh (Oxford, 1925), p. 152.

From mere inferiority nothing can be inferred; in the productions of wit there will be inequality. Sometimes judgment will err, and sometimes the matter itself will defeat the artist. Of every author's works one will be the best, and one will be the worst. The colours are not equally pleasing, nor the attitudes equally gracefull, in all the pictures of *Titian* or *Reynolds*.

The trilogy is, moreover, "ascribed to *Shakespeare* by the first editors, whose attestation may be received in questions of fact, however unskilfully they superintended their edition." [32] Yet Johnson went further than his predecessors in denying the presence even of Shakespearean touches in *Titus Andronicus*.

While Johnson's *Shakespeare* was in press, Edward Capell was putting the finishing touches to his own edition, which appeared in 1768. Of Capell's abilities Johnson reputedly declared that they were "just sufficient . . . to select the black hairs from the white ones, for the use of the periwig-makers." [33] But Capell's *Shakespeare* was a precedent-shattering achievement. All previous editions trace their descent from Rowe, who based his text on the unauthoritative Fourth Folio. Capell went back to the early quartos and the First Folio, and built on new foundations. In his discussion of canonical problems, he displays the same intellectual rigor that distinguishes his handling of the text. He is the first authority to challenge on all fronts the disintegrators of his day, and the eleven pages of his preface devoted to refuting them comprise the most elaborate discussion of the canonical question yet to appear. The "sum of what is brought

32. *Plays of William Shakespeare*, V, 225; *Johnson on Shakespeare*, pp. 144, 145.

33. *Johnsonian Miscellanies*, ed. George Birkbeck Hill (Oxford, 1897), II, 316. The source of the anecdote, Steevens, is (as Joseph Epes Brown observes) sometimes untrustworthy—and Steevens elsewhere expresses hostility towards Capell's scholarship (*The Critical Opinions of Samuel Johnson*, ed. Brown [Princeton, 1926], p. 303).

against them [the contested plays]," he remarks at the outset,

> . . . may be all ultimately resolv'd into the sole opinion of their unworthiness, exclusive of some weak surmises which do not deserve a notice: it is therefore fair and allowable, by all laws of duelling, to oppose opinion to opinion; which if we can strengthen with reasons, and something like proofs, which are totally wanting on the other side, the last opinion may chance to carry the day. . . .[34]

Capell recognized—as others had not—the relevance of chronological succession to questions of authenticity. He suggested rightly that the *Henry VI* plays, *Love's Labor's Lost, The Taming of the Shrew,* and *Titus Andronicus* were all early productions, and that their weaknesses might derive from inexperience on the dramatist's part. Capell had read more widely in Elizabethan literature than his predecessors, and he was in a position to note—as they were not—that special features of the disputed works (e.g., the prevalence of rhyme in *Love's Labor's Lost*) were also features of the earlier drama as a whole.

At the same time, Capell refused to grant that the plays were unworthy of Shakespeare. His defense is spirited. Of the *Henry VI* trilogy he notes that

> . . . one circumstance there is that runs through all the three plays, by which he is as surely to be known as by any other that can be thought of; and that is, —the preservation of character: all the personages in them are distinctly and truly delineated, and the character given them sustain'd uniformly throughout. . . .[35]

34. *Mr William Shakespeare His Comedies, Histories, and Tragedies,* ed. Capell [London, 1767–68], I, Preface, 35.
35. *Ibid.,* p. 38.

He cites as an example "the enormous Richard." Capell remarks on the "sprightliness of the dialogue" of *Love's Labor's Lost* and the stageworthiness of the *Shrew*. *Titus Andronicus* presents him with his greatest challenge, as the whole weight of contemporary orthodoxy is against him. The play is universally condemned "as a very bundle of horrors, totally unfit for the stage, and unlike the Poet's manner, and even the style of his other pieces; all which allegations are extreamly true, and we readily admit of them, but can not admit the conclusion—that, therefore, it is not his. . . ." [36] Capell gives the evidence for an early date and goes on to argue from the standpoint of theatrical fashion. The tragedians of the day,

falling in with that innate love of blood which has been often objected to *British* audiences, and choosing fables of horror which they made horrider still by their manner of handling them, they produc'd a set of monsters that are not to be parallel'd in all the annals of play-writing; yet they were receiv'd with applause, and were the favourites of the publick for almost ten years together ending at 1595. . . . [37]

To this class of plays, which includes *Tamburlaine* and *The Spanish Tragedy*, *Titus Andronicus* belongs, and it is the work of a professional dramatist indifferent neither to popular taste nor to financial profit. Capell concludes by returning to the contested plays as a group, and his most telling argument is his last: the First Folio editors, "seemingly honest men," included all these works in their volume, and ". . . it had behov'd those gentlemen who have question'd the plays to have got rid of it [this argument] in the first instance, as it lies full in their way in the very entrance upon this dispute." [38]

36. *Ibid.*, p. 41.
37. *Ibid.*, p. 43.
38. *Ibid.*, pp. 45-46.

Elsewhere Capell, in his most idiosyncratic lapse, defends the Shakespearean authorship of the apocryphal plays of the Third Folio, which he takes to be early productions designed for provincial tours;[39] but he has sufficient prudence not to insist upon this extremist position. It remains to mention that Capell in his *Prolusions* (1760) reprints the anonymous *Edward III* as *"a Play, thought to be writ by* SHAKESPEARE." There is no external evidence; "something of proof arises from resemblance between the stile of his earlier performance and of the work in question; and a more conclusive one yet from consideration of the time it appear'd in, in which there was no known writer equal to such a play."[40] Capell further notes that both Shakespeare and the author of *Edward III* drew upon Holinshed's *Chronicle* and Painter's *Palace of Pleasure,* but he ends by confessing his assignment to be "conjecture only, and matter of opinion; and the reader must form one of his own. . . ."[41] The hypothesis that Shakespeare participated in the composition of *Edward III* has had reputable advocates to this day.[42]

Capell's performance, taken as a whole, is remarkable. He argues from style but does not ignore the claims of external evidence. He tends to see a questioned play in

39. *Ibid.,* pp. 14n–17n.
40. *Prolusions; or, Select Pieces of Antient Poetry,* ed. Capell (London, 1760), p. ix.
41. *Ibid.,* p. x.
42. The most recent support has come from Kenneth Muir; see *Shakespeare as Collaborator* (London, 1960), pp. 31–55, and below, pp. 126–127, 188. Not all the backing has been responsible. Earlier comment includes Alexander Teetgen's *Shakespeare's "King Edward the Third," Absurdly Called, and Scandalously Treated as, a "Doubtful Play:" An Indignation Pamphlet* (London, 1875), which is as eccentric as the title suggests. Yet Teetgen won the endorsement of Tennyson, who wrote him: "I have no doubt a good deal of it [*Edward III*] is Shakespeare's. You have given me a great treat" (Teetgen, p. 20).

relation to the author's acknowledged works and the facts of theatrical history. Moreover, Capell has the ability to label speculation as such. These virtues may appear commonplace—indeed, they *should* be commonplace—but later students have neglected them again and again, and it is a sad fact that they still do. Capell's hope that his defense of the contested plays would carry the day of course proved illusory. His edition fared poorly, suffering not only from Johnson's formidable competition but also from his own peculiarities (it was published without explanatory notes).[43] Until very recently Capell has truly been, as Miss Alice Walker argues, "a neglected Shakespearian," to whom indeed we owe the very word "Shakespearean."[44]

No comparable neglect clouded the achievement of the last and greatest of eighteenth-century Shakespeareans. Of Edmond Malone, Caldwell remarked to Bishop Percy, "No writer, I think, ever took more pains to establish facts and detect errors."[45] Malone's great work in the exposure of forgeries, the augmentation of our knowledge of Elizabethan stage history, and the elucidation of Shakespeare's biography and writings lies outside the province of this study. His findings with regard to the canon were—apart from some isolated sniping—accepted as authoritative for almost a century. Malone placed inquiries into authenticity on a more secure footing than in the past by giving prior consideration to

43. Capell's undisciplined prose style also caused displeasure. "If the man would have come to me," Johnson remarked to Boswell, "I would have endeavoured to endow his purposes with words; for, as it is, he doth gabble monstrously" (James Boswell, *Life of Jonson,* ed. Hill [Oxford, 1887], IV, 5).

44. Alice Walker, "Edward Capell and His Edition of *Shakespeare,"* *Proceedings of the British Academy 1960* (London, 1961), pp. 131, 145. Miss Walker provides a judicious appraisal of Capell's achievement.

45. James Prior, *Life of Edmond Malone* (London, 1860), p. 268.

chronological sequence, which he was the first to treat in systematic fashion. In 1778 he published his *Attempt to Ascertain the Order in Which the Plays of Shakspeare Were Written,* the conclusions of which were modified when he reprinted the essay in his 1790 edition of Shakespeare. With *A Dissertation on the Three Parts of King Henry VI* (1787), Malone produced the most elaborate study up to that time of the authenticity of an Elizabethan play. Together, the *Attempt* and the *Dissertation* brought about a new orthodoxy.

Following a lead from Farmer's influential *Essay on the Learning of Shakespeare,* Malone accepted Shakespeare's part-authorship of *Pericles* and restored the play to collected editions of Shakespeare's works. On the basis of a tortuous line of reasoning he assigned *Henry VIII* to the year 1601 and, after Johnson and Farmer, postulated later revisions, possibly by Jonson. He denied Shakespeare *Titus Andronicus* on several grounds, including "dissimilitude of style," but was guided chiefly by the tradition reported by Ravenscroft. Having decided that *Titus* could not be Shakespeare's, he used this exclusion as support for his theories regarding the authenticity of *Henry VI*—thus providing an ominous early illustration of the tendency of canonical investigators to set forth a hypothesis, then urge it as a fact in support of a subsequent hypothesis.

In his discussion of the *Henry VI* plays, Malone defends the value of internal—largely stylistic—evidence as a guide to authorship, and he quotes approvingly Upton's rhetorical questions: "How does the painter distinguish copies from originals but by manner and style? And have not authors their peculiar style and manner, from which a true critick can form as unerring a judgment as a painter?" [46] On the basis of internal evidence Malone denies Shakespeare *1 Henry VI:* the play differs from his other works in diction, versification, employment of classical allusions, and treatment of historical fact. Heminges and Condell admitted the play to the First Folio because Shakespeare perhaps contributed the Talbot scenes of the fourth act, "which are for the most part written in rhyme, and appear to me somewhat of a different complexion from the rest of the play." [47] Malone accepts Shakespeare's responsibility for *2* and *3 Henry VI,* which he takes to be revisions (respectively) of *The Contention of the Two Houses of York and Lancaster* and *The True Tragedy of Richard Duke of York.* These conclusions derive from the most "minute examination" of the quartos of the *Contention* and *True Tragedy,* and "careful comparison" of them with the corresponding Folio texts.

So persuasive was Malone's argument that for 150 years it enjoyed the status of dogma. In the very lecture in which Chambers turned the tide against the disintegrators of Shakespeare, that great scholar could assume that Malone had "worked out the relation of 2 and 3 *Henry VI* to the *Contention* plays." [48] But Malone was almost certainly wrong, and Johnson and Capell were almost certainly right. Malone was misled by the assumption (derived from Farmer) that Shakespeare had begun his theatrical career as a refurbisher of the writings of experienced playwrights. This unwarranted supposition

46. Malone, "Dissertation," in *The Plays and Poems of William Shakespeare* (London, 1790), VI, 382.
47. *Ibid.,* p. 424. Malone also suggests that the editors' memory may have faltered or that they possibly thought the first part essential for the reader's understanding of the two sequels.
48. "Disintegration of Shakespeare," p. 26.

led to the probable—and crucial—misinterpretation of the ambiguously allusive "upstart crow" passage in Greene: a passage which is (as Malone grants) "the chief hinge of my argument." [49] The *Contention* and *True Tragedy* are, in truth, not independent plays, but Bad Quartos of *2* and *3 Henry VI*. That such was the case, Peter Alexander demonstrated in 1929 in his *Shakespeare's Henry VI and Richard III*.

In marshaling all his formidable resources as a scholar to substantiate a hypothesis deriving from a mistaken premise, Malone places himself in the unenviable position of being the Ptolemy of attribution study. He is our first great cautionary case, illustrating the pitfalls attendant upon violation of the fourth principle of attribution study, that *textual analysis logically precedes stylistic analysis.*[50] But to regard Malone solely in this light would be to do a gross disservice to the most eminent Shakespearean of the age. Malone, as to a lesser extent Capell before him, anticipates the modern approach by his application of knowledge and reason—rather than mere impressionism—to problems of authorship, and by his consistent willingness to set forth the evidence on which his conclusions rest. His performance is placed in striking relief by that of Joseph Ritson, one of the few voices the authority of Malone failed to silence. Ritson, a great and quarrelsome antiquarian, denies the substantial Shakespearean authorship not only of the *Henry VI* plays and *Titus Andronicus,* but also of *The Comedy of Errors, Two Gentlemen of Verona, Love's Labor's Lost* and *Richard II,* "in all which pieces Shakspeare's new work is as apparent as the brightest touches of Titian would be on the poorest performance of the veriest canvas-spoiler

49. Malone, p. 397.
50. See below, Part Three, pp. 172-175.

24

that ever handled a brush." [51] On *Titus* he smugly concludes: "Future editors will, doubtless, agree in ejecting
a performance by which their author's name is dishon-
oured, and his works are disgraced." [52] How tiresome
it all sounds by now; Ritson might at least have recalled
Dr. Johnson's reference to Titian. Of *Troilus and Cressida* Ritson conceives the epilogue and (in part) the
dialogue to be "interpolated by some *Kyd* or *Marlowe* of
the time." [53] The telltale *some* affords a revealing clue
to the quality of the sensibility which could venture upon
such nice discriminations of style. Reliance upon taste as
final arbiter of authenticity was foreign to Malone's
modus operandi as a scholar. He stands as a great bul-
wark against all casual, uninformed, or prejudiced speculation on authorship.

Nevertheless, by a curious irony, Malone is himself
responsible for a method which a later generation of
scholars used as the basis for speculation on a scale that
he could scarcely have envisaged. When the pioneers of
Gower Street embarked upon their adventurous path in
1874, they paid Malone homage—although it was qualified—as "the discoverer and applier of the Ryme-
Test." [54] In a footnote to the section on *Love's Labor's
Lost* in his essay on the Shakespeare chronology, Malone
had observed:

Whether in process of time Shakspeare grew weary of the bond-
age of rhyme, or whether he became convinced of its impropriety
in a dramatick dialogue, his neglect of rhyming (for he never
wholly disused it) seems to have been *gradual*. As, therefore,
most of his early productions are characterized by the multitude

51. *The Plays of William Shakspeare,* ed. Johnson and Steevens (London, 1793), VII [209].
52. *Ibid.,* XIII, 280n.
53. *Ibid.,* XI, 214n.
54. *New Shakspere Society Transactions,* 1874, p. ivd.

25

of similar terminations which they exhibit, whenever of two early pieces it is doubtful which preceded the other, I am disposed to believe, (other proofs being wanting) that play in which the greater number of rhymes is found, to have been first composed.[55]

Malone's advocacy of the rhyme test is hedged with reservation, and it never occurred to him that this test— or other verse tests—could be systematically applied to determine the authorship of plays. That imaginative discovery belongs to the century which followed.

» IV «

BETWEEN THE TIME OF MALONE, whose conclusions regarding the canon provided the basis for a new orthodoxy, and Fleay, who found in Malone a method by which to launch a sweeping assault on that orthodoxy, a few dissenting voices may be noted. Of these the most extreme is E. H. Seymour, who in 1805 published his *Remarks Critical, Conjectural, and Explanatory, upon the Plays of Shakespeare.* Seymour makes the not inconsiderable assumption *"that interpolation does exist, and is frequent"* [italics Seymour's].[56] Apart from *A Midsummer Night's Dream,*

. . . we shall not, perhaps, find a single play that is not evidently corrupted; and there exists no other rule whereby we can distinguish the genuine from the spurious parts, but that internal evidence which critical discernment may be able to extract from a patient and minute examination of the earliest copies, the consciousness of a peculiar and predominating style, and the sagacious perception of an original design, howsoever adulterated or deranged by innovation or unskilfulness.[57]

55. "Attempt," in *Shakspeare,* ed. Malone, *op. cit.,* vol. I, Part I, p. 294n.
56. *Remarks,* I, Introduction, p. 5.
57. *Ibid.,* I, Introduction, p. 2.

Seymour reveals the caliber of his critical discernment throughout his two substantial volumes, and not least when he finds *Hamlet* a muddled anomalous drama full of "egregious improprieties." The following passage on the first scene of *Macbeth* will serve to illustrate his sagacity:

The witches here seem to be introduced for no other purpose than to tell us they are to meet again; and as I cannot discover any advantage resulting from such anticipation, but, on the contrary, think it injurious, I conclude the scene is not genuine.[58]

In attaching usefulness to the double-ending test for discriminating between styles, Seymour anticipates later students. The *Remarks* made little impression in his own time; seldom has obscurity been more richly merited. A century later Seymour was resurrected by another wholesale disintegrator, J. M. Robertson, who credits him with rare gifts of perception.[59]

Seymour's contemporary, S. T. Coleridge, has needed no resurrecting. "Any work which claims to be held authentic," Coleridge wrote in *The Morning Post* (February 3, 1800), "must have had witnesses, and competent witnesses; this is external evidence. Or it may be its own competent witness; this is called the internal evidence." Coleridge went on to distinguish interestingly between direct and indirect testimony, and then, on the basis of his criteria, to expose as forgeries certain supposed "copies of original letters from the French army in Egypt." The demonstration is acutely reasoned and aptly illustrated. By contrast, Coleridge's reflections on problems of the Shakespeare canon are laconic, fragmentary, or random.

58. *Ibid.,* I, 172.
59. Robertson, *The Shakespeare Canon, Part II* (London, 1923), p. 128.

In the *Table-Talk* he claimed that he could "point out
to a half line what is really Shakspere's in Love's Labour's
Lost, and some other of the not entirely genuine plays." [60]
As Chambers drily remarks, "Coleridge being Coleridge,
it is needless to say that he never performed this task." [61]
He did, however, assign to Shakespeare Act I and Act II,
scene i, of *The Two Noble Kinsmen.* He questioned
whether any of *Richard III* was Shakespearean apart
from the character of Richard himself. In his famous
comment on the Porter in *Macbeth,* Coleridge's wish
governs his reasoning with delicious transparency. "This
low soliloquy of the Porter," Coleridge declares,

and his few speeches afterwards, I believe to have been written
for the mob by some other hand, perhaps with Shakspeare's con-
sent; and that finding it take, he with the remaining ink of a pen
otherwise employed, just interpolated the words—

I'll devil-porter it no further: I had thought to have let in
some of all professions, that go the primose way to th' everlasting bonfire.

Of the rest not one syllable has the ever-present being of Shakspeare.[62]

The scene, with its sexual references and innuendoes, is
gross, hence bad; therefore Shakespeare did not write it.
But because the passage about the everlasting bonfire is
pure gold amidst the dross, the bard must somehow be
credited with it. A theory of interpolation and revision
(never mind the total want of evidence!) serves conveniently to rationalize criteria for authenticity which
are subjective and anachronistic. "This is the very ecstacy

60. Samuel Taylor Coleridge, *The Table Talk and Omniana,* ed. T.
Ashe (Bohn's Standard Lib. [London, 1884]), p. 204.
61. "Disintegration of Shakespeare," p. 26.
62. Coleridge, *Notes and Lectures upon Shakespeare,* ed. Mrs. H. N.
Coleridge (London, 1849), I, 249.

of criticism," objects Raleigh.[63] No doubt it is; but the ecstasy has been widespread since Pope's day. From Coleridge's rejection of a single scene it is an easy step to the broader challenge of Clark and Wright, the Clarendon editors, who see extensive interpolations by Middleton in *Macbeth* and who label as spurious, in whole or in part, no fewer than six scenes.

Because Coleridge was the most celebrated critic of the day, his pronouncements on the Shakespeare canon carried weight and were cited with respect. But being brief and clairvoyant, they gave little assistance to investigators in quest of a methodology for determining authorship. Of greater practical value were the contributions of three lesser men: William Spalding, Samuel Hickson, and James Spedding. In 1833 Spalding published anonymously his *Letter on Shakespeare's Authorship of "The Two Noble Kinsmen."* Fourteen years later, in the April 1847 number of the *Westminster and Foreign Quarterly Review,* Hickson reviewed Spalding's *Letter* in an article on the same play. Spedding's paper, "Who Wrote Shakespeare's *Henry VIII?*"—the most substantial effort of the three—appeared in *The Gentleman's Magazine* for August 1850. It prompted the publication, in *Notes and Queries* for the same month, of Hickson's independent findings with regard to the same problem. Spedding in turn responded with a letter in the October issue of *The Gentleman's Magazine.* For a quarter of a century these documents gathered dust, until reread and publicized by the admiring founders of the New Shakspere Society. The Hickson and Spedding essays were reprinted in the *Transactions* for 1874; Spalding's *Letter* reappeared in 1876 as one of the Society's miscellaneous publications.

63. Walter Raleigh, quoted by Alexander, "Conjectural History," p. 97.

The *Letter* reveals a refreshing interest in general principles as well as in the specific case. Spalding accepts the preeminence of external evidence; attribution questions arise only when the external proof is fragile, "and the internal evidence has therefore to be continually resorted to for supplying the defects of the external." [64] He anticipates many twentieth-century investigators in stressing the importance of the cumulative impression:

> In forming your opinion, you will be careful to view the circumstances, not singly, but together, and to give each point of resemblance the support of the others. It may be that every consideration suggested may not affect your mind with equal strength of conviction; but numerous probabilities all tending the same way are sufficient to generate positive certainty. . . .[65]

In practice Spalding does not escape inherited prejudices. The fact that *The Two Noble Kinsmen* was not included in the First Folio he explains away by denying the authority of the Folio— "It was just a speculation for profit; designd to put down the Quartos, which yet it copies." [66] In his division of the play Spalding exempts Shakespeare altogether from responsibility for the underplot. The internal evidence for Shakespeare is all stylistic. Spalding discusses in very general terms such aspects of the dramatist's art as versification, imagery, classical allusions, and thought; he offers no statistics. His argument is not especially effective, as Spalding himself seems to have recognized in later years (he was only twenty-four when the *Letter* was published). By 1840 his opinion was "not now so decided as it once was"; in 1847 he declared that

64. Spalding, *Letter,* Pubs. of New Shakspere Society, Ser. VIII, No. 1 (London, 1876), p. 3.
65. *Ibid.,* p. 108.
66. *Ibid.,* p. 7. I have quoted the marginal glosses, which succinctly summarize Spalding's position.

"The question of Shakespeare's share in this play is really insoluble." [67]

While Spalding was experiencing second thoughts, Hickson was setting out to demonstrate the presence in *The Two Noble Kinsmen* of "two writers, of dissimilar and unequal powers." [68] Like Spalding's, his pace is leisurely; he strolls through the play, pausing at every turn in his argument to pluck a specimen from the text and share its scent with his readers. In certain scenes he finds one or more traits—usually several in combination—that indicate Shakespeare's hand: straightforward exposition, philosophical utterances, high moral purposes, nice discrimination of characters, bold metaphor, a distinctive metrical pattern. Other scenes regrettably lack these felicities. They are Fletcher's. Thus, in Act III, scene iii,

Arcite brings "food and files" to Palamon; and, after some patter of early reminiscences between them utterly out of character, they separate. The fourth scene introduces the jailor's daughter again: she is now mad. She fancies she sees a ship, and there is some affectation of nautical language, (why, Heaven only knows) ; and the rest is mere incoherent nonsense.[69]

It comes as no surprise that "The . . . scene, without any doubt, is by Fletcher"—although one must in fairness add that Hickson is capable of assigning to Fletcher passages "of a much higher character." [70]

Hickson cites parallels: a mad scene of the jailor's daughter (IV, iii) recalls *Lear* (IV, vi, 126–132). "The

67. Italics are Spalding's. The revised judgments were expressed in the *Edinburgh Review*, July 1840, p. 468, and July 1847, p. 57; Furnivall cites them in his "Forewords" to the New Shakspere Society reprint of the *Letter,* pp. vii–viii.
68. Hickson, "The Shares of Shakspere and Fletcher in *The Two Noble Kinsmen*," in *Transactions,* 1874, Appendix, p. 26*.
69. *Ibid.,* p. 44*.
70. *Ibid.* Hickson regards Act III, scene iv, as Fletcher work of "higher character."

resemblance . . . is striking, but rather in style or structure, which go to prove identity of writer, than in either
sentiment or imagery." [71] Although Hickson sees the
need to distinguish between an author's unconscious self-
repetition and the imitation of him by another writer, he
underestimates the difficulties. He isolates certain characteristics of the verse as Shakespearean but is without
apparent awareness of flux and development in the poet's
art: the verse is described as though its peculiarities were
once and forever fixed. Hickson also notes similarities
between characters in *The Two Noble Kinsmen* and personages in the canonical plays; perhaps the high point of
the essay occurs when he supposes that "the doctor who
attended the jailor's daughter was afterwards called to
King Lear and Lady Macbeth." [72]

Hickson specifies no date for *The Two Noble Kinsmen,* but he sees it as preceding *Philaster* (*c.* 1609) and
thinks Fletcher's share that of "a young and inexperi-
enced writer." [73] It follows naturally from this line of
reasoning that Hickson should assign the framework of
the play and a majority of the scenes to Shakespeare. The
preceding summary has perhaps already sufficiently indicated Hickson's limitations, but further testimony may
be found in his cordial agreement with the view of a contemporary, Knight, that Fletcher suffered from "impure
thoughts," from which Shakespeare was happily exempt.[74] In discriminating, however, between two kinds
of verse in the play, Hickson made a contribution which
a later generation of scholars could readily follow up
with tests of their own. In 1874 metrical tables for *The*

71. *Ibid.,* p. 50*.
72. *Ibid.*
73. *Ibid.,* p. 59*.
74. *Ibid.,* p. 51*.

32

Two Noble Kinsmen, confirming Hickson's division, were provided by Fleay, who counted the double endings, and by Furnivall, who tabulated the end-stopped lines.[75] The path opened up by Hickson was to take many curious turns in the years following.

Spedding's inquiry into the authorship of *Henry VIII* provided one such turn. In an "Account of the History of the Verse-Tests" read at the New Shakspere Society's tenth meeting, John K. Ingram praised Spedding's essay as at once a classic—"a perfect model of Shaksperian criticism"—and a revolutionary document containing "the first example . . . of the application to Shaksperian metre of the strict numerical analysis, since advocated and practised with so much effect by Mr. Fleay." [76]

The play that occupied the distinguished editor of Francis Bacon's works and letters was included by Heminges and Condell in the 1623 Folio, where it appears last in the sequence of histories. Although a few of Spedding's predecessors had suspected interpolations, perhaps by Jonson—*vide* Dr. Johnson on the prologue and epilogue—no one had cast doubt upon the substantial Shakespearean authorship of the play, and no one had argued for Fletcher's intervention. Earlier critics had, however, noted "something peculiar either in the execution, or the structure, or the general design of it." [77] Idiosyncrasies of a more technical character had been observed by Roderick, who pointed to the frequency, unprecedented in Shakespeare, of feminine endings, and by Knight, who

75. Fleay, "Mr Hickson's Division of the *Two Noble Kinsmen,* Confirmed by Metrical Tests," *Transactions,* Appendix, pp. 61*–64*; Furnivall, "Mr Hickson's Division of *The Two Noble Kinsmen,* Confirmed by the Stopt-Line Test," *Transactions,* Appendix, p. 64*.
76. "On the 'Weak Endings' of Shakspere, with Some Account of the History of the Verse-Tests in General," *Transactions,* 1874, p. 444.
77. James Spedding, "On the Several Shares of Shakspere and Fletcher in the Play of *Henry VIII,*" in *Transactions,* Appendix. p. 1*.

remarked on the abnormally high percentage of run-on lines. In conversation with Spedding several years before the essay was written, Tennyson had expressed the view that the style in some portions of *Henry VIII* resembled Fletcher's. Finally, Hickson's essay on *The Two Noble Kinsmen* had opened the door for further speculation on the possibility of Shakespeare-Fletcher partnerships.

Spedding's point of departure, like that of so many disintegrators before and since, is the ineffectiveness of the play as it stands. He finds the impression left by the drama *"as a whole . . .* weak and disappointing." [78] Characters and events are introduced without preparation in the last act, and we are invited to rejoice in "the ultimate triumph of wrong" (the coronation of Anne Bullen and the birth of Elizabeth).[79] These "defects" cannot be blamed upon intractable historical source materials—a point which Spedding supports by giving his own recipe for a more edifying play on Henry's reign. This "great historical drama" would take in "the divorce of Katharine, the fall of Wolsey, the rise of Cranmer, the coronation of Anne Bullen, and the final separation of the English from the Romish Church, which, being the one great historical event of the reign, would naturally be chosen as the focus of poetic interest. . . ." [80] One can only regret that Shakespeare suffered the disadvantage of being born several centuries too soon to profit from Spedding's assistance.

Spurred on by his bardolatry, Spedding subjected *Henry VIII* to a minute examination which led to his firm conviction that in the composition of the play "at least two different hands had been employed . . . if not

78. *Ibid.,* p. 2*.
79. *Ibid.,* p. 3*.
80. *Ibid.,* pp. 16*–17*

34

three; and that they had worked, not together, but alternately upon distinct portions of it." [81] In his demonstration, Spedding avoids citing parallel passages: "The only satisfactory evidence . . . is to be found in the general effect produced on the mind, the ear, and the feelings by a free and broad perusal. . . ." [82] On the basis of such a perusal, he assigns to Shakespeare the scenes in which he finds vigor, reality, impassioned language, and figurative richness; those scenes which are, in a word, *excellent*. To Fletcher he gives the episodes that are conventional, diffuse, languid—in short, *inferior*. The design of the play, with all its inconsistency and moral incoherence, is Fletcher's, whose characteristic defect is the "want of a just moral feeling." [83]

These *aperçus* of the higher criticism Spedding reinforces with prosaic but reassuringly concrete numerical tabulations. He provides a table of the frequency and proportion of feminine endings, which range from 1 in 2.6 to 1 in 3.5 lines in the Shakespearean scenes, and from 1 in 1.3 to 1 in 2 in the passages assigned to Fletcher. "A distinction so broad and so uniform, running through so large a portion of the same piece," Spedding asserts, "cannot have been accidental." [84] Moreover, the division of scenes called for by these results coincides with one based upon another verse test, that of run-on lines, which vary in inverse proportion to the feminine endings.

The possible objections to his premises and methods did not much trouble Spedding. There is no external proof for Fletcher, but the strongest evidence for Shakespeare: inclusion of *Henry VIII* in the First Folio. The task of

81. *Ibid.*, pp. 6*–7*.
82. *Ibid.*, p. 7*.
83. *Ibid.*, p. 17*.
84. *Ibid.*, p. 15*.

undermining the Folio had, however, been so well accomplished by Spedding's time that he had merely to point to *Titus Andronicus* and *1, 2,* and *3 Henry VI* to demonstrate that "The editors were not critics." [85] (But if Heminges and Condell were not "critics," they did, as Alexander observes, manage the King's men in 1612–13, and thus would have paid Fletcher for his share in *Henry VIII* and, presumably, received from him the manuscript.) [86] To answer the "curious question" as to why Shakespeare entered into a partnership which spoiled his play, Spedding theorizes that *Henry VIII* was begun by the master and hurriedly altered and completed by Fletcher to satisfy the company's urgent need for a suitable new play to honor Princess Elizabeth's marriage to the Elector Palatine on February 14, 1613. But no such performance is recorded in the Lord Treasurer's accounts, which show payments for performances of five other plays by Shakespeare before the royal newlyweds. *Henry VIII* may have been first acted on June 29, 1613, the famous occasion when the Globe Theatre burned down.[87]

85. *Ibid.,* p. 10*.
86. "Conjectural History," p. 118. J. C. Maxwell offers a rejoinder: What [he asks] does Alexander think that Heminge and Condell would have done if Spedding's analysis of the play were correct? Omitted it altogether? But it must have been well known, it contained a substantial body of Shakespearian work, and it rounds off one of the three sections of the Folio. But, it might be argued, they would have said that it *was* a collaborative work. Here, I think, the only tenable position is a completely agnostic one. If Shakespeare was responsible for some collaborative works, there is no way of telling *a priori* what, if anything, Heminge and Condell were likely to say about them (*Henry VIII*, ed. Maxwell [Cambridge, 1962], Introduction, pp. xviii–xix).

But, as Maxwell goes on to acknowledge, they *did* exclude *Pericles, Sir Thomas More,* and the apocryphal plays; the external evidence, while not ruling out Shakespeare-Fletcher collaboration, gives comfort only to the advocates of single authorship.

87. Spedding's "bold conjecture" about the circumstances of the play's composition elicited a vigorous rejoinder from Delius when the essay was reprinted by the New Shakspere Society; see "Fletcher's angebliche

Spedding's stylistic evidence is also vulnerable. Where he sees disunity, others have discerned throughout "a unified, if special, conception and spirit." [88] The arguments from metrical data fail to satisfy the requirements of sound statistical procedure, for Spedding ignores the possibility of an alternative explanation. As Alexander remarks,

Spedding has not isolated the essentials of the problem, for the vital question of how modifications arise in the development of Shakespeare's verse is never seriously considered by him. He merely assumes, contrary to evidence, that such a modification as is found in *Henry VIII* could not arise. Nor has he considered the question of variation within the individual plays.[89]

Such doubts did not arise to dampen the enthusiasm of Spedding's early readers. His findings received the immediate endorsement of Hickson, who had arrived independently at the same scene assignment. In 1874 further confirmation came from the New Shakspere Society. Fleay applied the rhyme test to *Henry VIII*, and Furnivall the stopped-line test; in both cases, the results justified Spedding.[90] His essay remained the basis for subsequent commentary until challenged by Alexander in 1930. Opinion since has been divided, with the hypothesis of Fletcher-Shakespeare collaboration receiving

Betheiligung an Shakespeare's King Henry VIII," *Jahrbuch der deutschen Shakespeare-Gesellschaft*, XIV (1879), 180–206. Delius also rejected the arguments of Hickson and the New Shaksperians that *Two Noble Kinsmen* is a Shakespeare-Fletcher collaboration ("Die angebliche Shakespeare-Fletcher'sche Autorschaft des Drama's 'The Two Noble Kinsmen,'" *Jahrbuch*, XIII [1878], 16–44).

88. Foakes, Introduction to new Arden ed., p. xxiv; see also pp. xlv–lvi, devoted to showing the "careful organization" of the play.

89. "Conjectural History," p. 117n.

90. Fleay, "A Fresh Confirmation of Mr Spedding's Division and Date of the Play of *Henry VIII*," *Transactions*, 1874, Appendix, p. 23*; Furnivall, "Another Fresh Confirmation of Mr Spedding's Division and Date of the Play of *Henry VIII*," *Transactions*, 1874, Appendix, p. 24*.

powerful new support in the form of linguistic data.[91] The weaknesses of Spedding's demonstration do not rule out the strong possibility that his original intuition was correct. His early essay must be credited with providing an impetus for all subsequent investigation of what is perhaps the most intriguing puzzle of the Shakespeare canon.

» V «

ALTHOUGH THE ATTRIBUTION of Elizabethan plays on internal grounds has a history reaching back to the eighteenth century, and although (as we have seen) Spedding's essay on *Henry VIII* provided an authentic model for subsequent investigators, early work was sporadic and limited to select questions concerning the Shakespeare canon. Spedding and his predecessors were solving problems, or trying to solve them, rather than establishing a school. The modern movement in authorship study, taking as its province the whole sweep of Tudor and Stuart drama, properly begins with the establishment of the New Shakspere Society. Its advent has, of course, larger significance. The first generation of Victorian Shakespeareans—the antiquarian school of Collier, Dyce, Cunningham, and Halliwell-Phillipps—was on the way out; ". . . a new School [in John Munro's words] was arising which took up its work, and applied itself to . . . the study of Shakspere's contemporaries, of his times, and the growth and development of his art." [92] That school centered in the meetings and publications of the New Shakespere Society.

91. See below, Part Two, pp. 128–130.
92. *Frederick James Furnivall: A Volume of Personal Record* (Oxford, 1911), p. lii.

38

The Society's work was made possible by the energy and zeal of its founding director, Frederick James Furnivall (1825–1910), who in the course of his long career tirelessly devoted himself to the formation of societies and, through them, the advancement of literary and philological learning. All students owe him an everlasting debt of gratitude for his extraordinary contribution— as organizer, editor, and contributor—to the *Oxford English Dictionary,* and for his dedicated labors in behalf of the Early English Text Society, the first of his literary societies and the only one to survive to our own day. Furnivall's reliance on cooperative effort to achieve scholarly goals proceeded naturally from his Christian Socialist persuasion; a disciple of Ruskin, he had in 1854 helped to found the Working Men's College in Red Lion Square. It is a curious fact that the great organizer was anything but an organization man. "Devoid of tact or discretion in almost every relation of life," observes his long-time associate Sir Sidney Lee, "he cherished throughout his career a boyish frankness of speech which offended many and led him into unedifying controversies. He cannot be absolved of a tendency to make mischief and stir up strife." [93] Furnivall's abusive attacks on Swinburne and Halliwell-Phillipps led in 1881 to the resignation of many of the New Shakspere Society's eminent vice-presidents and some ordinary members—a blow from which it never fully recovered. Furnivall's unyielding temper, not without its paranoiac overtones, is revealed in his letter to the departing members. "I regard as an impertinence," he wrote, "your intrusion of yourselves into a dispute declared by me to be private between Mr. Hl.-Phillipps and myself, and I am now glad to be rid

93. *D.N.B.,* 2nd Supp., II, 65.

of you, whose return for the faithful work I have given you (and others), is this present censorious caballing against me." [94]

During the Society's heyday in the seventies, however, its work proceeded apace. The list of active members included such lights of Victorian literary scholarship as P. A. Daniel, Dowden, Lee, Brinsley Nicholson, and Spedding. Above all, the Society provided a forum, at its regular meetings and in the published *Transactions,* for the irrepressible Frederick Gard Fleay (1831–1909), the first of the great fantastics of attribution study.

The son of a linen draper, Fleay took his B.A. and M.A. degrees at Trinity College, Cambridge. "The industrious flea," as he was unappreciatively known to fellow undergraduates, distinguished himself by placing in four tripos lists: classics, moral science, mathematics, and natural science. A true contemporary of Taine and Herbert Spencer, Fleay found the last of these disciplines particularly valuable for his later experiments with metrical tests. "The great need for any critic who attempts to use these tests," he insisted, "is to have had a thorough training in the Natural Sciences, especially in Mineralogy, classificatory Botany, and above all, in Chemical Analysis. The methods of all these sciences are applicable to this kind of criticism, which, indeed, can scarcely be understood without them." [95] Fleay took orders in 1857, but was drawn to an academic career. For years he taught in

94. Quoted by Munro in *Furnivall,* pp. lviii–lix. For an appreciative estimate of Furnivall, discounting (while recognizing) the eccentricities and stressing "those qualities of breadth, humility, and humanity, characteristic of the more genial and expansive scholarship of his age," see Beatrice White's delightful paper, "Frederick James Furnivall," in *Essays and Studies 1952,* ed. Arundell Esdaile (London, 1952), pp. 64–76. If it is perhaps sentimental to speak of the scholarship of Furnivall's day as being genial, there can be no question of its expansiveness.

95. Fleay, *Shakespeare Manual* (London, 1876), p. 108.

grammar schools, mainly on the scientific side, and in time he came to cherish the illusory hope of being appointed to a university post in English literature.

Isolated in the North and burdened with teaching duties that he found increasingly uncongenial, Fleay nevertheless set for himself—and completed—an extraordinary program of scholarly investigation. By 1876 he could boast that he had ". . . reduced the theory of such [i.e., metrical] tests to a system, established the canons for their use, assigned special distinctive tests to each of the Elizabethan dramatists and worked out the results for the whole of their plays." [96] Fleay had been working on the metrical tests for five or six years when he came forward to share his results with the other founding members of the New Shakspere Society. Although his first paper was on the chronology of Shakespeare's writings, he left no doubt that, so far as he was concerned, the principal end of the tests would be "the determination of the genuineness of the works traditionally assigned to a writer." [97] The novelty of the method was that it replaced impressionism with science. With missionary ardor Fleay urged the merits of the new and (was it possible?) infallible tool:

. . . our analysis, which has hitherto been qualitative, must become quantitative; we must cease to be empirical, and become scientific: in criticism as in other matters, the test that decides between science and empiricism is this: "Can you say, not only of what kind, but how much? If you cannot weigh, measure, number your results, however you may be convinced yourself,

96. *Ibid.* Fleay also found time to apply the tests to Aeschylus and Sophocles with "satisfactory results"; his metrical analysis of Homer led him to conjecture the existence of an *Achilleis* "completed afterwards by the author of the *Odyssey* into the present form of the *Iliad.*"
97. Fleay, "On Metrical Tests as Applied to Dramatic Poetry," Part I, *Transactions*, 1874, p. 6.

you must not hope to convince others, or claim the position of an investigator; you are merely a guesser, a propounder of hypotheses."[98]

From the outset, however, impartial science led Fleay down strange paths. On the basis of quantitative data—counts of rhymes, double endings, Alexandrines, and broken lines—he concluded that *Macbeth* preceded *Hamlet, Othello,* and *Lear;* he assigned *The Taming of the Shrew* to the year 1600, *Cymbeline* to 1604, and *Julius Caesar* to 1607. The minutes of the discussions following Fleay's inaugural paper indicate that gratitude for his toilsome labor was from the first mingled with skepticism regarding his methods and findings. Some of the reservations and objections voiced in 1874 by Furnivall, Simpson, Ellis, and the rest might well have given pause to subsequent metrical analysts; but these early strictures (taken into account in a later section of this study) went unheeded. In a paper read at the Society's sixth meeting, on June 12, 1874, Fleay himself offered ten "canons of method" for the guidance of investigators using the tests.[99] One or two of these "canons" are reasonable enough, but the rest, with their assumptions offered as facts and their irrelevant analogies from the physical sciences, serve as little more than Fleay's rationalizations for his own procedures.

Fleay took special pride in his second paper, on Fletcher, Beaumont, and Massinger.[100] It is indeed a pioneer effort: Fleay must be credited with having undertaken the first systematic analysis of the entire Beaumont and Fletcher corpus with a view to determining the re-

98. *Ibid.,* p. 2.
99. "On Certain Plays of Shakspere," Part III, *Transactions,* 1874, pp. 312–317.
100. "On Metrical Tests as Applied to Dramatic Poetry," Part II, *Transactions,* 1874, pp. 51–72.

spective shares of the several participating dramatists. Fleay provides tables of attribution and metrical statistics for plays by Beaumont and Fletcher, by Fletcher alone, by Fletcher and Massinger, and by Fletcher in collaboration with Middleton, Rowley, or Shirley. For good measure he includes several plays not in the 1647 or 1679 Folios (e.g., *The Old Law*) : plays in which neither Beaumont nor Fletcher took any part. Although Fleay offers his paper as a preliminary survey, he shows no false modesty about his accomplishment:

> The matters I believe to be absolutely fixed in it by the application of metrical tests are, the part authorship of Massinger . . . ; the relative amount of Beaumont's work; and the classification of these plays. . . . I am certain that no one can go through the detailed evidence in the way I have done, and remain unconvinced.[101]

Those familiar with even a portion of the voluminous twentieth-century literature on the Beaumont and Fletcher canon may be inclined to regard Fleay's claims as premature.

His remaining papers for the Society are on Shakespeare. In "On the Authorship of the *Taming of the Shrew*," [102] he begins inauspiciously by misquoting an opinion that Collier had formulated but subsequently withdrawn. Fleay in this study argues that Shakespeare is responsible only for the characters of Katherine and Petruchio. The usual metrical statistics are buttressed by other kinds of evidence: the diction and the manner of introduction of classical quotations and allusions. But Fleay himself does not guarantee the accuracy of his word-lists, and Furnivall, lamenting the absence from the paper of the author's "firm dividing hand," easily showed

101. *Ibid.*, pp. 65–66.
102. *Transactions*, 1874, pp. 85–101.

how vulnerable were Fleay's generalizations about Shakespeare's use of the classics.[103] In his article on *Timon of Athens*,[104] Fleay offers the remarkable theory that the play was begun by Shakespeare about 1606, left unfinished, and finally completed in 1623, probably by Cyril Tourneur, who was commissioned by Heminges and Condell "to make it up to 30 pages" in order to fill a gap in the First Folio. The essay is followed in the *Transactions* by Fleay's edition of *The Life of Tymon of Athens*, "As Written by W. Shakspere," with the additions by an "inferior hand" excised. In a similar investigation of *Pericles*,[105] Fleay denies Shakespeare all of Acts I and II, the brothel scenes of Act IV, and the Gower chorus. The explanation, offered as "certain," is that Shakespeare wrote the Marina story (except for the indicated omissions), but finding it too short, laid it aside. It was taken up by George Wilkins, who supplied the first two acts, and by William Rowley, who provided the brothel scenes and the Gower chorus of Acts III–V to lengthen out the play. Having separated the true Shakespearean grain from the chaff of Wilkins and Rowley, Fleay made the "authentic" *Pericles* available in his old-spelling text of *The Strange and Worthy Accidents in the Birth and Life of Marina*.[106] With these papers on *Timon* and *Pericles*, and the accompanying editions of the dismembered plays, the disintegration of Shakespeare moves into high gear.

Yet these assaults upon orthodoxy appear mild in comparison with the theories which Fleay evolves in his last two papers for the New Shakspere Society. In "On Certain Plays of Shakspere of Which Portions Were

103. Discussion on Third Paper, *Transactions*, 1874, p. 112.
104. "On the Authorship of *Timon of Athens*," *Transactions*, 1874, pp. 130–151.
105. "On the Play of *Pericles*," *Transactions*, 1874, pp. 195–209.
106. In *Transactions*, 1874, pp. 211–241.

Written at Different Periods of His Life," [107] he develops a hypothesis of coexistent textual strata: in several periods of his career Shakespeare wrote nothing but unfinished fragments of plays which he abandoned for a number of years but ultimately picked up again and completed. Thus, the dramatist began *Troilus and Cressida* in 1593 or 1594, resumed work on it after an interval, and finished it in *c.* 1607. But the "spurious part of the last Act is probably débris from Dekker and Chettle's *Troylus & Cressida,* written in 1592, and reproduced in a revised form as *Agamemnon* in 1599." [108] The statement illustrates Fleay's penchant for offering his assumptions as facts. Dekker and Chettle wrote their lost *Troilus and Cressida* for Henslowe not in 1592 but in 1599; no evidence exists to link it with the *Agamemnon,* also lost. In his paper "On Two Plays of Shakspere's," [109] Fleay maintains that *Macbeth,* as we have it, is a Middleton adaptation of Shakespeare, and that *Julius Caesar,* in its present state, represents Jonson's reworking of Shakespeare's original. The following statement is indicative of the quality of Fleay's "evidence": "Shakspere and Jonson probably worked together on Sejanus in 1602–3. . . . He having helpt Jonson then in a historical play, what more likely than that Jonson should be chosen to remodel Shakspere's history, if it needed to be reproduced in a shorter form than he wrote it originally." [110]

107. *Transactions,* 1874, pp. 285–317.
108. *Ibid.,* p. 308n.
109. "On Two Plays of Shakspere's, the Versions of Which as We Have Them Are the Results of Alterations by Other Hands," *Transactions,* 1874, pp. 339–366. The curious assumption that Shakespeare collaborated with Jonson on *Sejanus* derives from the latter's prefatory reference to "so happy a *Genius"* who "had good share" in the play as originally produced. The happy genius was more likely Chapman; see Jonson, *Works,* ed. Herford and P. and E. Simpson (Oxford, 1925–52), II, 3–5; IX, 592–593.
110. "On Two Plays of Shakspere's," p. 359.

Brief summary can scarcely do justice to Fleay's dizzying flights in these last papers, in which strictures on method, statistical tables, and the sequential enumeration of points of "evidence" give an air of rationality to the high and mirthless fantasy of Fleay's propositions.

It was too much even for those who had applauded his earlier contributions. Fleay was forced to withdraw and modify part of the paper on stratification of texts. He retracted also his assault on the authenticity of the Porter scene from his *Macbeth* study, but Furnivall, unappeased, went ahead with publication of a rebuttal. "When attacks on the genuineness of Shakspere's text are made rashly," he snarled, "it is well to note their failure as a warning for the future." [111] The minutes for the discussions of Fleay's last two papers record no voice raised in his behalf.

After dominating the sessions of the New Shakspere Society during its first months, Fleay dropped out completely. In 1876 he gave up his headmaster's post at Skipton Grammar School, and in 1884 he relinquished orders. In the seclusion of his home in Upper Tooting he devoted his enormous energy to larger projects: *A Chronicle History of the Life and Work of William Shakespeare* (1886), *A Chronicle History of the London Stage, 1559–1642* (1890), and the *magnum opus, A Biographical Chronicle of the English Drama, 1559–1642* (2 vols.; 1891). In his introduction to the *London Stage* Fleay complained querulously about the Society "which so soon forgot, and still refuses to recognise, me," and in the *Biographical Chronicle* he alluded bitterly to Furnivall as the Præpositus Imperio Generalis "of these numerous Societies (for they, like the Jesuit seminaries, are all

111. Discussion of Mr Fleay's *Macbeth* and *Julius Caesar* Paper, *Transactions*, 1874, p. 498.

subject to one General)." [112] He countered vehemently A. H. Bullen's disparagement of him in the introduction to his edition of Middleton.[113] After completing his labors on the drama, Fleay turned to more recondite investigations: Assyriology and Egyptology claimed his attention. The chronicler of the English stage now produced an *Egyptian Chronology;* his last paper, published in 1905, is on the Great Pyramid.

Fleay is easily disparaged. The limitations and excesses that disfigure the later volumes, no less than the early papers, are only too apparent. He embraces an extraordinary range of contradictions. As a historian of the stage Fleay is by occupational necessity committed to the factual; yet fact and fancy, scholarship and romance, jostle confusedly together in his pages. He prides himself on being a pioneer of scientific criticism but displays none of the scientist's patient determination to gather, sift, and evaluate all the available data; instead he rushes impetuously ahead to his conclusions. Relying on statistics, Fleay is continually guilty of simple errors of arithmetic and oversights that would discourage a less intrepid investigator. Thus he published his "Metrical Table of Shakspere's Plays" in the New Shakspere Society *Transactions* without the essential Table of Proportions, which he had misplaced while type was being set. The table having reappeared, he printed it elsewhere, in *The Academy;* then again, in revised form, in the *Transactions,* with the confession that *Cymbeline* had been "misplaced through another cause, a numerical blunder." [114] He further altered the table and published it out-of-the-way,

112. *London Stage*, p. 8; *Biographical Chronicle*, II, 373n.
113. *Biographical Chronicle*, II, 373–375. Remarks on Bullen are scattered through the *Chronicle;* Fleay was evidently hurt by the censure of a younger scholar whose work he admired.
114. Postscript to Paper I, *Transactions*, 1874, p. 39.

in someone else's book; [115] Chambers checked the revised figures and found them "still inaccurate, but less so." [116] To these oddities must be added a streak of childlike capriciousness. Bullen recalls, in a delicious anecdote, that

. . . on one occasion, when I objected to some peculiarly far-fetched theory of his, he protested that it was not to be taken seriously but was "intended as a skit on the New Shakspere Society;" whereupon I reminded him of the fact (which he had forgotten) that he originally announced this theory in a school-edition of *King John* (when he was headmaster of Skipton Grammar School) ; and I mildly expostulated with him for mystifying schoolboys.[117]

Fleay rarely had the last word.

Despite these disabilities and the opposition incurred by his extravagances, Fleay's confidence never faltered; such words as *certain, conclusive, infallible, absolutely,* and *unquestionably* loom large in his vocabulary. When forced to retreat, he would revise his theory and present it with no less dogmatism than before. As often he changed his own mind. If in 1874 Fleay thought Shakespeare assisted Jonson with *Sejanus,* he believed otherwise in 1891, when the role of collaborator was given to Chapman. Irreconcilable views of this kind are sometimes propounded with equal conviction in different parts of the same work; conscious of an element of "apparent contradiction" in the *Biographical Chronicle,* Fleay in his "Afterword" offers the unlikely excuse that he "thought it better to send forth the arguments for rival hypotheses, and leave the decision to the reader. . . ." [118]

115. The table appeared in C. M. Ingleby, *Shakespeare, the Man and the Book* (London, 1877–81), Part II, pp. 99–141.
116. "Disintegration of Shakespeare," p. 34.
117. Preface to H. Dugdale Sykes, *Sidelights on Shakespeare* (London, 1919), p. vii.
118. *Biographical Chronicle,* II, 405.

Often he withholds evidence altogether. In the *Biograph-ical Chronicle* he merely records his conclusions with regard to authorship and assures readers that "every play that I possess has been metrically analysed, and I hold the results ready for reference at the service of any critic who may desire to avail himself thereof." [119] Care-less, arbitrary, quixotic, and irresponsible, he is the de-spair of the sober historian of the stage.

But to dismiss Fleay without further ado would be unfair not only to his memory but also to English dra-matic scholarship. He is sometimes right. His scene-by-scene allocation of *The Changeling* to Middleton and Rowley, offered without evidence in the *Biographical Chronicle* (II, 101), corresponds exactly with the divi-sion made by Pauline Wiggin six years later in her pains-taking *Inquiry into the Authorship of the Middleton-Rowley Plays*. The analysis of the collaboration has won unanimous acceptance from all responsible subsequent authorities—a rare phenomenon in this line of inquiry. When (to cite another example) Bullen reprinted the anonymous *Sir Giles Goosecap* in the third volume of his *Old English Plays* (1884), he suspected it was by an imitator of Chapman. Fleay, who had examined the proofsheets of the edition, immediately proposed in a letter to *The Athenæum* (June 9, 1883) that Chapman himself was the sole author, and he repeated the attribu-tion in the *Biographical Chronicle* (II, 322–323). While insisting that the internal evidence for Chapman was conclusive, Fleay characteristically neglected to provide it. Twenty years after the *Athenæum* letter, T. M. Par-rott summed up the case for Chapman in a persuasive article. Once again, Fleay had pointed the way. He did so on numerous other occasions and on a wide range of

119. *Ibid.*, I, 6.

problems, for his interest extended to every aspect of theatrical history. His labors, moreover, provided a stimulus to the succeeding generation. Few serious students in the first quarter of the present century failed to acknowledge a debt—sometimes a large one—to Fleay. Sir Edmund Chambers and Sir Walter Greg are among the distinguished Elizabethan scholars who profited from his researches and ultimately relegated them to obscurity. Even Fleay's guesses and hunches have won deserved tribute from the most rigorous theatrical historian of our own day. G. E. Bentley, for whom Fleay has so often been a nuisance or distraction, nevertheless links him with W. J. Lawrence when he writes of those men who had "so much experience with the plays and the theatrical records of the time that at their best they instinctively, or subconsciously, set up for themselves limits of probability more precise and valid than less experienced scholars can set with fully developed arguments." [120]

» VI «

With Fleay's departure, the New Shakspere Society no longer dwelled obsessively on attribution problems, although the subject remained one of its special concerns. In 1875 Richard Simpson contributed to the *Transactions* his paper "On Some Plays Attributed to Shakspere." The essay, concerned primarily with *Mucedorus* and *Fair Em,* is not without fanciful speculation—Simpson discerns in the latter harmless romance an allegory on Shakespeare, Greene, and Kempe, and he conjectures that the play, as it survives, may be a reported version of a Shakespearean original. On *Mucedorus* he comments, more

120. *The Jacobean and Caroline Stage* (Oxford, 1941—), III, Preface, p. x.

rationally, that the "critic who should attribute any of it to him [Shakespeare] on internal evidence would be crazy," and he goes on to take a skeptical view of the growing enthusiasm for stylistic tests of authorship:

... if I may venture a remark in the face of critics, I should say that the internal evidence on which they rely holds about the same proportion to external evidence that evidence of character bears to evidence of fact in a criminal trial. In spite of all the array of witnesses to character, I fear an impartial jury must find Shakspere guilty of *Titus Andronicus*.[121]

It is noteworthy that thus early in the day Simpson should regard himself as upholding a minority view.

No such qualms deter Jane Lee in her paper, "On the Authorship of the Second and Third Parts of *Henry VI*, and Their Originals," published in the *Transactions* for 1876. This was one of the most detailed inquiries into the question since Malone (see Postscript), to whom she admittedly owes much. Miss Lee maintains that the *Contention* and *True Tragedy* were by Marlowe and Greene, possibly aided by Peele, and that *2* and *3 Henry VI* represent alterations of the earlier plays by Shakespeare, with the probable assistance of Marlowe. It is "the strange likeness" of form and fashion that leads Miss Lee to link the *Contention* and *True Tragedy* with the plays of Marlowe and Greene, but she bases her case on "the further and surer ground" of similarities of grammatical structure, diction, phraseology, and thought. Unfortunately, the firm ground turns out to be shifting sand; Miss Lee's strange study is of no value.

In the same year the Society republished Spalding's *Letter on Shakspere's Authorship of "The Two Noble Kinsmen"* and in 1876–85 issued Littledale's reprint of

121. *Transactions,* 1875, p. 160.

the 1634 quarto of the play, together with his critical old-spelling edition. The result of years of devoted study, Littledale's edition has not yet been superseded. In his elaborate introduction he provided—after all allowance has been made for the prejudices, untenable assumptions, and methodological deficiencies he shared with other scholars of his day—the most thorough single study of an authorship problem to appear in the nineteenth century. Littledale believed that Shakespeare wrote approximately two-fifths of the play (all or part of I, i–iv; II, i; III, i–ii; IV, iii; V, i, iii–iv), that he gave up the project, and that Fletcher filled in the fragmentary sketch, supplying—in addition to much else—the "trash" of the underplot. Littledale thought, further, that Beaumont may have lent Fletcher a hand with a few scenes, but he refrained from pressing the conjecture.

Littledale's evidence consists partly of the by now familiar metrical data. He provides the results of no fewer than four tests (rhymes, light and weak endings, end-stopped lines, and double endings); his tabulations include the ratios which Fleay was censured for omitting. These data are, at best, as reliable as the lineation they are based on—and the lineation may be questioned. But Littledale devotes most of his space to the scene-by-scene citation of parallels between passages in *The Two Noble Kinsmen* and words, phrases, and speeches in Shakespeare. This material is, moreover, supplemented by other parallels listed in Littledale's voluminous commentary on the play. Such a *"systematic* comparison," he observes, ". . . has never before been carried out"; [122] Littledale is the first of the great parallel-hunters of Elizabethan authorship studies. Although conscious

---

122. William Shakspere and John Fletcher, *The Two Noble Kinsmen,* Pubs. of New Shakspere Soc., Ser. II, No. 15 (London, 1885), Part II, Introduction, p. 29*. Italics Littledale's.

of the need for distinguishing between plagiarisms and self-imitations, he underestimates the complexity of the problem and makes no attempt to set up standards for the admissibility of evidence. With regard to a particular parallel (as Muir notes, citing I, ii, 11, *"Mary-golds, on death-beds blowing"*), one cannot be certain whether Shakespeare is echoing himself (in this instance *Pericles,* IV, i, 16–18), or Fletcher is echoing Shakespeare, or the similarity is accidental. But half a century would pass before scholars began to address themselves to the task of establishing criteria for the evidential value of parallel passages. Although the problem of the authorship of *The Two Noble Kinsmen* remains unsettled, Littledale has always enjoyed the respect—if not necessarily the agreement—of subsequent investigators, and he has not wanted advocates. Kittredge included the *Kinsmen* in his edition of Shakespeare's complete works; most recently, Kenneth Muir, while taking exception to some of Littledale's methods, finds the metrical evidence persuasive and accepts his conclusions.[123]

» VII «

ALTHOUGH THE NEW SHAKSPERE SOCIETY continued operations until 1892, it did not again sponsor an attribution study of the stature of Littledale's work on *The Two Noble Kinsmen.* For a brief period in the 1880's, however, authorship discussion again bulked large in the pages of the *Transactions.* This flurry of interest must be credited—if that is the right word—to a "certain Boyle," as T. S. Eliot contemptuously referred to Robert Boyle in his essay on Massinger.[124] The papers Boyle

123. Muir, *Shakespeare as Collaborator,* pp. 98–99.
124. "Philip Massinger," in *Selected Essays* (London, 1951), p. 210.

published in the *Transactions* concern such favorite topics as the authorship of *Pericles, The Two Noble Kinsmen,* and *Henry VIII;* the fourth and last is on Massinger's share in the Beaumont and Fletcher plays. Tutor to the unprecocious Czar Nicholas II, Boyle was no doubt the most assiduous student of Massinger in St. Petersburg during the latter part of the nineteenth century. The zeal and amplitude of his investigations can be appreciated only when one studies his New Shakspere Society papers (as Boyle recommends) in conjunction with the series he contributed, from 1881 until 1887, to *Englische Studien,* which had recently been established by Professor Eugen Kölbing of the University of Breslau.[125]

In these papers Boyle alternately scolds Fleay for his dogmatism, carelessness, and bad manners, and pays tribute to him for his pioneering explorations. Boyle may be said to have, in a sense, inherited the mantle of the scholar towards whom he had such divided feelings. Boyle has Fleay's persistence, his love of the old drama, his faith (although less exclusive) in metrical tests, his eccentricity; but unhappily he lacks Fleay's intelligence, breadth of knowledge, and gifts of intuition. When he

---

125. To the New Shakspere Society he gave "On Wilkins's Share in the Play Called Shakspere's *Pericles,*" *Transactions,* 1880–86, pp. 323–340; "On Massinger and *The Two Noble Kinsmen,*" *Transactions,* 1880–86, pp. 371–399; "*Henry VIII.* An Investigation into the Origin and Authorship of the Play," *Transactions,* 1880–86, pp. 443–487; and "Beaumont, Fletcher, and Massinger," *Transactions,* 1880–86, pp. 579–628. In *Englische Studien,* Boyle published "Shakespeare und Die Beiden Edlen Vettern," IV (1881), 34–68; "Pericles," V (1882), 363–369, and "Beaumont, Fletcher and Massinger," in five installments: V (1882), 74–96; VII (1884), 66–87; VIII (1885), 39–61; IX (1886), 209–239; X (1887), 383–412. Some years later, after Swaen had edited two Daborne plays in *Anglia,* Boyle wrote on "Daborne's Share in the Beaumont and Fletcher Plays," (*Englische Studien,* XXVI [1899], 352–369). In "*Troilus and Cressida,*" published in the same journal in 1901 (XXX, 21–59), Boyle gives a large share of the play to Marston, whom he sees as indulging his fondness for "filth and froth."

54

turns to *Pericles,* Boyle contents himself with supporting, on the basis of numerous Wilkinisms (the neologism is Boyle's), Fleay's division of the play among Shakespeare, Wilkins, and Rowley. But on the subject of *Henry VIII* he makes his controversial predecessor appear to be caution itself; he removes Shakespeare from the play altogether and substitutes for him his hero Massinger. The "evidence" is, of course, all internal—meter, language, imagery, tone, and thought. The authenticity of the First Folio is thus rejected outright. To explain away the inconvenient external facts, Boyle offers the fantastic theory that Fletcher and Massinger collaborated to replace a Shakespeare original, *All Is True,* unfortunately lost in the conflagration that destroyed the Globe in 1613. In his paper on *The Two Noble Kinsmen,* Boyle again deposes Shakespeare in favor of Massinger, and on similar grounds.

With the exception of his article on *Pericles,* Boyle devoted himself singlemindedly to what he took to be the Beaumont, Fletcher, and Massinger plays. In a remote corner of the world, aided by a few fellow members of the St. Petersburg Shakespeare Circle and encouraged (he tells us) by a friend "whose name is honoured and revered wherever Shakespeare is known," [126] he made the rigors of the long Russian winters more endurable for himself by compiling his metrical statistics and an immense collection of parallel passages—a thousand in all, he boasts more than once. Nor did Boyle restrict himself to the minutiae of style; he looked also for larger correspondences between Massinger's writings and the plays of the Beaumont and Fletcher corpus. The results of his laborious inquiry are rarely trustworthy,

126. "Beaumont, Fletcher and Massinger," *Englische Studien,* X (1887), 412.

and they are occasionally startling. Not only does Boyle find Massinger in *Henry VIII* and *The Two Noble Kinsmen*, but he also discerns Fletcher in *A New Way to Pay Old Debts*—despite the fact, not unknown to him, that the play was composed just about or shortly after the time of Fletcher's death. Boyle's work need not detain the present-day student of Massinger; Bentley makes no mention of him in *The Jacobean and Caroline Stage.*

Why did Boyle fail, and so absurdly? For one thing, many of his parallels are unparallel. Thus Silvia's declaration in *The Elder Brother*—

> in that word,
> A noble husband, all content of woman
> Is wholly comprehended—

is compared with Arnoldo's lamentation for the loss of Zenocia in *The Custom of the Country:*

> In that alone all miseries are spoken.[127]

Often Boyle cites the merest commonplaces; he is not above pointing out that Massinger, *mirabile dictu,* is fond of classical allusions. He failed to see, moreover, that the value of any collection of Massinger parallels would be impaired by the derivative character of his art—the numerous echoes of Shakespeare, Jonson, and other Jacobeans. Then, Boyle is remarkably naive. Citing as an example of Fletcher's allusiveness the passage in *Henry VIII* about "some strange Indian with the great tool come to court" (V, iii, 34), he apparently misses the bawdy reference, which he interprets as a topical allusion to a comical Irishman named O'Toole![128] At

127. This particular "parallel" astonished Greg; see his introduction to *The Elder Brother,* Variorum *Beaumont and Fletcher* (London, 1905), II, 4.

128. *"Henry VIII,"* Transactions, 1880–86, p. 464. Years later, in a review of Pauline Wiggin's *Inquiry into the Authorship of the Middleton-*

the same time he is a prude. To Boyle the most striking feature of Massinger's work—"the cloven hoof that always betrays him"—is that his women are sensual and look forward to the felicities of matrimony. It is "a terrible example of . . . moral deterioration" [129] to which Boyle returns again and again with energetic revulsion; apparently he had not read *Romeo and Juliet* very carefully. When Eliot sneered at Boyle, it was in response to a sensibility so impoverished as to prefer *The Atheist's Tragedy* to *The Revenger's Tragedy*. Boyle is indeed capable of odd judgments. He seems not to have understood very clearly that *The Faithful Shepherdess* is a play ("It is a pastoral poem in rhyme"). [130] With characteristic humorlessness he dismissed *The Knight of the Burning Pestle* as of "so little literary value that the matter [of authorship] is of comparatively no consequence." [131] Little wonder that in the papers of Boyle the authorship inquiries of the New Shakspere Society conclude on a note of ludicrous anticlimax!

Yet Boyle received some recognition in his own day (he was commissioned to provide the article on Massinger in the *Dictionary of National Biography*), and a few later students, such as Oliphant, have recognized the originality of his efforts and treated him with respect. But perhaps the most useful purpose served by Boyle's work, apart from standing as another cautionary

Rowley Plays, Boyle protested, rather too strenuously, that he had understood the passage all along (*Englische Studien,* XXVI [1889], 63–64). The obscenity, he insists, was not discussed because of the presence of the "fair sex" in the hall! Boyle does not explain why it is not mentioned in his printed paper.

129. "On Massinger and *The Two Noble Kinsmen,'" Transactions,* 1880–86, p. 385.

130. "Beaumont, Fletcher and Massinger," *Englische Studien,* VIII, (1885), 50.

131. *Ibid.,* VII (1884), 86.

example, was in directing scholarly attention to problems of attribution in playwrights other than Shakespeare. He was conscious of the novelty of his program and the loneliness of his position, a loneliness not solely geographical in origin. He laments the exclusive preoccupation of Oxford and Cambridge with the heritage of Greece and Rome. "All the work," Boyle complains, "that has been done towards the preservation and illustration of the monuments of our literary past has been done by private, special societies, or by individuals"; inevitably that work has been unplanned and uncoordinated. Consequently, certain authors and periods have been neglected. The basic materials for the beginning student are, moreover, widely scattered, and unlike his counterpart at a German university, he has no experienced guide to help him through the initial stages of a project. Instead he "must stumble on, comparatively in the dark, must work out a method for himself, and painfully grope his way from error to error, till the fire of his enthusiasm becomes, in most cases, quenched." Should he somehow manage to produce something valuable, he must have the means to publish his findings at his own expense, unless a literary society exists which shares his interests.[132]

Of all the relatively unexplored literary terrain in England, the post-Shakespearean drama is to Boyle the most scandalously neglected. He pleads, with good reason, for new directions in research:

The study of Shakespeare has always engrossed, and must continue to engross, the lion's share of the attention of scholars. But it has been only too often forgotten, that the proper way to understand Shakespeare is to become thoroughly conversant with the spirit of his age, and this spirit of the age cannot be gathered from the pages of any one author, however great. It must be laboriously

132. *Ibid.,* VII (1884), 67.

collected from a thousand sources, its development must be studied, its direction ascertained, its forces weighed, ere we can estimate its general character. . . . A good deal has been done towards the study of Shakespeare's immediate predecessors, and more remains to be done. But, in order to come to a trustworthy result, it is not only necessary to study Shakespeare's predecessors and contemporaries. We must also study his successors, if we will measure with any degree of exactness the forces which were at work in his time, under the influence of which his mind was formed. Whilst acknowledging the great amount of good done by the New Shakspere Society, I consider it a great mistake that they are, with the exception of some few articles, so exclusively Shakespearean.[133]

Change, a new emphasis, was already in the air; indeed, Boyle's work is symptomatic of it.

» VIII «

THAT NEW EMPHASIS was made possible by the extraordinary editorial labors of the nineteenth century. In 1808 Charles Lamb contributed to the burgeoning interest in the old drama with his celebrated *Specimens of English Dramatic Poets Contemporary with Shakespeare*.[134] As the century progressed, editions of the playwrights multiplied rapidly. William Gifford, best known as editor of the *Quarterly Review,* published the collected works of Massinger (1805; rev. 1813), Jonson (1816), and Ford (1827). His notes on Shirley were used posthumously by the Rev. Alexander Dyce, who brought out the first and still the only complete edition in 1833. Dyce also edited Peele (1828, 1839), Webster (1830), Greene (1831),

133. *Ibid.,* VII (1884), 68–69.
134. See, however, Robert D. Williams, "Antiquarian Interest in Elizabethan Drama before Lamb" (*PMLA,* LIII [1938], 434–444) for a useful corrective to the more excessive claims made for Lamb as a champion of the non-Shakespearean drama.

Middleton (1840), Beaumont and Fletcher (1843–46), and Marlowe (1850). His last editorial project was a revision of Gifford's *Ford* (1869). A booksellers' hack, R. H. Shepherd, is responsible for the so-called Pearson reprints, issued in 1873 and 1874, of Brome, Chapman, Dekker, Glapthorne, and Thomas Heywood. W. C. Hazlitt's third edition of Robert Dodsley's *Select Collection of Old English Plays* (1874–76), in fifteen volumes, furnished a heterogeneous sampling. Hazlitt also edited the *Poems and Plays of Thomas Randolph* (1875). Collins edited Tourneur (1878); Maidment and Logan, Cokayne (1874), Marmion (1875), and Tatham (1879). In a single decade, from 1881 until 1890, A. H. Bullen prepared collected editions of Davenport, Day, Marlowe, Marston, Middleton, Nabbes, and Peele, as well as the first volumes of *Old English Plays,* comprising sixteen plays, four of which are printed for the first time from manuscript.

Every one of these editions—and the list is far from complete—falls short of present-day standards; some, such as the Pearson series, are beneath contempt. But they introduced the plays and playwrights to an increasingly large audience and promoted that interest in attribution which was to become so widespread in the next century. Speculation about the authorship of certain plays, and the shares of participants in collaborations, entered naturally enough into the prefatory memoirs to these editions. Usually impressionistic, these comments provided starting-points for more elaborate investigations. In his first *Old English Plays* collection, to cite but one instance, Bullen made a number of interesting ascriptions. With absolute certainty he gave *Barnavelt* to Fletcher and Massinger, *Captain Underwit* to Shirley, *The Lady Mother* to Glapthorne, and *The Captives* to Heywood.

On *Underwit* he came a cropper, for the play turned out to be Cavendish's *The Country Captain,* published in 1649 at the Hague. All the other assignments have stuck —not a bad average by most standards—and even the *Underwit* blunder is not as ghastly as might at first appear: Shirley apparently did have something to do with the play.[135]

With the advent of learned journals in the modern languages in the latter part of the century, new outlets became available for publishing the results of investigation. The Germans led the field. The *Jahrbuch der deutschen Shakespeare-Gesellschaft* (called *Shakespeare Jahrbuch* after 1925) was begun in 1865. From the standpoint of the present inquiry, perhaps the most interesting article published in the *Jahrbuch* during the nineteenth century was Wilhelm Wendlandt's "Shakespeare's *Timon von Athen"* (1888), in which it was suggested, apparently for the first time, that the Folio text of *Timon* was set from the dramatist's unfinished draft. The paper unfortunately did not put an end to the search for Shakespeare's nonexistent collaborator. *Englische Studien,* which made its debut in 1877, was more broadly conceived than the *Jahrbuch,* and from the first attracted English-language contributions. In addition to articles and reviews by the prolific Boyle, it carried the work of Fleay, Grosart, and others; a young Australian scholar, E. H. C. Oliphant, established his reputation with three papers on the Beaumont and Fletcher canon.[136] *Anglia* commenced publication in 1878. In the United States, *Modern Language Notes* was founded in 1886; the Modern Language Association, organized in 1883,

135. See Bentley, *Jacobean and Caroline Stage,* III, 148.
136. "The Works of Beaumont and Fletcher," *Englische Studien,* XIV (1890), 53–94; XV (1891), 321–360; XVI (1892), 180–200. On Oliphant see below, Part Two, pp. 84–88, 101–103.

issued the first of its quarterly *Publications* in 1889. *Modern Philology,* in whose pages so many authorship studies were to appear, got under way in 1903. When doctoral programs on the Teutonic model, culminating in a published dissertation, became part of the American academic scene, universities offering the Ph.D. instituted monograph series. Pauline Wiggin's study of the Middleton-Rowley collaborations, already cited, is an early (1897) Radcliffe doctoral dissertation.

England lagged behind. A gentlemanly amateur interested in the old drama might publish his reflections in *The Retrospective Review* or enter the correspondence columns of *The Athenæum* or ruminate in any one of a number of other *belles-lettristic* periodicals that came and went as the century progressed. But only *Notes and Queries* (established in 1850) consistently served antiquarian needs, although it was, of course, restricted to short pieces. Not until 1905, when *Modern Language Review* appeared on the scene, did England have a truly professional literary and philological journal. By then sufficient facilities were at the disposal of Elizabethan scholars to make possible the Golden Age of attribution study.

II

The
Golden Age
and After

» I «

THE TEMPO OF SCHOLARLY ACTIVITY quickened as the new century got under way. Articles, editions, monographs, and comprehensive studies flowed from the presses in ever-increasing numbers; histories of the Elizabethan stage, on a scale previously undreamt of, were planned and executed. In this vast outpouring of the fruits of learning and speculation, attribution study—an exciting and as yet untarnished sphere of investigation—played no inconsiderable part.

Of the new journals, the University of Chicago's *Modern Philology,* under the editorial direction first of Philip S. Allen and afterwards of the great John M. Manly, seems particularly to have encouraged articles on authorship. In its pages, between 1904 and 1910, Gaud discussed the rival claims of Peele and Greene for *Locrine;* Garnett made a case for Jonson's responsibility for Act IV, scene ii, of *The Bloody Brother;* Parrott gave Chapman *Sir Giles Goosecap;* Thomas took away *Revenge for Honor* from the same dramatist; Howe divided *The Birth of Merlin* between Middleton and Rowley; and Miss Hibbard reasserted Heywood's claim to *The Fair Maid of the Exchange.*[1] At last the non-Shakespearean

1. W. S. Gaud, "The Authorship of Locrine," *Mod. Phil.,* I (1904), 409–422; Richard Garnett, "Ben Jonson's Probable Authorship of Scene

Elizabethan drama was receiving sustained attention in its own right. Most of this work proceeded from the pens of a new breed of scholars: American academicians at Princeton University or Mount Holyoke College or Los Angeles State Normal School; content more often than not to track down the author of a single anonymous play rather than to attempt the subduing of an entire canon; without Fleay's dogmatism and instability, but also without his extraordinary knowledge and gifts of intuition.

Gaud's article on *Locrine,* the first in the series, illustrates the methods favored by the new school. *Locrine* was published in 1595 as "Newlie set foorth, ouerseene and corrected, by *W. S."* Reprinted in the Shakespeare Third Folio of 1663, it thus became part of the Apocrypha. Only a few critics (mostly Germans) have found Shakespeare guilty of this lamentable play, even to the limited extent of being an accomplice in its perpetration —although Richard Simpson did offer the entertaining hypothesis that the dramatist, having been accused of stealing from Peele and Greene, interpolated passages from their work into an older tragedy in order "to show what manner of plays his would be if he imitated those models." [2] Other conjecturists prior to Gaud had generally favored either Greene or Peele as author of *Locrine.* Gaud, building upon these guesses, has as his purpose the enthronement of Peele.

His method is to demonstrate how in imagery, versification, theme, characterization, thought and phrasing, *Locrine* resembles the undoubted work of Peele and dif-

2, Act IV, of Fletcher's Bloody Brother," II (1905), 489–495; T. M. Parrott, "The Authorship of 'Sir Gyles Goosecappe,'" IV (1906), 25–37; D. L. Thomas, "Authorship of *Revenge for Honour,"* V (1908), 617–636; Fred Allison Howe, "The Authorship of 'The Birth of Merlin,'" IV (1906), 193–205; Laura A. Hibbard, "The Authorship and Date of the *Fayre Maide of the Exchange,"* VII (1910), 383–394.

2. Simpson, review of Wolfgang Bernhardi's *Robert Greene's Leben*

fers from the accepted plays of his fellow University Wits, Greene in particular. Gaud provides statistical tables of certain metrical peculiarities and grammatical constructions (e.g., *for to* followed by an infinitive). Unfortunately for his purposes, the grammatical tables reveal considerable fluctuation within the work of each playwright. *For to,* employed four times in *Locrine,* appears with equal frequency in Greene's *Orlando Furioso* but sixty-five times in the same playwright's *Alphonsus;* Peele eschews the construction in his *David and Bethsabe* but uses it six times in *Edward I.* It is not easy to see how these figures help or hinder the case for either candidate. Gaud does not fare much better with his other evidence. The metrical data he cites as an argument for Peele are taken by Tucker Brooke to favor Greene, whose verse Gaud apparently did not trouble to analyze.[3] Both Peele and the author of *Locrine,* Gaud finds, favor the adjectives *latest, fell, coal-black, ugly,* and *grim*—commonplace words every one. His definition of theme ("the attitude of the author to his plot") is scarcely reassuring, and he is equally unprofound on imagery, the modern analytical study of which had not yet begun. Gaud concludes with a series of parallel passages, but the "very large number of verbal parallels" with which he has been credited[4] amounts to no more than a dozen. The value of parallel passages—disputable even under more favorable conditions—cannot be great in determining the authorship of the work of (in Chambers' phrase) "an abnormal plagiarist."[5]

und Schriften, in *The Academy,* V (March 21, 1874), 310.

3. *The Shakespeare Apocrypha,* ed. C. F. Tucker Brooke (Oxford, 1908), Introduction, p. xviii. Brooke points to "the extreme rarity of run-on lines" in *Locrine* and Peele.

4. By Baldwin Maxwell, *Studies in the Shakespeare Apocrypha* (New York, 1956), p. 66.

5. E. K. Chambers, *The Elizabethan Stage* (Oxford, 1923), IV, 27.

Gaud's other deficiencies are no less serious. Nowhere does he consider the possibility that someone other than Greene or Peele may have written *Locrine,* or that the play may be a collaboration or a revision or both. That the surviving text reflects an adapter's intervention is suggested not only by the title-page declaration, but also by an allusion in the epilogue to Elizabeth's thirty-eight years of reign, which were not completed until after *Locrine* appeared in print.[6] Nor does Gaud take into account another anonymous play, *Selimus,* which stands in a special and uncertain relation to *Locrine.* The main peculiarity is that several passages in the two works are almost identical, and some of these lines have been appropriated from Spenser's *Complaints.*

Were Gaud's performance atypical or uninfluential, it might be dismissed with less flogging as one of those weak efforts which in any period and in any branch of scholarship editorial misjudgment sometimes allows to creep into print—even into the pages of as distinguished a journal as *Modern Philology.* But "The Authorship of Locrine" does not differ materially from a host of articles (all on single plays) produced around the same time or in the decades following. The metrical tables, the word-lists, the impressionistic comments on theme, character, and plot, the final brandishing of the parallels—all designed to create a "cumulative impression"—were to constitute a durable formula. When, as with *Locrine,* the play under discussion is simultaneously minor and bris-

6. "So let vs pray for that renowned mayd, / That eight and thirtie yeares the scepter swayd" (V, iv, 268–269, in *Shakespeare Apocrypha,* ed. Brooke). Elizabeth's thirty-eighth regnal year began on November 17, 1595, and ended on November 16, 1596. To be chronologically accurate, the passage must postdate the Stationers' Register entry for the play (July 20, 1594). There are other internal indications that *Locrine,* originally written in *c.* 1591, underwent adaptation, presumably for a revival.

tling with complicated, perhaps insoluble, problems, the apparent weight of evidence tends to disarm criticism, and the danger exists that the investigator's conclusions will receive insufficient scrutiny. Schelling accepted Gaud's case in the *Elizabethan Drama*.[7] As recently as 1956, the conscientious Maxwell gave his argument respectful notice in *Studies in the Shakespeare Apocrypha*.[8]

Where Gaud fails, Parrott succeeds. Since the course of attribution study cannot be fairly described as a succession of triumphs, his achievement deserves savoring. Some of his success Parrott undoubtedly owes to the avoidance of high-pressure tactics. No passion to bestow a neglected masterpiece upon his hero urges him heedlessly on; "*Sir Gyles Goosecappe*," he confesses, "is by no means a comedy of remarkable merit." [9] Nevertheless, as he goes on to note, the play—if indeed Chapman wrote it—holds interest for several reasons: it foreshadows a finer romantic comedy, *The Gentleman Usher;* it testifies to the influence of Lyly and Jonson upon Chapman's dramatic art; it provides a link between the playwright's early work for Henslowe and his later efforts on behalf of the boy actors.[10]

Sir Giles Goosecap was written sometime between 1601 and 1603, printed anonymously in 1606 as presented by the Children of the Chapel, and reprinted in 1636 with a dedicatory epistle by the publisher, who refers to the author as deceased. These meager facts—the sum of our external information about the play—serve to narrow down the field of authorial candidates in a most extraordinary fashion. Parrott, modifying a suggestion by Fleay,

7. Felix E. Schelling, *Elizabethan Drama, 1558–1642* (Boston and New York, 1908), I, 256.
8. Maxwell, *Studies,* p. 66.
9. Parrott, "Authorship of 'Sir Gyles Goosecappe,' " p. 27.
10. *Ibid.*

remarks that the only known dramatists associated with the Chapel children in 1601 and dead by 1636 are Marston, Middleton, and Chapman. But Parrott errs: in the first years of the century Marston, so far as we can tell, wrote exclusively for Paul's boys, and Middleton for Paul's and the Admiral's men. After 1601, with the departure of Jonson, Chapman appears to have singlehandedly provided his company with its comic repertory. But the external evidence, although more powerful than Parrott realized, is not conclusive; theatrical records for the period are incomplete, and the play might conceivably be the work of some unknown. In this case, internal evidence confirms an assignment already likely on external grounds.

That internal evidence consists of the small details of style—particular words, phrases, images—and also larger literary correspondences: thought, characterization, incident. Parrott notes that the word *Eternesse* (II, i, 9),[11] apparently a Chapman coinage, appears also in *The Tragedy of Byron* (V, iii, 191); another unusual word, *mankindly* (= *cruelly*), at II, i, 38, is paralleled by Chapman's use of the adjective *mankind* in the unusual sense of *cruel* in *All Fools* (IV, i, 235) and *The Gentleman Usher* (IV, i, 49). The lofty and labored rhetoric given to the idealized Clarence in *Goosecap* recalls the philosophical Chapman at every turn. Clarence's defense of cosmetic paint as imparting "A lawful and a commendable grace" is unusual in a period when feminine make-up was a commonplace object of satirical derision; but it sorts well with the idiosyncratic temper of a dramatist who defends dueling and has a good word to say for the St. Bartholomew Day massacre. The "humour" of

11. Act, scene, and line references are to *The Comedies of George Chapman,* ed. Parrott (London, 1914).

Sir Giles, who speaks backward as though a crabfish had bitten his tongue, resembles that of Poggio—"cousin Hysteron Proteron"—in *The Gentleman Usher*. Lady Furnifall, described as "never in any sociable vein till she be tipsy," brings to mind the "humours of the cup" of Cortezza in the *Usher,* a shrew sober but when drunk an affable and amorous companion. These and other similarities between *Goosecap* and Chapman's acknowledged plays acquire a special persuasiveness in view of his well-known tendency to repeat himself. The most striking verbal parallels, moreover, concern two plays—*All Fools* and the *Usher*—still unpublished when *Goosecap* appeared in the 1606 quarto, although both were written earlier. Thus the possibility of imitation evaporates.

Unwilling to press too hard, Parrott claimed strong probability rather than mathematical certainty ("by the nature of things, impossible") for his attribution. Support in the form of additional scraps of internal evidence was forthcoming from F. L. Schoell in his University of Paris thesis, *George Chapman as a Comic Writer* (1911). Parrott strengthened his own case when he edited *Goosecap* with Chapman's accepted comedies in 1914. In the same year, Schoell remarked: "His [Parrott's] twofold evidence—precise, striking parallels between *Sir Gyles Goosecappe* and Chapman's other works, special likeness between *Sir Gyles Goosecappe* and Chapman's romantic comedy, *The Gentleman Usher*—carries absolute conviction to the unbiased mind. *Sir Gyles Goosecappe* is now universally acknowledged as Chapman's authentic work. . . ." [12] Schoell was right. In the most recent general study of the poet, Jacquot flatly declares that "cette pièce est certainement l'œuvre de

12. "A New Source of *Sir Gyles Goosecappe,*" *Mod. Phil.,* XI (1914), 548.

Chapman." [13] It is noteworthy that Parrott makes his case without recourse to a single metrical table.

» II «

ATTRIBUTION STUDIES of Elizabethan plays appeared sporadically in other journals in the first decade of the new century. Charles Crawford pointed out, in the *Jahrbuch der deutschen Shakespeare-Gesellschaft* (1903), that both Kyd and the author of *Arden of Feversham* were acquainted with servant life and the law, and that both playwrights imitate Lyly and Marlowe; that the character of Black Will in *Arden* resembles Basilisco in *Soliman and Perseda;* that numerous similarities of vocabulary, phraseology, and figures of speech link *Arden* with Kyd's accepted writings. [14] On the basis of such parallels—most of them commonplace—Crawford confidently proclaimed that he had solved the difficult problem of the play's authorship. The confidence was unwarranted. In *Modern Language Notes* in 1905, James E. Routh, Jr., applied rhyme tests to Kyd as an argument for the authenticity of *Soliman and Perseda* and the spuriousness of *The First Part of Jeronimo*. [15] *Notes and Queries,* ever hospitable to antiquarian speculation of any kind, in 1906 carried Bertram Dobell's article advancing George Wilkins' title to *A Yorkshire Tragedy*. [16] In the

13. Jean Jacquot, *George Chapman (1559–1634), sa vie, sa poésie, son théâtre, sa pensée* (Paris, 1951), p. 89.

14. "The Authorship of Arden of Feversham," *Jahrbuch,* XXXIX, 74–86; reprinted in Crawford's *Collectanea,* 1st Ser. (Stratford-on-Avon, 1906), pp. 101–130. Crawford assumes, unjustifiably, that the anonymous *Soliman and Perseda* is Kyd's unaided work.

15. "Thomas Kyd's Rime Schemes and the Authorship of *Soliman and Perseda* and of *The First Part of Jeronimo*," *Mod. Lang. Notes,* XX, 49–51.

16. "The Author of 'A Yorkshire Tragedy,'" *Notes and Queries,* 10th Ser., VI (1906), 41–43.

first number of *Modern Language Review* (1906), the young Walter Greg discussed "The Authorship of the Songs in Lyly's Plays," and in the course of his article rejected the dramatist's claim to the anonymous *Maid's Metamorphosis*. O. L. Hatcher, in "The Sources and Authorship of *The Thracian Wonder*" (*Modern Language Notes,* 1908), noted resemblances between that play and Greene's writings other than the *Menaphon,* which is its source. After triumphantly demonstrating that the plot of *The Thracian Wonder* (which bears a title-page ascription to Webster and Rowley) is "practically compounded from Greene's accepted works," Hatcher arrives at the novel conclusion that the play is not his: Greene is unlikely to have "thus fully . . . duplicated his own material, fond as he was of repeating himself. . . ." [17] Hatcher perhaps underestimates Greene, but her reluctance to assume that stylistic similarities between works necessarily imply common authorship is healthy skepticism. In any event, the play may date from some years after Greene's death.

Studies during this period vary greatly in the elaborateness of the arguments used to support attributions. Kittredge, in the *Journal of Germanic Philology,* suggests that Thomas Preston, the author of *Cambyses,* is responsible for *Clyomon and Clamydes.* "The general resemblance in style and method," he declares, "is remarkable." [18] Kittredge finds Subtle Shift in *Clyomon* similar to Ambidexter in *Cambyses* (it apparently does not occur to him that the Vices of Tudor moralities may be expected to share generic traits). But he rests his case primarily on a single parallel passage "which shows such an

17. Hatcher, p. 19.
18. G. L. Kittredge, "Notes on Elizabethan Plays," *Jour. of Germ. Phil.,* II (1898–99), 8. In 1903 the periodical was rechristened *The Journal of English and Germanic Philology.*

identity of style between the two plays as almost to settle the question." [19] Edgar Coit Morris, on the other hand, takes an inordinate number of pages in *PMLA* to divide *The Old Law* line by line between Middleton, Massinger, and Rowley.[20] His chief distinction is to be as ineffective in seventy pages as Kittredge is in two.

Book-length general studies of individual dramatists are, for all practical purposes, a twentieth-century phenomenon, the one significant exception being G. C. Macaulay's *Francis Beaumont* (1883). Macaulay devoted almost half his space to an effort to distinguish, on simple impressionistic grounds, between Beaumont's work and Fletcher's. In critical studies produced in the first decade of the new century, the degree of attention given to authorship questions varies from the brief footnote remarks of Albert Feuillerat in his huge *John Lyly* (1910) to the considered evaluations of E. E. Stoll in his comparatively slender *John Webster* (1905). O. L. Hatcher's *John Fletcher: A Study in Dramatic Method* (1905) contains a useful first chapter surveying previous work on the Beaumont-Fletcher collaborations.

The two large-scale histories of the Elizabethan stage produced in this decade constitute, understandably enough, bastions of orthodoxy. Ascriptional commonplaces strew the vast gray desert of Felix Schelling's *Elizabethan Drama* (1908); few surprises enliven the essays by divers hands comprising the volumes on the drama to 1642 in *The Cambridge History of English Literature* (1910). These syntheses remain useful, if at all, primarily for their bibliographies.

A pair of monographs, American doctoral dissertations

19. *Ibid.*
20. "On the Date and Composition of *The Old Law,*" *PMLA*, XVII (1902), 1–70.

in origin, require notice. Frederick Erastus Pierce's *The Collaboration of Webster and Dekker* (1909) is an attempt to determine the respective shares of the two dramatists in *Westward Ho, Northward Ho,* and *Sir Thomas Wyatt.* Pierce makes use of a number of tests, including one of his own devising: the "three-syllable Latin word-test." Webster, he finds, employs many polysyllabic words of Greek or Latin derivation; Dekker, on the other hand, introduces such words sparingly. The elaborate tables of frequency and proportion, intended to put the test on "a scientific basis, and free it from the rambling guesswork of vague impressionism," is in fact impressionism rationalized. In a fine display of pointless effort, Pierce estimates the number of prose lines which each scene—whether in verse or prose—*would have* occupied in Dyce's edition of Webster, and on this basis calculates his averages; relationships between subject matter and vocabulary are not considered. Pierce's other evidence includes metrics, dialect passages (favored by Dekker), and similitudes of incident, characterization, and atmosphere; but parallel passages figure most prominently, occupying almost half the book. "The value of parallel passages as a test of authorship," Pierce sanguinely remarks, "has been almost universally recognized." [21] Uncertain as to which parallels are evidentially significant and which not, he hospitably admits all, including some he acknowledges to be virtually worthless. Other passages, he grants, owe their parallelism to proverbial or literary commonplaces, but Pierce maintains—

21. *Collaboration,* p. 29. A few years later, in "The Collaboration of Dekker and Ford," *Anglia,* XXXVI (1912), 140–168, 289–312, Pierce speaks with less confidence on the same issue: "Great as are the dangers involved in this much abused form of evidence, most scholars, I believe, feel that a large number of close parallelisms have some value when they fall in line with other testimony" (151). His methods, however, remain the same.

without explanation—"that nevertheless the parallelism seems valuable as proof." [22] His chapter on *Sir Thomas Wyatt* is an object lesson in futility, for the text which he so painfully analyzes is an extremely corrupt memorial reconstruction.[23] Pierce offers his dissertation to the public "not as a piece of hackwork, but as a sympathetic, although necessarily accurate, study of two great poets" [24] (the *although* is an endearing touch). His conclusions on the Dekker-Webster collaborations, arrived at on so insecure a methodological foundation, were accepted by Lucas in what remains, for want of a successor, the standard edition of Webster.

In the second monograph, *The Authorship of Timon of Athens* (1910), Ernest Hunter Wright essays to distinguish between Shakespeare's share in the play and the interpolations of an unknown but recognizably inferior hand. Wright's scene-by-scene analysis of *Timon* is lavishly detailed, and of course he provides the tables, by now almost *de rigueur,* of verse characteristics: feminine endings, run-on lines, rhymes, and irregular lines. They inspire little confidence in Wright's fantastic hypothesis that the chief dramatist for the King's men produced a drama of insufficient length—approximately seventeen hundred lines—which some unidentified hack was then commissioned to eke out. Wright never seriously considers the possibility, favored by present-day scholarship, that *Timon* is not in fact a composite work but Shakespeare's unaided draft of a play which he abandoned.

Editions of plays and playwrights during these years are concerned often enough with matters canonical. F. S. Boas, in his *Works of Kyd* (1901), warily sifts problems

22. *Collaboration,* p. 31.
23. See *The Dramatic Works of Thomas Dekker,* ed. Fredson Bowers (Cambridge, 1953), I, 399.
24. *Collaboration,* Preface, unpaged.

which, before and since, have prompted much reckless conjecture; he prints *Soliman and Perseda,* which few students of Kyd now accept as authentic. In his edition of Lyly (1902), R. W. Bond suggests, with undisguised lack of conviction, that *The Maid's Metamorphosis* is a Day comedy patched up by Lyly; at the same time he ushers into the canon a half-dozen entertainments on the basis of dubious parallels. Churton Collins attempts to justify on stylistic grounds the inclusion of *George a Greene* in his edition of Greene's *Plays and Poems* (1905). In a substantial introduction to *The Shakespeare Apocrypha* (1908), Tucker Brooke leans towards Boyle's division of *The Two Noble Kinsmen;* on the other plays he is much more prudent. The dependably undependable Morris, editing *All's Lost by Lust* and *The Spanish Gypsy* for the Belles-Lettres Series (1908), undertakes a preposterous line-by-line division of the latter play between Middleton and Rowley. R. M. Alden deals more intelligently with the problem of Beaumont-Fletcher collaboration and furnishes a comparative view in his Belles-Lettres edition (1910) of *The Knight of the Burning Pestle* and *A King and No King.* The same problem occupies the several editors of the Variorum *Beaumont and Fletcher* (1904–12), abandoned after four volumes and twenty plays. After rejecting Chapman's claim to *Alphonsus, Emperor of Germany,* Parrott nevertheless includes the play in his edition of the *Tragedies* (1910). Of more far-reaching significance than the appearance of these individual editions is the inauguration in the same decade of two large-scale scholarly ventures concerned with the publication of texts.

In 1902, Willy Bang, Professor of English Philology at the University of Louvain, issued the first installment of *Materialien zur Kunde des älteren englischen Dramas,* a collection which was to achieve, in its two series, seventy volumes of documents, concordances, monographs, and editions of plays.[25] Among the early publications in the *Materialien* was Bang's edition of *The Queen, or The Excellency of Her Sex* (1906). In a short introduction, he attributed the tragi-comedy, printed anonymously in 1653, to John Ford, and he pointed out general resemblances to the dramatist's accepted work. This evidence Bang supplemented by the detailed citation of parallels in his notes to the text. Greg, reviewing the edition, was unimpressed with the parallels but nevertheless supported the ascription. "It cannot be a case of imitation," he shrewdly observed, "for some of it is Ford at his worst, and that no sane man would imitate." [26] All modern Ford scholars have accepted *The Queen* as his. Bang's success is remarkably similar in its ingredients to Parrott's successful assignment of *Goosecap* to Chapman; both scholars had devoted many years to the close study of their respective dramatists (Bang's interest in Ford harks back to his Gymnasium days), both came to attribution study via editing, and both disdained metrical and other quantitative tests.

Four years after Bang initiated the *Materialien,* A. W. Pollard proposed the formation of the Malone Society to Greg and a small group of dedicated Elizabethan scholars. Pollard pointed out that, although "every generation will need to make its own critical editions to suit its own critical taste, . . . work of permanent utility can be done by placing in the hands of students at large such reproductions of the original textual authorities as

25. The *Materialien* was discontinued in 1914 and resumed in 1927 as *Materials for the Study of the Old English Drama,* under the general editorship of Henry de Vocht. The undertaking is apparently now defunct.

26. *Mod. Lang. Rev.,* III (1908), 292.

may make constant and continuous reference to those originals themselves unnecessary." [27] The Society was established at an inaugural meeting held at University College London on July 30, 1906. In the same year, at the first general meeting, Chambers was elected President, and Greg General Editor. From 1907 until 1914, the Society published annually six volumes of plays or dramatic records. Operations were suspended temporarily from 1915 through 1919 and again from 1940 through 1947; otherwise the Society has maintained a continuous program of publication.

With the passage of the years, Bang's *Materialien* and the Malone Society publications have made accessible a large number of previously unfamiliar plays (e.g., *John of Bordeaux, The Soddered Citizen,* and *The Welsh Embassador,* all first printed by the Society from manuscript), thus providing new materials for the investigator. At a time when firsthand consultation of early texts was often impracticable, and when microfilm facilities were unavailable and Xerox unknown, the service performed by the Malone Society and (to a lesser extent) by the *Materialien* can scarcely be overvalued. That service has, of course, not been limited to the provision of texts of previously unedited plays. Most of the authorship studies noticed thus far in Part Two were based on inaccurate modern reprints, despite the fact that the internal evidence adduced often emphasized the most minute particulars of style.[28] The textual originals went unconsulted, one charitably imagines, because of their inaccessibility. When better editions appeared, responsible

27. Recalled by Greg in "Type-Facsimiles and Others," *The Library,* VI (1926), 321; see also F. P. Wilson, "The Malone Society: The First Fifty Years: 1906–56," Malone Soc. *Collections, Volume IV* (Oxford, 1956), p. 2.
28. See below, Part Three, pp. 169–172.

scholars discovered the inadequacies of the reprints to which they had rather naively trusted. Ashley Thorndike, assigned for review Bang's edition of Chettle and Day's *Blind Beggar of Bednal Green,* the first volume in the *Materialien,* collated the new text with Bullen's and was astonished to find over two hundred textual variants unexplained in the notes to either edition. "Bullen apparently corrects misprints and occasionally alters spelling without comment," Thorndike observed, "and he is presumably less painstaking than Professor Bang in reproducing the original text; but a large number of the variations seem due to grave faults in editing." [29] Such an awakening is salutary: the pity is that so many still slept.

» III «

THE EXACTING EDITORIAL STANDARDS for which we owe so much to Greg, McKerrow, and Pollard were not necessarily carried over to other branches of Elizabethan dramatic scholarship; similar rigor was, for the time, neither demanded nor forthcoming in attribution study. Even the incomparable Greg is in his youthful work vulnerable. Thus, in the commentary to his epoch-making edition of Henslowe's *Diary* (1908), he speaks of *"Edward IV,* on internal evidence, as unquestionably Heywood's." [30] This despite the absence of any record linking Heywood with the Earl of Derby's men, who, according to the title-page of the 1600 quarto, acted the play. Where the conclusive evidence resides, Greg does not reveal—he

---

29. *Mod. Lang. Notes,* XVIII (1903), 82. Bang's edition, although more accurate than Bullen's, is by no means impeccable; see William Peery, "Notes on Bang's Edition of 'The Blind Beggar of Bednal-Green,' " *English Studies,* XXVII (1946), 152–155.

30. *Diary,* II, 173.

80

has scarcely the space—and his unwarranted confidence brings to mind Fleay.[31]

Like others of his generation, Greg did not escape the baleful influence of that great eccentric, with whom he corresponded on a number of points while preparing the *Henslowe*. Greg's lucid analytical intelligence of course prevented him from being blind to the elder scholar's most grievous shortcomings, but much of his early work admittedly stems from the *Chronicle History of the London Stage* and the *Biographical Chronicle of the English Drama*. In his preface to the *Diary*, Part II, he offers homage to his literary godfather. "By means of a number of ingenious, and sometimes daring, arguments, founded upon a singularly minute and at the same time wide examination of the existing evidence," Greg declares, "Mr. Fleay has revolutionized the methods of theatrical history." [32] Revolutions, alas, rarely have entirely beneficent results.

How Greg's acceptance of some of Fleay's assumptions affected, not always for the better, his evaluation of Henslowe and his interpretation of stage history between 1584 and 1613 lies beyond the scope of the present study.[33] But Greg was influenced also by Fleay's assertions regarding authorship and by his identification of plays mentioned in the *Diary* with extant pieces. A single illustration—perhaps the most spectacular—must suffice.

In *Diary* entries between November 21 and December 6, 1599, Henslowe records payments to Day and Haughton for a play variously referred to as *Merry* or *Thomas*

31. Fleay, however, was on this particular issue more cautious than Greg! He questioned whether the play should be assigned to Heywood (*Biographical Chronicle*, I, 288).
32. *Diary*, II, Preface, p. ix.
33. On these questions see Henslowe's *Diary*, ed. Foakes and Rickert (Cambridge, 1961), Introduction, pp. xxv–xl.

Merry or *Beech's Tragedy*.[34] Its subject must have been the sensational murder of Robert Beech by Thomas Merry in Norfolk in 1594. Now, a play entitled *Two Lamentable Tragedies* was published in 1601 with Robert Yarington's name on the title-page and following the "Finis." One of these "Two Tragedies in One," which are dramatized in alternate scenes, deals with the Beech murder; the other is a rendering of the babes in the wood story against an Italian setting. Greg notes that while Day and Haughton were receiving advances from Henslowe for *Merry*, Henry Chettle—according to the *Diary*—was working on the *Orphan's Tragedy*, and Day on an unnamed "Italian tragedy." Greg suggests that the "Italian tragedy" is in fact the *Orphan's Tragedy*, and he goes on to make the "obvious inference" that the printed play combines the latter with *Merry*. It is "evident" that the two plots of the extant work are by different writers, although Greg "cannot trace more than one hand in each as one would expect to from Henslowe's entries." Much matter, he conjectures, must have been dropped when the two Admiral's company plays were welded together, and this matter consisted of the separable underplot which Day had contributed to each work in its original form: "There is certainly no trace of his hand now remaining." Greg rather cavalierly assigns the Merry story to Haughton and the babes in the wood story to Chettle. From still another Henslowe payment he deduces that Chettle effected the amalgamation. The Induction to the *Two Lamentable Tragedies* suits the play as it stands and should therefore be by the putative reviser, but since it "rather resembles the Merry part

34. For the relevant entries, see the *Diary*, ed. Greg, I, ff.65^v–66, 67. Greg discusses the play in his Commentary to the *Diary*, II, 208–209.

in style," Greg is driven to still more elaborate conjectural reconstruction. The Induction, he reasons, originally belonged to *Merry* and was adapted by Chettle to fit the composite tragedy. How did Yarington become associated with the play? He was the scribe whose existence is necessitated by the appearance of the same unusual stage direction in both parts and by peculiarities of spelling consistent throughout the two plays.[35]

This fantastically complicated chain of speculation owes a good deal, as one would suspect, to Fleay (*Biographical Chronicle,* II, 285–286); but Greg surpasses his predecessor in ingenuity. Greg's reconstruction of the history of the *Two Lamentable Tragedies* was effectively challenged by his friend, Robert Adger Law.[36] Law pointed to stylistic similarities between the two stories of the play, and he noted a common indebtedness to *King Leir.* He took polite issue with Greg's interpretation of the Henslowe entries—an interpretation which may be described, not unfairly, as arbitrary. Allusions in the Induction seem to imply, moreover, that Beech's murder and Merry's execution were recent occurrences rather than events recalled after an interval of five years. Law was right. In the introduction to his edition of Haughton's *Englishmen for My Money* in 1917, A. C. Baugh showed that the *Two Lamentable Tragedies* must have been written before 1598 and therefore could not represent an amalgamation of *Beech's Tragedy* and the

---

35. Greg may have been right in guessing that Yarington was the scribe rather than the author. Bernard M. Wagner later discovered a record of "Robt. Yarrington jun^r." in the *Catalogue . . . of the Company of Scrivenors* ("Robert Yarrington," *Mod. Lang. Notes,* XLV [1930], 147–148). Apart from this possible identification, we know nothing about Yarington.

36. "Yarington's 'Two Lamentable Tragedies,'" *Mod. Lang. Rev.,* V (1910), 167–177.

Orphan's Tragedy of 1599–1600. Greg, reviewing Baugh's edition, admitted his error.[37] The episode does not augur well. If the greatest Elizabethan scholar of his generation could wander down so strange and deviously winding a path, what, one may ask, is reasonably to be expected of lesser mortals?

» IV «

"THE SCHOLAR who commits himself on the authorship of an anonymous old play takes his life in his hands," Stuart P. Sherman declared in 1908; "there are few more daring things that he can do, and there is no more searching test of his scholarship." [38] Sherman was himself up to nothing more audacious than a demonstration of support for Bang's ascription of *The Queen* to Ford. His melodramatic pronouncement seems uncalled for; the fatality rate (at least so far as reputations were concerned) was not so high as to discourage many daredevils. Although a few dissidents grumbled about evidence that was merely internal, the journals, as we have seen, were receptive to articles relying upon such evidence. The Edwardian years, regarded by many today with a not entirely justifiable nostalgia, offered golden prospects for the attribution student. With conditions so favorable, it was desirable—perhaps inevitable—that someone should furnish a guide to the opportunities.

That ambitious task was undertaken by E. H. C. Oliphant. An Australian scholar then residing in London, Oliphant (as noted in Part One of this study) had contributed a series of articles on Beaumont and Fletcher to *Englische Studien* in the nineties. He had published

37. *Mod. Lang. Rev.*, XIII (1918), 101.
38. "A New Play by John Ford," *Mod. Lang. Notes*, XXIII, 246.

an unmemorable novel, *The Mesmerist,* and most recently had engaged in some unspectacular Shakespeare disintegration in *Modern Language Review.* Now, in the January 1911 number of *Modern Philology* he published a long article, "Problems of Authorship in Elizabethan Dramatic Literature." In it Oliphant surveys the land and finds it good.

His coverage takes in the period from the publication of Whetstone's *Promos and Cassandra* in 1578 until the closing of the theaters in 1642. Within these chronological limits and restricting himself to plays in English exclusive of translations, Oliphant finds himself faced with a corpus of roughly six hundred dramatic or quasi-dramatic works. His object is "not to attempt the settlement of questions of authorship, but to state what those questions are, and to classify them according to the value of the external evidence." [39] Unfortunately, Oliphant has little aptitude for classifying—a fairly serious limitation in a classifier. His categories, subjectively rather than logically determined, overlap. Too numerous for his needs, they dwindle from thirteen in the essay proper to eight in the summing up! There are other weaknesses. Some of the plays on which Oliphant must comment he has not read, as he freely confesses. Repeatedly he breaks his pledge not to obtrude his own views. Yet, despite these and other weaknesses, the article provides a valuable comprehensive view of the subject and—because of its very lack of sophistication—equally valuable insight into the mood and mentality of the investigator as the century entered its second decade.

Oliphant's opinions sometimes have a symptomatic interest; on other occasions he speaks with the voice of prophecy. Of "plays unclaimed but having possibilities

39. "Problems of Authorship," p. 413.

of specific authorship which have first to be considered," he gives pride of place to *Sir Thomas More:* "This drama is particularly worthy of attention, for, though scarcely a great play, [it] has some magnificent passages." [40] He discerns a likeness to Shakespeare's manner in the great insurrection scene, and suggests that the drama is of composite authorship. In the category of "plays claimed on altogether inadequate grounds," he bestows extravagant praise on *Arden of Feversham.* "As one of the finest and most effective tragedies of the period," Oliphant writes, "there is scarcely any Elizabethan play more recommendable than *Arden* to anyone wishing to consider questions of authorship; but he must first steep himself in Marlowe, Kyd, Greene, and their contemporaries." [41] He gives Shakespeare a larger share in *Edward III* than that claimed for him by previous conjecturists. Middleton, he believes, is responsible for *The Second Maiden's Tragedy,* with possible help from the author of *The Revenger's Tragedy.* Of the latter work Oliphant remarks:

To accept Tourneur as the writer of *The Revenger's Tragedy* we have to suppose that he alone of the Elizabethan dramatists did not develop but absolutely revolutionized his manner of writing. That the author of this tragedy was not a one-play dramatist may be inferred by his mastery of his medium, but I know of no one among the named writers of the time to whom I would attribute it, unless it be Middleton, to whose verse alone the swing of the verse of *The Revenger's Tragedy* makes some approximation. . . . I prefer, however, to consider *The Revenger's Tragedy* as the greatest work of its period of that prolific writer "Anon," and look upon the establishment of the identity of the author as one of the chief problems to be tackled by students of Elizabethan drama.[42]

40. *Ibid.,* p. 416. See the discussion of *More* below, pp. 104–107.
41. *Ibid.,* p. 420.
42. *Ibid.,* pp. 427–428.

Thus Oliphant launches the most durable authorship controversy of the century—a controversy in which he was himself later to play a major role.

Elsewhere in his essay Oliphant questions Webster's part-authorship of *A Cure for a Cuckold,* published in 1661 as *"Written* by John Webster *and* William Rowley." He is unconventional enough to call for a reexamination of the orthodox attributions of *1* and *2 Tamburlaine* to Marlowe, *Alphonsus, King of Aragon* to Greene, and *Fortune by Land and Sea* to Heywood and Rowley. He suggests that the initials "T. D." on the title-page of *The Bloody Banquet* stand for Thomas Dekker—a motion which no responsible scholar has seen fit to second. Other titles in Oliphant's ample list of recommendations for study include *Swetnam the Woman-Hater, The Rare Triumphs of Love and Fortune, 1 Richard II (Woodstock), The Wisdom of Doctor Dodypoll, The Taming of a Shrew, George a Greene, A Match at Midnight,* and *Thorney Abbey.* About the authorship of most of these plays we are today, fifty years afterward, little the wiser. A few still call for more adequate attention than they have received—most notably, *A Match at Midnight, Thorney Abbey,* and the collection to which the latter belongs (the *Gratiae Theatrales* of 1662, including also *Grim the Collier of Croydon* and *The Marriage Broker*).[43]

With the optimism usually associated with pioneers, Oliphant manages not to foresee the hazards of the quest and the stubborn infertility of the promised soil. He sets forth a vast array of authorship problems and, with the delicious casualness of a departed age, leaves their

---

43. The collection is described by Alfred Harbage in "A Choice Ternary: Belated Issues of Elizabethan Plays," *Notes and Queries,* CLXXXIII (1942), 32–34.

solution to "students with time and inclination for such pursuits." [44] It never occurs to Oliphant that some problems may be insoluble. Nor does he envisage methodological difficulties; nowhere in his essay does he indicate an awareness of the need to work out general principles according to which the investigation of specific cases might more safely proceed.[45] Fleay and the New Shaksperians had at least occasionally worried about such matters.

» V «

WITH SO MANY OPPORTUNITIES beckoning and so agreeable an atmosphere for conjecture, it is little wonder that a number of students found time and inclination for attribution studies. Oliphant himself turned to *Arden* and other plays, and brought to completion his *magnum opus* on the Beaumont and Fletcher corpus; his name will reappear in this narrative. No scholar of the Golden Age, however, applied himself to authorship problems with more single-minded devotion than H. Dugdale Sykes. Using *Notes and Queries* as his principal outlet, he produced a steady flow of articles in which he sought to identify the writers of anonymous plays or to work out the shares of known participants in collaborations. His principal studies were gathered together in two volumes: *Sidelights on Shakespeare* (1919) and the more influential *Sidelights on Elizabethan Drama* (1924).

The former was published by A. H. Bullen's Shakespeare Head Press. Bullen, who provided an appreciative preface, saw Sykes as a dispassionate seeker after truth: fair-minded, sincere, a persuasive attorney; he was

44. "Problems of Authorship," p. 413.
45. See below, Part Three, p. 148.

contrasted favorably with the wayward Fleay. The methods which won Bullen's admiration stand clearly revealed in his first book, and Sykes never thereafter altered his course in subjecting fifty plays to diligent examination. Although he mentions external evidence and larger issues of style and matter (usually in the introductory paragraphs to his essays), Sykes depends mainly on a minutely detailed analysis of language. In isolating the elements that go to the making of a style, he focuses on rare words, on common words employed with exceptional frequency, on characteristic word formations (e.g., polysyllabic nouns ending in -*tion*), and on grammatical constructions (e.g., omission of the relative pronoun). Above all he trusts to parallels of phraseology and thought, attaching supreme importance to those parallels in which the two coincide. There can be little doubt that Sykes qualifies as leader of what Greg called "the parallelographic school." That Bullen should so enthusiastically champion his cause is perhaps surprising in view of the elder scholar's previous skepticism regarding just the sort of evidence that constituted Sykes's stock in trade. "The testimony of parallel passages," Bullen remarked in 1887 in the introduction to his edition of *Arden of Feversham,* "is like the evidence given by experts in handwriting before a jury: it is always expected, it is always produced, and it is seldom regarded." [46] One of Sykes's papers in *Sidelights on Shakespeare* concerns *Arden,* which (following Crawford) he assigns to Kyd—largely on the evidence of parallels. Bullen accepted the argument. Such were Sykes's powers of advocacy!

His first book is curiously misnamed. Of the seven plays discussed, Sykes finds Shakespeare's hand in but one, *Pericles,* which he conceives to be Wilkins' work

46. *Arden of Feversham,* ed. Bullen (London, 1887), p. xiii.

revised and expanded by Shakespeare. To Wilkins he also gives the *Yorkshire Tragedy*. Reviving the justly neglected theories of Boyle, Sykes assigns *The Two Noble Kinsmen* and *Henry VIII* to Massinger and Fletcher. (The editors of the First Folio, he holds, perpetrated a deliberate fraud in admitting the latter play.) Finally, Sykes argues that *King Leir* and both parts of *The Troublesome Reign of King John* are the work of Peele.

In *Sidelights on Elizabethan Drama* Sykes continued his relentless inquisition. As in the previous volume, several essays are given over not to promoting new authorial candidates, but to strengthening familiar hypotheses; Sykes is no revolutionary. He supports Peele's title to *Alphonsus, Emperor of Germany,* Webster's to *Appius and Virginia,* Ford's to *The Queen.* He follows Collier, Fleay, and Swinburne in identifying *Lust's Dominion,* published as Marlowe's in 1657, with *The Spanish Moor's Tragedy* for which Henslowe paid Dekker, Haughton, and Day in 1599–1600. If Sykes strikes out on his own in proposing, in his most elaborate paper, that *Timon of Athens* is Shakespeare's "imperfect recast" of a Day-Middleton original, his views about the play are no more extravagant than those which earlier disintegrators had less skillfully argued. The remaining essays, however, offer more novel theories. Sykes maintains that *The Fair Maid of the Inn* (printed in the Beaumont and Fletcher folios) is by Webster and Massinger, that *Anything for a Quiet Life* (published as Middleton's) is mostly Webster's, and that *The Spanish Gypsy* (assigned on the title-page to Middleton and Rowley) is substantially the work of Ford. In his last article Sykes traces the spoor of Nathan Field (whom he confuses with Nathaniel) in three Beaumont and

Fletcher pieces: *Four Plays in One, The Queen of Corinth,* and *The Knight of Malta.* An appendix summarizes findings with regard to thirty-six additional plays, on sixteen of which Sykes had published articles.

His productivity tapered off after the second collection. He wrote an occasional review. In 1925 he supported Heywood's claim to *Edward IV,* and in 1926 he attempted to disentangle the shares of Ford, Dekker, and Rowley in *The Witch of Edmonton;* both articles appeared in *Notes and Queries.* Sykes's last essay, on *George a Greene,* in *Modern Language Review* in 1931, was designed to strengthen the case for Greene.[47] He died in 1932.

In its day Sykes's work impressed the impressionable and won the cautious approval of many of the best judges, among them Boas, Chambers, Greg, and Dover Wilson. A notable exception was Baldwin Maxwell who, in a major review-article, leveled all his ammunition at a single vulnerable target: Sykes's flimsy case for Massinger's part-authorship of *Henry VIII.*[48] But most of those unprepared to accept all of Sykes's conclusions paid tribute nevertheless to his knowledge and retentive memory, his sobriety and critical discernment. His ability to marshal data and present the dry results of his labors with succinctness, lucidity, and force earned just praise.[49]

---

47. A letter by Sykes to J. Le Gay Brereton citing additional Greene parallels was published posthumously ("Robert Greene and *George a Greene, the Pinner of Wakefield," Rev. of Eng. Stud.,* IX [1933], 189–190).

48. *Mod. Phil.,* XXIII (1926), 365–372; reprinted in Maxwell, *Studies in Beaumont, Fletcher, and Massinger* (Chapel Hill, N.C., 1939), pp. 63–73.

49. Thus, William Dinsmore Briggs, reviewing *Sidelights on Elizabethan Drama* in *Modern Language Notes,* wrote: "Of the diligence and acuteness which he displays in assembling his materials and of his ingenuity in arranging them clearly and forcibly, students of the Elizabethan drama hardly need to be reminded" (XLII [1927], 545).

Unlike Fleay before him, Sykes gives little appearance of eccentricity. He issues no manifestoes; he does not brandish the magical word *science*. But he does share with Fleay what may be described as the vocabulary of confidence; Sykes favors such terms as *conclusive, unquestionable, indubitable, unequivocal* and *unmistakably.* He is, however, tactful in their deployment. Austerely surrounded by word-lists and parallel passages, they contribute to the persuasive effect.

Yet even a superficial probing of Sykes's work raises disturbing questions. Why, one wonders, did he not in 1924 revise his 1914 *Appius and Virginia* paper to take into account the appearance of Clark's article on the play's authorship? [50] Should Sykes have reprinted his 1920 paper on Samuel Rowley without acknowledging the important point, made subsequently, that four of the plays concerned were probably not, in their extant form, connected with the Admiral's men—the only company with which Rowley had any known association? If in 1924 Sykes felt that Ford was implicated in *The Fair Maid of the Inn,* why did he permit his 1915 article to stand unaltered? [51] And is he not unjustified in interpreting as authorship clues the borrowings in that play from Sidney's *Arcadia* and the 1615 Overbury *Characters* —sources readily available to any writer? In explaining away as Websterian imitation the presence in *Appius and Virginia* of unusual words employed by Heywood (e.g., *infallid, strage,* and *thrill* in the sense of *hurl*), surely Sykes is opening the door to doubts about the validity of his method? The same problem arises with *Alphonsus,* where he shrugs off evidence for traces of

50. Arthur M. Clark, "The Authorship of 'Appius and Virginia,' " *Mod. Lang. Rev.,* XVI (1921), 1–17.
51. *Sidelights on Elizabethan Drama,* p. 150.

other playwrights by remarking: "but then Peele was an imitative writer." [52] This sword has two edges. Several critics, most notably Greg, expressed uneasiness, but their doubts did not yet impel them to question whether "Mr. Sykes's really brilliant qualities"—the phrase is Greg's —were in truth so brilliant.

By 1932 the case had altered. In a remarkable paper read before the Bibliographical Society on February 15 of that year, Miss M. St. Clare Byrne picked Sykes apart with devastating effect.[53] Faced with the task of editing Chettle and Munday's *Downfall* and *Death of Robert Earl of Huntingdon,* she had consulted Sykes's essay on these plays and submitted his evidence to negative checks in order to see whether the words, images, and phrases cited as characteristic of Chettle or Munday were duplicated in the writings of their contemporaries. She found that the parallels, taken one by one, "are either cancelled by the negative test, or else their significance is so whittled away as to make them practically valueless." [54] Sykes's method, she discovered, was methodless. His arrangement of material was misleading, he was inconsistent, he violated logical imperatives, and at crucial junctures he abandoned his objective techniques for simple impressionism. Sykes had no opportunity to reply—he died while Miss Byrne's paper was in proof—but he could scarcely have effectively answered the unanswerable. His authorship attributions, except where he confirms assignments already likely on other grounds, have failed to stick.

52. *Ibid.,* p. 96.
53. "Bibliographical Clues in Collaborate Plays," published in *The Library,* 4th Ser., XIII(1932), 21–48.
54. *Ibid.,* p. 28.

» VI «

OTHER PLAYERS swelled the scene. In William Wells, a friend of Sykes, the parallelographic school produced one of its more colorful practitioners. In a Nissen hut in France during the First World War, Wells turned to the *Timon* question. The play, he decided, was early Middleton revised by Shakespeare. Having sorted out this puzzle to his satisfaction, Wells moved to the next play in his borrowed edition of Shakespeare's tragedies. "It was *Julius Caesar,*" he records, "and I had not read very far when I found myself listening to the voice of Francis Beaumont." [55] In 1920 Wells published his findings on *Timon* in an article that moved Sykes to modify his views.[56] Then, in the afterhours of days regretfully devoted to gainful employment, he pursued his investigation of *Julius Caesar*. Libraries, Wells complained, cater in their hours only to the leisured; a few furtive visits excepted, he managed without them. Determined to bring out his book, he set it in type with his own hands, directly as he wrote. Wells delivered his work to the stereotyper two pages at a time, after which he distributed type and continued. It is hardly surprising, under the circumstances, that one of Wells's later chapters is devoted entirely to his own errors and omissions. The completed book he dedicated "(without authority) to the Shade of Francis Beaumont." One hopes the tribute won recognition in the proper quarter, but it is to be feared that the spirit which spoke to Wells and beckoned him towards—and over—the brink was a goblin damned.

55. William Wells, *The Authorship of Julius Caesar* (London, 1923), Foreword, p. [v].
56. Wells, " 'Timon of Athens,' " *Notes and Queries,* 12th Ser., VI (1920), 266–269; Sykes, *Sidelights on Elizabethan Drama,* p. 19.

Wells concluded that *Julius Caesar* was an old Marlowe play revised by Beaumont and then overhauled by Shakespeare, who contributed only the opening fifty-seven lines.[57] In an appendix Wells argued that *The Faithful Shepherdess* is a Beaumont and Fletcher collaboration. Wells produced several articles besides the *Timon* piece. In 1921 he maintained that *The Birth of Merlin* was largely the work of Beaumont and Fletcher, and in 1928 he urged Chapman's part-authorship of *The Bloody Brother*.[58] Years later, in 1939, another voice whispered in his ear, and in a series of papers he proclaimed Kyd's presence in a number of plays.[59]

The abundance of articles in the second and third decades of the century suggests exceptional interest in authorship problems. The evidence on which investigators relied consisted—by and large—of general resemblances of matter and manner, metrical statistics, and phraseological parallels; increasingly the parallel-passage test tended to displace verse tests as the favored tool. A bare enumeration of titles will suffice to indicate the range of exploration and also the persistence of familiar obsessions: Joseph Quincy Adams, Jr., *"Every Woman in Her Humor* and *The Dumb Knight," Modern Philology* (1913), "The Authorship of *A Warning for Fair Women," PMLA* (1913), and "Captaine Thomas Stukeley," *Journal of English and Germanic Philology* (1916); C. E. Andrews, "The Authorship of *The Late*

57. For these findings Wells was congratulated by J. M. Robertson, who was, however, unwilling to concede that Shakespeare might have written lines 1–57 (*Shakespeare Canon, Part II,* Preface, pp. xix–xx). On Robertson, see below, pp. 107–119.
58. " 'The Birth of Merlin,' " *Mod. Lang. Rev.,* XVI (1921), 129–137; " 'The Bloody Brother,' " *Notes and Queries,* CLIV (1928), 6–9.
59. "The Authorship of 'King Leir,' " *Notes and Queries,* CLXXVII (1939), 434–438; "Thomas Kyd and the Chronicle History," *Notes and Queries,* CLXXVIII (1940), 218–224, 238–243; " 'Alphonsus, Emperor of Germany,' " *Notes and Queries,* CLXXIX (1940), 218–223, 236–240.

Lancashire Witches," *Modern Language Notes* (1913); A. H. Cruickshank, "Massinger and *The Two Noble Kinsmen,"* Elizabethan Literary Society Lecture (1922); Cyrus L. Day, "Thomas Randolph's Part in the Authorship of *Hey for Honesty,"* *PMLA* (1926); W. D. Dunkel, "The Authorship of *The Puritan,"* *PMLA* (1930); Walter Graham, "The *Cardenio-Double Falsehood* Problem," *Modern Philology* (1916); Henry David Gray, "Greene as a Collaborator," *Modern Language Notes* (1915); "Heywood's *Pericles,* Revised by Shakespeare," *PMLA* (1925), "Shakespeare's Share in Titus Andronicus," *Philological Quarterly* (1926), " 'Appius and Virginia': by Webster and Heywood," *Studies in Philology* (1927), and " '*A Cure for a Cuckold'* by Heywood, Rowley and Webster," *Modern Language Review* (1927); F. L. Jones, *"The Trial of Chivalry,* a Chettle Play," *PMLA* (1926); Marjorie H. Nicolson, "The Authorship of *Henry the Eighth,"* *PMLA* (1922); Oliphant, " 'The Bloodie Banquet'. A Dekker-Middleton Play," *Times Literary Supplement* (1925), "The Authorship of 'The Revenger's Tragedy,' " *Studies in Philology* (1926), and "Marlowe's Hand in 'Arden of Feversham': A Problem for Critics," *New Criterion* (1926); Parrott, "The Authorship of *Two Italian Gentlemen,"* *Modern Philology* (1915), "Shakespeare's Revision of 'Titus Andronicus,' " *Modern Language Review* (1919), and "The Problem of Timon of Athens," *Shakespeare Association Papers* (1923); and Albert W. Upton, "The Authorship of *The Woman Hater,"* *Philological Quarterly* (1930). The list might be extended.

More ambitious and hence more interesting are the articles summarizing and evaluating knowledge of a writer's entire *œuvre:* Tucker Brooke, "The Marlowe

Canon," *PMLA* (1922); T. Larsen, "The Canon of Peele's Works," *Modern Philology* (1928), and "The Growth of the Peele Canon," *The Library* (1930); and G. C. Moore Smith, "The Canon of Randolph's Dramatic Works," *Review of English Studies* (1925).

Still more arresting are the few studies making use of new or comparatively untried tests. Of these the first and perhaps most important is Willard Farnham's "Colloquial Contractions in Beaumont, Fletcher, Massinger, and Shakespeare as a Test of Authorship" in *PMLA* in 1916. Farnham suggested that certain linguistic preferences—*t*-contractions (*in't, to't, for't,* etc.), *the*-contractions (*i'th, o'th,* etc.), and *s*-contractions (*on's, in's,* etc.) —had evidential significance, and he applied these criteria to *The Captain, Henry VIII,* and *The Two Noble Kinsmen.* Farnham did not represent himself as a great innovator. Thorndike, in *The Influence of Beaumont and Fletcher on Shakspere* (1901), had devised and employed the *'em-them* test for the purpose of isolating the work of Fletcher, Massinger, and Shakespeare in several plays. In 1905 McKerrow and Greg, while editing plays for the Variorum *Beaumont and Fletcher,* had pointed to Fletcher's preference for *ye,* the more colloquial form of the pronoun *you.* Farnham's investigation stands, however, as the most elaborate and carefully considered attempt up to that time to employ linguistic criteria of authorship. Forty years would pass before the same test was revised, refined, and systematically applied to the whole body of Beaumont and Fletcher's work.[60]

At a meeting of the Bibliographical Society on January

60. In 1930 Helena Franklin Miller employed *has-hath* and *does-doth* tests to distinguish between Shakespeare's work and Massinger's; her article, "The Use of the Third Person Singular of *Have* and *Do* in the Works of Shakespeare and Massinger," *Phil. Quar.,* IX (1930), 373–378, is of no value.

15, 1923, Pollard invited attention to "the possibility of testing attributions of authorship in the case of any writer with whom peculiar habits of spelling can be connected." [61] On the same day Miss Byrne read her paper on "Anthony Munday's Spelling as a Literary Clue." [62] She cited Munday's consistent preference, shown in the autograph manuscripts, for doubled medial *o* in such words as *doone, looue,* and *woorthy.* These unusual spellings support Munday's claim to *Fedele and Fortunio,* the 1584 print of which preserves 101 instances out of a possible 230. They point also to Munday's possible responsibility for *Love and Fortune.* Thus the spelling test may not only strengthen a doubtful attribution but also suggest likely authorial candidates for anonymous works.

In 1932 W. J. Lawrence proposed that an idiosyncrasy of Massinger's punctuation—the use of full stops in stage directions where normally one would expect commas —might help in locating the dramatist's "revising hand" in plays where his presence was suspected on other grounds.[63] But would the printed copy preserve an author's peculiar habits of pointing? Lawrence recognized the danger of "infiltration" by prompter or compositor. He thus raised, however casually, the overwhelming question regarding tests—whether of punctuation, spelling, or linguistic preference—that have the outstanding merit of objectivity. The question will arise again in these pages.

In the same year a mechanical test of a quite different

---

61. Andrew W. Pollard, "Elizabethan Spelling as a Literary and Bibliographical Clue," *The Library,* 4th Ser., IV (1923), 8.

62. Published in *The Library,* 4th Ser., IV (1923), 9–23.

63. "Massinger's Punctuation and What It Reveals," *The Criterion,* XI (1932), 214–221; reprinted in Lawrence, *Those Nut-Cracking Elizabethans* (London, 1935), pp. 194–205.

nature was applied to Massinger by F. L. Jones.[64] Jones counted blank verse lines ending in the insignificant words *of* and *to* in 172 plays by 33 known and several anonymous dramatists. He found that Massinger favored *of* and *to* terminations (even at the expense of splitting prepositional phrases), but that other dramatists (for example, Fletcher) disdained them. Preference or abhorrence, however, was not always so clear cut. Jones administered his test to plays which Massinger supposedly collaborated on or revised, and also to so-called "doubtful works" (e.g., *Two Noble Kinsmen*). The test is admittedly valueless for anonymous plays, and Jones did not claim more for his figures than that they were "suggestive." He concludes with a modesty which, under the circumstances, is entirely appropriate: "Alone, such evidence can never be convincing; with other metrical tests, qualities of style, ideas, and methods of phrasing, the data of the *of* and *to* test may be found useful as corroborative proof."[65]

Authorship problems of necessity continued to occupy editors. Parrott, in his edition of Chapman's *Comedies* (1914), attempted to work out the dramatist's part in *Eastward Ho;* he discussed and printed *Goosecap* and, while denying Chapman's involvement, *The Ball*. In an edition of the anonymous *Charlemagne* (1920), Schoell produced many parallels to support the view, first expressed by Bullen, that the play is by Chapman; but Schoell's elaborate case has won little acceptance.[66] Wilhelmina P. Frijlinck, in her edition of *Barnavelt* (1920), divided the anonymous manuscript tragedy between Massinger and Fletcher, as others before her had

64. "An Experiment with Massinger's Verse," *PMLA*, XLVII (1932), 727–740.
65. *Ibid.*, p. 740.
66. See below, Part Three, p. 173.

done. In 1926 Julia Hamlet Harris defined the shares of Chapman, Jonson, and Marston in *Eastward Ho* with a precision that the evidence, however amply presented, did not warrant. F. L. Lucas' *Complete Works of John Webster* (1927) is misnamed, for the three Webster-Dekker collaborations are omitted; swayed by Sykes, however, Lucas compensated for his omissions by including two plays with which the dramatist is doubtfully associated: *Anything for a Quiet Life* and *The Fair Maid of the Inn*. In an edition of Tourneur's *Works* (n.d., 1929?), Allardyce Nicoll contributed to the swelling controversy over *The Revenger's Tragedy* by defending Tourneur's claim. Rollins and Tannenbaum reaffirmed Randolph's title to *The Drinking Academy* (1930).

Comprehensive studies of individual dramatists became more numerous during this period. Those in which canonical problems received more than passing notice included C. M. Gayley, *Beaumont the Dramatist* (1914); Rupert Brooke, *John Webster and the Elizabethan Drama* (1916); A. H. Cruickshank, *Philip Massinger* (1920); and A. M. Clark, *Thomas Heywood, Playwright and Miscellanist* (1931).

The monographs of these decades sometimes make for curious reading today. In a dubious act of piety, Tucker Brooke offered up the *Contention* and *True Tragedy* at the shrine of his idol Marlowe (*The Authorship of the Second and Third Parts of "King Henry VI,"* 1912). Alexander's *Shakespeare's Henry VI and Richard III* (1929), already mentioned, would serve in future to curtail—if by no means to eliminate—such misplaced ascriptional zeal. The shadows of Fleay, Boyle, and the young Oliphant fall across the pages of Maurice Chelli's *Étude sur la collaboration de Massinger avec Fletcher et son groupe*, published posthumously in

1926 but completed by 1914; Chelli trusts too much to metrical tests in a study notable for its Gallic clarity of organization. More noteworthy is *The Plays of Beaumont and Fletcher: An Attempt to Determine Their Respective Shares and the Shares of Others* (1927) by Oliphant himself. This five-hundred-page book covering the whole ground—fifty-nine plays in all—deserves a closer look.

When Oliphant's crowning achievement, almost forty years in the making, appeared, he was praised for his learning, integrity, and openmindedness, for his acute sensibility, and for the unwavering dedication with which he had pursued his task to a successful termination. The book indeed reflects these admirable qualities, but it has also some eccentricities which are less attractive. Oliphant mars his first chapter by stridently attacking the conservative position of Sir Edmund Chambers. Oliphant insists that no personal grievance moves him—his wrath has been aroused by Chambers' sneers at Fleay—but for once Oliphant either deceives himself or is less than candid; there can be little doubt of the personal character of the onslaught or of the essential incompatibility of his position with that of Chambers.[67] The attack, in the course of which Oliphant makes the quaint suggestion that Chambers is not a scholar, fails to convince. Then there is

67. Oliphant quotes Chambers' unfavorable judgment on his evidence for dating *The Woman's Prize* (*Plays of Beaumont and Fletcher*, p. 151). As early as 1908 Chambers had remarked, after summarizing the conclusions of Oliphant and several other disintegrators on the authorship of *The Laws of Candy:* "I do not propose to enter further into this welter of critical opinion than by disclaiming any confidence in the methods by which it is achieved" (Variorum *Beaumont and Fletcher,* III, 469). In *The Elizabethan Stage* he refers slightingly to Oliphant's unsupported conjectures (III, 218). Oliphant could hardly have been unmindful of this disparagement, and he appears to be disingenuous in claiming, "[I] have no particular reason to object to any mention he [Chambers] has made of my work" (*Plays of Beaumont and Fletcher,* p. 11).

Oliphant's rather startling confession that the work on which he rested his reputation was written "under enormous disadvantages, far away from my books"; [68] hence the meager list of authorities cited in the "Bibliographical Note."

But more fundamentally disabling is the essential subjectivism of his entire method. Oliphant writes:

It is not by the mental or the moral or the dramatic that we may best judge, but by the literary—the language employed (vocabulary of word and phrase), the form into which that language is put (that is to say, the construction of the sentences), the facture of the verse into which those sentences are moulded (that is to say, the outward and obvious qualities of it, such as the frequency of rhyme, the proportion of double endings, and the percentage of end-stopt lines), and the indefinite music that permeates it all (the rise and fall of the melody, proceeding one hardly knows whence, but mainly doubtless from the distribution of stresses). This last may well be the most subtle, the most elusive, the most insecure, the most perilous, of these four means; but the importance of it is enormous. [69]

Of the last test, which admits of no tabulation of results, Oliphant makes full use, although he does not ignore more conventional criteria, such as the *ye–you* test. *The Plays of Beaumont and Fletcher* is, therefore, not a work of objective, disciplined scholarship, but of avowed impressionism, however rationalized with tangible evidence.

Oliphant frankly prefers Beaumont to Fletcher, who

68. *Plays of Beaumont and Fletcher*, p. 524. This state of affairs becomes the more curious in view of Oliphant's similar admission in his 1892 article on Beaumont and Fletcher (*Englische Studien*, XVI, 186). The latter confession prompted Boyle to ask, reasonably enough, "how come Mr. Oliphant to write such a paper without having a copy of Massinger at his side?" ("Mr. Oliphant on Beaumont and Fletcher," *Englische Studien*, XVIII [1893], 293). Oliphant appears to have been without access to his books for some time.

69. *Plays of Beaumont and Fletcher*, pp. 30–31.

"delights to wallow in the mud," [70] and this personal bias leads him, no doubt unconsciously, to discern the hand of his hero in a score of plays, as opposed to the dozen or less usually assigned him by the disintegrators. This despite the fact that the Beaumont-Fletcher collaboration presumably lasted no more than five years (Beaumont retired from the stage by 1613), and despite Sir Aston Cokayne's lines on the 1647 collection of thirty-four plays:

> that whole
> Volume of plays being almost every one
> After the death of *Beaumont* writ.[71]

Oliphant produces other oddities. His delicately attuned ear leads him to detect Shakespeare and Fletcher in Theobald's *Double Falsehood*. Influenced by Wells, he finds Beaumont and Fletcher (as well as Rowley) in *The Birth of Merlin* and Beaumont and Marlowe (in addition to Shakespeare) in *Julius Caesar*. Of this last aberration Parrott remarked, "It can not but make the judicious grieve to observe that so brilliant and, as a rule, so independent, an investigator . . . as [E. H. C.] Oliphant should have allowed himself to be misled by the rash assumptions and incorrect statements of such a sciolist as William Wells." [72] To which, amen.

At the same time it must in fairness be said that Oliphant does not ignore external evidence, that he customarily gives the reasons for his opinions, and that on many

70. *Ibid.*, p. 41. The onslaught against Fletcher is continuous, and Oliphant acknowledges that the dramatist's methods inspire him with resentment (p. 39). All of Fletcher's comedy heroes and heroines "are alike despicable and disgusting" (p. 43n).

71. *Poems by Sir Aston Cokaine*, ed. A. E. Cokayne (Congleton, 1877), p. 103. Sykes points to this passage in an important notice of Oliphant's book in *Rev. of Eng. Stud.*, IV (1928), 456–463.

72. "Marlowe, Beaumont, and *Julius Caesar*," *Mod. Lang. Notes*, XLIV (1929), 69.

plays (e.g., *The False One, The Knight of Malta, The Lover's Progress*) he is in general accord with other investigators. Always willing to modify a conclusion in the light of reason or new evidence, Oliphant subsequently recanted his advocacy of Massinger as reviser of *The Two Noble Kinsmen*, and altered or clarified his views on a number of other plays.[73] Intuitive, erratic, passionately involved in his material, Oliphant remains, despite his limitations, one of the more remarkable figures of the generation after Fleay.

» VII «

ONE CAN HARDLY CONCEIVE of a work more different from Oliphant's huge volume in scope, methods, and effectiveness than the remarkable symposium edited by Pollard in the tercentenary year of the First Folio. *Shakespeare's Hand in the Play of Sir Thomas More* is concerned entirely with the Addition of 147 lines, identified by Greg as hand D, occupying three pages of Harleian manuscript 7368.

Sir Thomas More was first edited by Dyce in 1844. Twenty-seven years later Richard Simpson queried whether Shakespeare's hand was not present in two sections,[74] and in the following year the question was taken up by Spedding.[75] In 1911 Greg's classic Malone Society edition, with its brilliant introduction, provided the basis for all subsequent work. In his monograph on *Shakespeare's Handwriting* (1916), the greatest paleog-

---

73. Oliphant, "The Plays of Beaumont and Fletcher: Some Additional Notes," *Phil. Quar.*, IX (1930), 7–22.

74. "Are There Any Extant MSS. in Shakespeare's Handwriting?" *Notes and Queries*, 4th Ser., VIII (1871), 1–3.

75. "Shakespeare's Handwriting," *Notes and Queries*, 4th Ser., X (1872), 227–228.

rapher of his day, Sir Edward Maunde Thompson, gave his reasons for believing the Addition to be in the dramatist's hand. There the matter rested until 1923 and the appearance of Pollard's collection.

Pollard himself contributed an introductory chapter describing the play and its background and summarizing previous work. Greg discussed the distribution of the hands in *More* and the identification of those labeled S, E, and C. In a masterful essay providing a letter-by-letter paleographical analysis, Thompson compared the hand of D with the six authentic Shakespeare signatures. Of the peculiarities to which he directed attention, most striking is the open *a* formed with a horizontal spur at the back; Thompson could find this spur in no other document of the period save the Addition and Shakespeare's signature No. 3. The two occurrences remain to this day (in Greg's words) "unchallenged and unparalleled." In the essay on bibliographical links contributed by Dover Wilson to the symposium, he assembled correspondences between handwriting characteristics in the three pages and misprints in the Good Quartos; he pointed, moreover, to the extraordinary spelling *scilens* (for *silence*) which occurs in line 50 of the Addition, eighteen times in *2 Henry IV,* and nowhere else during this period.

The final chapter, by R. W. Chambers, deals with correspondences of thought and style between *More* and canonical plays. Drawing chiefly upon *2 Henry VI, Troilus and Cressida,* and the Roman plays, Chambers emphasizes Shakespeare's passionate commitment to the values inherent in the concept of "degree," his equally intense apprehensions regarding chaos, and his complexly ambivalent attitude towards the mob. All these concerns Chambers discovers in the crucial three pages, but he does not merely cite parallels; he explores, rather, "those subtle links of thought by which ideas are associated in one mind." [76] More's metaphoric identification of the mob with a surging flood recalls the "bounded waters" lifting "their bosoms higher than the shores" in *Troilus;* his apocalyptic vision of the consequences of rebellious insolence—his prophecy of a time when "men like ravenous fishes, / Would feed on one another,"—brings to mind the universal wolf devouring himself in the same speech of Ulysses. [77] When Chambers revised and elaborated his paper in 1931, he turned once again to these great passages and found in the words of More and Ulysses a still richer and subtler correspondence of thoughts: a sequence moving from the idea of the neglect of degree to the overflowing irresistible waters, thence to infanticide and parricide, and, finally, to actual cannibalism. The same sequence occurs, in part, in *Hamlet, Lear,* and *Coriolanus.* Chambers' final statement on *More* appears as Chapter VII of *Man's Unconquerable Mind* (1939), but the essential argument is present in the first version. Its force, like that of the symbolic flood, is not to be denied.

The varieties of evidence presented in the Pollard collection—paleographic, bibliographical, and critical—converge upon a single destination; all roads lead to Shakespeare. One or two diehards, it is true, cried out in protest. Schücking rejected Chambers' literary evidence, [78]

76. "The Expression of Ideas—Particularly Political Ideas—in the Three Pages, and in Shakespeare," *Shakespeare's Hand in the Play of Sir Thomas More* (Cambridge, 1923), p. 165.

77. Apparently Chambers did not recall that the specific image likening devouring men to the devouring fishes is a commonplace which can be traced to the Church Fathers; see F. P. Wilson, "Shakespeare's Reading," *Shakespeare Survey 3* (Cambridge, 1950), pp. 19–20. This fact perhaps weakens slightly—but only very slightly—an argument based on larger and more complex considerations. Wilson assumes Shakespeare's authorship of the scene in *More.*

78. L. L. Schücking, "Shakespeare and *Sir Thomas More*," *Rev. of Eng. Stud.,* I (1925), 40–59.

and Tannenbaum took issue with the handwriting analysis of Greg and Thompson.[79] In neither instance was the opposition damaging. Support for the thesis of Pollard and company has been overwhelming, as the recent reviews of the *More* problem by Bald and Jenkins testify.[80] Alexander and Sisson included the Addition in their complete Shakespeares, and future editors may be expected to follow suit. The work on *Sir Thomas More* accomplished by a small band of distinguished scholars serves as a stunning vindication of the role of internal evidence in attribution study. Such triumphs have been few, however, and unfortunately overshadowed by the bedlamite antics of the wildmen.

» VIII «

CHIEF AMONG THESE is the Rt. Hon. John Mackinnon Robertson, prince of disintegrators. Alongside this mighty Tribulation, Wells dwindles into a puny Ananias and Sykes qualifies for membership in the established church. Largely self-educated (he left school at thirteen), Robertson began his career as a radical journalist. He entered politics and held high office in the Asquith government, but after defeat in the "coupon" election of 1918, devoted the remainder of his life to writing. His productivity astonishes and disheartens; the spirit quails before the nine columns devoted to Robertson in the British Museum catalogue of printed books. In his writings he ranges over such diverse topics as Home Rule,

79. S. A. Tannenbaum, *"The Booke of Sir Thomas Moore": A Bibliotic Study* (New York, 1927); *Shakspere and "Sir Thomas Moore"* (New York, 1929). Greg spoke of Tannenbaum's "idiotic bibliotics."

80. R. C. Bald, *"The Booke of Sir Thomas More* and Its Problems," *Shakespeare Survey 2* (Cambridge, 1949), pp. 44–61; Harold Jenkins, "A Supplement to Sir Walter Greg's Edition of *Sir Thomas More*," Malone Soc. *Collections, Volume VI* (Oxford, 1961 [1962]), pp. 177–192. See also A. C. Partridge's chapter on *More* in *Orthography in Shakespeare and Elizabethan Drama* (London, 1964), pp. 43–66.

tariff reform, the eight-hour day, Teutonic racial theories, the meaning and mission of liberalism, free trade and free thought, Christ and Krishna, rationalism, the dynamics of religion, and the historical Jesus. Yet Robertson could in 1919 speak with some justice of "a lifetime rather largely devoted to Shakespeare study." [81] That study was his great and final passion. Apart from pamphlets and a symposium on problems of *Macbeth,* he published twelve volumes on Shakespeare over the period of a quarter of a century, from 1905 until 1932. All are concerned directly or indirectly—most of them directly—with questions of authenticity.

"It is not improbable," wrote Robertson's memorialist, Harold Laski, "that his intellectual position will be much higher in the next generation than it was during his lifetime." [82] As praise the statement is equivocal; as forecast it proved incorrect. Robertson is today almost forgotten, remembered if at all as a great eccentric of Shakespearean scholarship and as one whose impact was felt by men of finer sensibility and more searching scholarship. His *Problem of "Hamlet"* (1919) provided the basis for T. S. Eliot's famous essay on *Hamlet* as an artistic failure, and his assault on the Shakespeare canon prompted Chambers' British Academy lecture, "The Disintegration of Shakespeare," which marked a turning point in the modern history of attribution study. Robertson's views on Shakespeare belong to a discarded past; his prolix and ungenial volumes gather dust on library shelves. Yet in his own day he created a considerable stir.

Sealed of the tribe of Fleay, Robertson offered homage to the sage of Upper Tooting in the Prologue to his first onslaught against the Folio: ". . . I must pay a special

81. *The Problem of "Hamlet,"* p. 7.
82. *D.N.B.,* 1931–40, p. 737.

tribute to the works of Mr. Fleay, to whom, though I have ventured on several points to differ from him, I feel I am indebted for more help to the critical study of the Elizabethan drama in general, and of Shakespeare in particular, than I have had from any other writer." [83] Like Fleay, Robertson sees himself as a pioneer. Scornful of mere impressionism, he raises aloft the banner of science; again and again he insists upon the inductive nature of his method. Like Fleay, he is assertive and dogmatic, but unlike his predecessor, he is incapable of hasty withdrawals from untenable positions. Like Fleay, he has a rare familiarity with the old drama, but on a much narrower basis; he knows best the anonymous plays of the decade preceding the publication of *Titus Andronicus* in 1594. He is, moreover, well versed in Shakespearean scholarship and criticism in England, Germany, and America. Unlike his master and guide, however, Robertson never withholds evidence. Rather he documents his arguments with exhausting thoroughness in a clotted prose that lends itself to condensation. "The truth is," Dover Wilson complained in an open letter, "that . . . you have built up a style which is occasionally incomprehensible to a mere 'academic' nourished on the simplicities of Newman and Matthew Arnold, of Lowes Dickinson and Bertrand Russell." [84]

Robertson's humorless pages bristle with contention. Sensitive regarding his lack of formal training, irritably conscious of being outside the academic establishment, he tirelessly controverts the donnish opposition, hurling his thunderbolts against Collins, Nicoll, and Pollard; Wilson, Chambers, and Alexander; the English

---

83. *Did Shakespeare Write "Titus Andronicus"?*, Prologue, p. x.
84. "Idolatry and Scepticism in Shakespearian Studies," *The Criterion*, IX (July, 1930), 631.

Association and the British Academy. Ultimately Robertson sees himself as a lone warrior pitted against the assembled hosts of orthodoxy. He deplores the low intellectual and moral state of Shakespeareology—a Robertson coinage—and revels in disorders in the enemy ranks. "Each academic, of course," he declares, "may repudiate the other. But it remains instructive to note the chaos in which the whole problem [of *Titus*] is left by the academic critics all round." [85] One suspects that Robertson's political radicalism, maintained to the end, informs and directs at least in part his animus against conservative scholarship, an impression that is reinforced by his uncivil treatment of Lord Balfour in the preface to Part III of *The Shakespeare Canon*.

If Robertson's vituperations against professors and academies are wearisome, his penchant for going over the same ground, with modifications and expansions, in successive volumes, also makes for heavy going. Thus he recast *Did Shakespeare Write "Titus Andronicus"?* (1905) as *An Introduction to the Study of the Shakespeare Canon* (1924); in the process the monograph doubled in size. The views he expressed in 1919 in *The Problem of "Hamlet"* (90 pages), Robertson in 1923 restated in *"Hamlet" Once More* (196 pages). Ideas sketched out briefly in *Shakespeare and Chapman* (1917) are developed fully, along with much new matter, in the enormous *Shakespeare Canon* in five volumes (1922–32). In 1930 Robertson summed up his main findings with respect to the entire canon in *The Genuine in Shakespeare*. The rehashings serve at least to make Robertson's productivity more humanly credible.

Despite his vehement denials, Robertson's iconolatrous campaign against the traditionists and their Foliolatry

85. *The Shakespeare Canon, Part IV*, Vol. II, p. 26.

(the unlovely neologisms are his) has its source in a familiar urge to cleanse the Folio of its rubbish—that is, of those lines, speeches, scenes, or whole plays which are aesthetically or morally unacceptable to the critic. Surely Shakespeare must not be held accountable for the degradation of Joan of Arc in *1 Henry VI* or the brutalities of *Titus Andronicus*. Surely he did not write:

> When I was mortal, my anointed body
> By thee was punched full of deadly holes.

Surely he cannot be held responsible for the internal inconsistencies and confusions that occur in even the greatest of his plays. The motive receives explicit statement in *Shakespeare and Chapman:* "So far as I know, no attempt at . . . elimination [of matter from the Folio] has ever touched any save inferior or second-rate work. . . . It is always by his [Shakespeare's] sheer superiority that he is or can be finally discriminated." [86]

Two crucial assumptions underlie Robertson's offensive. Universalizing Henslowe's *modus operandi,* he presupposes a habit of composite playwriting as standard Elizabethan theatrical procedure.[87] Robertson subscribes, secondly, to a theory of continual revision; plays were eked out, tinkered with, or wholly revamped "by way of freshening their appeal to the public, or giving new opportunities to actors." [88] These twin premises, which must sustain the burden of a whole edifice of argument, Robertson makes no real effort to justify in his voluminous pages. Needless to say, both points are highly questionable.

86. Pp. 274–275. In his preface to the first volume of *The Shakespeare Canon,* Robertson refers scornfully to those "excellent persons" who "see no difference of source between Shakespeare's gold and other men's copper . . ." (p. xvi).
87. *Did Shakespeare Write "Titus Andronicus"?*, pp. 30–31.
88. *Ibid.,* p. 31.

Robertson's grounds for rejecting the authority of the Folio are extraordinary. From Greene's deathbed pamphlet and a passage in *The Return from Parnassus,* he reconstructs a feud between the actors and the scholar-dramatists. By printing as Shakespeare's every possible play in their repertory, Heminges and Condell—mere players—were asserting their right to theatrical property that had become theirs; it was, in other words, a way of maintaining a hold on copyright. The claims made by the editors in their signed preface to the Folio need not be taken too seriously, for, as stylistic evidence clearly shows, the preface was written by Jonson.[89]

Robertson's program and methods are perhaps most clearly set forth in his early study of *Titus Andronicus,* "the most coarsely repulsive play in the entire Elizabethan drama." [90] After demolishing—as he believes—the external evidence for Shakespeare's authorship, Robertson goes on to discredit "alleged" Shakespearean verse, Shakespearean legal allusions, and Shakespearean parallels in *Titus.* To detect the "actual" authors, he relies on procedures already familiar: "The sound means of identification are, broadly speaking, *frequent* use of particular phrases, general or frequent notes of manner and mannerism, peculiarities of versification and vocabulary, tics of style, and forms of phrase which are not noticeably epigrammatic in character." [91] Any single bit of evidence counts far less than the collective impression towards which the scientific investigator inductively moves. Vocabulary and diction receive primary emphasis in *Who Wrote "Titus Andronicus"?;* Robertson is generous with word-lists for plays and dramatists. In later volumes he

89. This inspired suggestion was first made, Robertson notes, by Steevens in the Prolegomena to the Variorum *Shakespeare,* Vol. II.
90. *Did Shakespeare Write "Titus Andronicus"?,* p. 239.
91. *Ibid.,* p. 60.

would lay greater stress on verse criteria, especially on tests based upon the successive phases of Shakespeare's metrical technique, for discriminating between true and alien matter.

Robertson's range extends far beyond the play that is his point of departure and return. He sees, as an aspect of his task, the identification of the "unsigned work" of Peele, Greene, and Lodge. To each of these worthies Robertson devotes a chapter. As he moves along, assumption provides a basis for further assumption. Having accepted the anonymous *George a Greene* as Greene's, Robertson uses it as evidence for that playwright's participation in *Edward III*. After tracing Peele in *Titus*, he can say that the *Titus*-word *remunerate* points to his hand in the *Troublesome Reign*.

Considering the confidence of demonstration, Robertson's findings are surprisingly vague:

The probability is that between 1590 and 1592 Greene revised or expanded an older play, in which Peele had already a large share; but there is the alternative possibility that Peele revised an old play by Greene and Kyd. The fresh matter, or revision, which in 1594 caused the play to figure as new, may again have been by Peele, or by Kyd, or by Lodge; but the amount contributed by either of the two last named to the present play is small, though it is somewhat likely that Kyd had a hand earlier in shaping the plot.[92]

He is certain only that Peele and Greene wrote much of the play. A literary equation with five or six unknown quantities, as Chambers coldly observed, is not readily solved.[93] Nevertheless, Robertson's conclusion and the

92. *Ibid.*, p. 238.
93. *Titus Andronicus*, ed. E. K. Chambers (Red Letter Shakespeare [London, 1907]), Introduction, p. 11. Chambers reprinted the introduction in *Shakespeare: A Survey* (London, 1925), pp. 31–39.

processes leading to it received an encouraging welcome in the pages of *Modern Language Review*. "It is when we come to the internal evidence that the value of Mr Robertson's method becomes apparent," the notice declared. "The diligence with which he has sought out the use of rare words and distinctive expressions or turns of phrase as well as the occurrence of particular thoughts and metaphors in a large field of dramatic literature is beyond praise. It is scarcely necessary to say that his results are of the first importance." [94] The reviewer was Greg.

In impugning the Folio assignment of *Titus* to Shakespeare, Robertson was only endorsing, with unprecedented elaborateness, the majority opinion of his day, and it need not surprise us that his efforts won approval. But as he extended the baseless fabric of his vision to include half the plays of the canon, applause quickly gave way to consternation. For Robertson entered upon virgin realms of fantasy. It is sometimes difficult to extricate with certainty his findings from the later volumes, but in *Shakespeare and Chapman* he proposed that the latter wrote "The Lover's Complaint," originated *Timon of Athens*, planned or recast *Pericles*, and drafted the Grecian camp scenes of *Troilus and Cressida*. More tentatively Robertson suggested Chapman's part-authorship of *The Tempest, Hamlet, Julius Caesar, The Taming of the Shrew*, the *Henry VI* trilogy, *Henry V, The Comedy of Errors*, and *The Two Gentlemen of Verona*. With greater confidence he maintained that the same dramatist had a share in *All's Well That Ends Well*. The claim is a substantial one for a playwright not known ever to have had a connection with Shakespeare's company. Chapman and Marlowe loom large in the dozen plays Robertson discusses in the five volumes of *The Shake-*

94. *Mod. Lang. Rev.*, I (1906), 338.

speare Canon. Among the more entertaining theories put forward in "this exploratory pilgrimage" are those suggesting that *The Comedy of Errors,* with its sentiment and amiable farce, is substantially the work of Marlowe (Chapman having been deposed) and that Marlowe helped fashion the characters of Romeo and Juliet. Robertson recapitulated his views on Marlowe in *Marlowe: A Conspectus* (1931). In 1933 death put an end to further triumphs of the ascriptional imagination. By then the reaction against Robertson and the disintegrative impulse was in full tide.

In the demolition of Robertson and what he represented in Shakespeare studies, the principal role was taken by Sir Edmund Chambers, who had entertained doubts about Robertson from the beginning. Without ever naming him, Chambers subjected Robertson's early work to withering scrutiny in his introduction to the "Red Letter" edition of *Titus Andronicus.* Chambers insisted that the investigator must attend to certain preliminaries before proceeding to identify authors on the basis of style. The questions he raised in 1907 are so fundamental, and for their time so novel, as to deserve quotation at length:

You have to determine, on the side of Shakespeare, what portions of his early style were permanent and what passed away; and again, how far at the beginning he had a style of his own at all, and how far he reproduced, consciously or unconsciously, the style of his predecessors; and in the latter case, whether it was their printed works only, or his memory also of those that trod the stage, which influenced him. . . . And then, as regards the other dramatists, you have to ask, whether they also have distinctly recognizable styles of their own, and if so, what are the elements really characteristic of each, and what are the elements, if any, which belong to a common stock of vocabulary and metaphor upon which every writer of the time drew as a matter of course, and which therefore cannot be used as evidence of authorship at all. And are the known writers of the time sufficient to account for all its anonymous plays?. . . . And what were the methods of collaboration and revision? And what amount of revision was held to justify the reviser in claiming a play as a new play and as his play?. . . . And assuredly, if the investigation is to be undertaken at all, it must be undertaken . . . disinterestedly; in abstraction from each and all of the particular difficulties, which its results may ultimately help to clear up, and not in the light of this or that preconceived hypothesis about any one or more of these.[95]

If answers were to be had to these primary questions, the required labor would be considerable, as Chambers recognized; many would have to pool their energies collectively. Such disinterested cooperation is not easily enlisted.

Chambers' strictures were perhaps offered prematurely. Of concern only to an audience of specialist scholars, they were unstrategically presented in a popular edition of Shakespeare. In any event, they had little effect at the time. The impact of Chambers' position was fully felt only when, seventeen years later, he restated it in his British Academy lecture in which he mentioned Robertson by name. The supposedly austere rationalist is unmasked as the romantic he is; Chambers sees Robertson not as the iconoclast but as an idolator who, cloaked in the vestments of Fleay, performed rites of purification in the temple of his divinity. In a remorseless analysis, Chambers shows how Robertson starts from impressionistic judgments which are then rationalized with stylistic data. Chambers questions the evidential value of the verse tests and the vocabulary and phraseology clues; he dismisses as without foundation Robertson's peculiar

95. *Titus Andronicus,* Introduction, pp. 11–13.

idea of Elizabethan copyright. Under this sustained assault the whole structure collapses. Never again were Robertson's views to be regarded as intellectually respectable.

He had further blows to endure. In an introduction to Alexander's *Shakespeare's Henry VI and Richard III* (1929), Pollard endorsed the revolutionary new thesis that the *Contention* and *True Tragedy* represent debased versions of *2* and *3 Henry VI;* moreover, confessing his distrust of "literary connoisseurship," he announced his acceptance—much against his will—of the authenticity of *Titus Andronicus.* In his book Alexander added to Robertson's discomfiture. If all external authorial criteria are found wanting, he asks, how can we positively identify the true Shakespearean in order to use it as a measure for the rest? And how can we speak of Marlowe's unsigned work unless we have signed work? In his 1929 lecture to the British Academy, "The Elizabethan Shakespeare," Dover Wilson glanced tellingly at Robertson's ignorance of theatrical values, of plays as plays. Although Lascelles Abercrombie entitled his 1930 British Academy lecture "A plea for the Liberty of Interpreting," he made an exception in Robertson's case: the internal evidence on which the great disintegrator relies is subjective and circular, deriving its force only from the prejudice which prompts the quest.

Robertson flailed out wildly against his tormentors. Persuaded that a former sympathizer had betrayed him, he raged against Dover Wilson in *The Criterion* (January, 1930). Wilson, in an unembittered rejoinder, speculated on the Shakespeare of Robertson's dreams: "Someday," he addressed his wounded antagonist,

when your survey of the canon is complete, you will perhaps give us a collected edition of his [Shakespeare's] works—a slender volume, I should guess, an anthology of dramatic verse rather than a collection of plays—and write an introduction thereto in which we shall be permitted to catch sight of the Master's face as it has been revealed to you. Unless I am greatly mistaken, the features you display in such a mirror will not seem wholly unfamiliar to the gazing world. They will demonstrate what many Britishers have long suspected, that Shakespeare though no doubt born at Stratford was of Scotch origin, and having got so far the world will find no difficulty in admitting the rest, namely his radicalism and his rationalism, both—such is the prophetic power of genius 'dreaming on things to come'—of a late nineteenth century pattern.[96]

Further injured, Robertson reprinted his *Criterion* piece and added new diatribes in *The State of Shakespeare Study* (1931), which he "Dedicated with proper respect to that variously learned and magnanimous body the British Academy." The heavy sarcasm, the gestures of accusation and defense, reveal the acuteness of his distress and familiar patterns of conspiratorial thinking; just as clearly, the incoherent and tendentious arguments show Robertson's failure to grasp the true meaning of the criticism leveled against him. In his last book, in which he devoted long sections of abuse to Pollard and Alexander, he acknowledged a stampede back to the Folio.

Robertson's defeat was accomplished easily, and in one sense is hardly momentous; responsible scholars, even before Chambers destroyed him, had steered clear of (to use Boas' phrase) the "Robertsonian morass." Nor did this rejection of fantastical extremism put an end to the disintegration of Shakespeare. Chambers himself had in his youth drunk from the fountain of Fleay; he was not immune to infection, although he contracted the virus

96. "Idolatry and Scepticism," p. 641.

in a mild form.[97] And Dover Wilson could still say, in the very paper in which he censured Robertson, that "plays like *Measure for Measure* or *All's Well that ends Well* . . . are almost certainly the result of collaboration between Shakespeare and some second-rate dramatist to whom was entrusted the final shaping of the material." [98] The primary significance of the Robertson affair to this inquiry lies in the fact that it served to call into question the whole endeavor to establish authorship on the basis of style. In Abercrombie and other commentators the very word "internal" became a compromising epithet.[99] The Golden Age was over.

» IX «

The conservative counterthrust was not limited to the rigorous examination—and rejection—of the methods of the disintegrators and conjecturists. Theories about the authorship of individual plays were reviewed in a series of articles. Baldwin Maxwell in 1923 and Peter

97. Chambers acknowledged a debt to Fleay in the introduction to his Warwick Shakespeare edition of *Hamlet* (London, 1894), p. 4. Robertson was quick to note that Chambers had "put a disintegrating hand" to the *Henry VI* plays, *Titus, Macbeth, Timon, Cymbeline, Pericles,* and *Henry VIII* (*Shakespeare Canon, Part III,* pp. 4–9); see also below, pp. 166–167. That the great anti-disintegrator himself practiced disintegration has, not surprisingly, given comfort to more adventuresome spirits. Thus, Dover Wilson can write, ". . . Chambers himself admits the presence of a second or third hand in *I Henry VI, Titus* and *The Taming of the Shrew,* though he prefers the word 'collaboration' to 'revision' in describing Shakespeare's part" ("Malone and the Upstart Crow," *Shakespeare Survey 4* [Cambridge, 1951], p. 59).

98. "The Elizabethan Shakespeare," reprinted in *Aspects of Shakespeare* (Oxford, 1933), p. 203.

99. "There are prejudices, preferences, analyses, comparisons, statistics, verse-tests, word-counts, sense of style, poetical feelings, intuitions—but we must not call all this evidence, unless we add the compromising epithet 'internal'" (Abercrombie, "Plea for the Liberty of Interpreting," reprinted in *Aspects of Shakespeare,* p. 237). Note the sweeping inclusiveness of the indictment.

Alexander in 1930 defended the homogeneity of *Henry VIII* against mortar fire from the joint-authorship partisans.[100] In a monograph-length paper, E. P. Kuhl in 1925 replied to the disintegrators of *The Taming of the Shrew;* he found "no touches . . . of doubtful origin" but much evidence to indicate that the play is the unaided handiwork of an unrivaled master craftsman.[101] Arguing for "The Integrity of *The Tempest*" (*Review of English Studies,* 1925), E. K. Chambers countered those who saw the masque as a non-Shakespearean interpolation and those, most notably Dover Wilson, who held that the Folio text provides an abridged or revised version of Shakespeare's original. The article pursues the attack on the doctrine of continuous copy—the theory that theatrical manuscripts were periodically refurbished when plays were revived—which Chambers initiated in his lecture on the disintegration of Shakespeare. In a series of articles, S. R. Golding argued against Day's involvement in *The Maid's Metamorphosis,* the multiple authorship of *Two Lamentable Tragedies,* and attempts to distribute *Lust's Dominion* among three collaborators.[102] W. D.

100. Maxwell, "Fletcher and *Henry the Eighth," The Manly Anniversary Studies* (Chicago, 1923), pp. 104–112; reprinted, with revisions, in *Studies in Beaumont, Fletcher, and Massinger,* pp. 55–63. Alexander's paper, "Conjectural History, or Shakespeare's *Henry VIII,*" has been referred to in previous sections; see pp. 10n., 36, 37.

101. "The Authorship of *The Taming of the Shrew," PMLA,* XL (1925), 551–618. Kuhl's article did not put an end to debate; for subsequent work on *The Shrew* and its problems, see below, pp. 135–136.

102. "The Authorship of *The Maid's Metamorphosis," Rev. of Eng. Stud.,* II (1926), 270–279; "The Authorship of the 'Two Lamentable Tragedies,'" *Notes and Queries,* CLI (1926), 347–350; "The Authorship of 'Lust's Dominion,'" *Notes and Queries,* CLV (1928), 399–402. Golding's article on *Two Lamentable Tragedies* prompted Law to write again in support of single authorship ("Further Notes on 'Two Lamentable Tragedies,'" *Notes and Queries,* CLIII [1927], 93–94). It is sad to note that when Golding ventured upon positive authorship attributions of his own, as he did on several occasions, he equaled the worst excesses of the parallelographic school. His extravagances aroused the wrath of Oliphant; see below, Part Three, p. 192.

Dunkel, while not denying Webster a share in *Anything for a Quiet Life,* maintained that Sykes had "greatly overstated the case." [103]

These miscellaneous efforts, however salutary, seem minor indeed alongside the grandest achievements of this period: Chambers' *The Elizabethan Stage* (1923) and *William Shakespeare: A Study of Facts and Problems* (1930). These works sum up the conservative position on questions of authenticity and attribution, and provide a point of departure for all subsequent scholarship. In the sections of *The Elizabethan Stage* on Playwrights (volume III) and Anonymous Work (volume IV), Chambers records the views of his predecessors—Fleay, Sykes, Oliphant, Robertson, and the rest—generally without comment, although he compliments Sykes and permits himself more than once to express amusement or exasperation with the aberrations of Fleay. Not unexpectedly, those whose methods and findings came under fire complained that Chambers was merely the voice of consensus, never deviating from majority opinion on any question. This is, of course, unjust: he never bases a decision on the tabulation of votes. Yet one on occasion wishes that Chambers had taken a stand instead of objectively reporting (as he does in the case of Greg on *Two Lamentable Tragedies*), or that he had accepted the full consequences of his own reasoning; he regards as "very plausible" the arguments for Chapman's authorship of *Sir Giles Goosecap* but keeps the play in the anonymous category.[104] At the same time the impartial historian can only applaud Chambers for firmly keeping in that classification a number of disputed works, including *Arden of Feversham, Charlemagne, Edward IV,* and

103. "The Authorship of *Anything for a Quiet Life,*" *PMLA,* XLIII (1928), 793–799.
104. *Elizabethan Stage,* III, 518; IV, 15.

The Revenger's Tragedy. In concluding the last to be a play of "unknown or conjectural" parentage, Chambers provides an illuminating insight into the distinction between conservatism and traditionalism in literary scholarship. Tradition, which may or may not derive from legitimate authority, gives *The Revenger's Tragedy* to Tourneur; but the facts of the case, in Chambers' conservative evaluation, do not justify a positive ascription.

His conclusions were, of course, not impervious to the pressures of new facts and ideas. In *The Elizabethan Stage* he lists the *Contention* as an independent anonymous play which Shakespeare revised as *2* and *3 Henry VI*. But in his *Shakespeare,* published after the work of Alexander on *Henry VI* and Greg on *The Merry Wives of Windsor* and *Orlando Furioso,* Chambers admits his error and breaks with a tradition of scholarship going back to Malone.[105] The enlightened conservatism that distinguishes Chambers' monumental volumes is to be found, even more vigorously expressed, in the Plays and Playwrights section of Bentley's continuation, *The Jacobean and Caroline Stage* (1956).

» X «

THIRTY YEARS HAVE GONE BY since Sykes and Robertson passed from the scene, rather a long period in the modern history of a specialized discipline. Despite a general expansion—spectacular in recent years—of scholarly production, the sheer volume of attribution work has shrunk somewhat. So much might have been expected. In Shakespeare studies, moreover, a good part of the effort has gone into repairing the damage done by the previous generation; Kenneth Muir, in a survey of "Fifty Years of

105. Greg's analyses of *Merry Wives* and *Orlando* persuaded Chambers that memorization could produce texts with the characteristics exhibited by the Bad Quartos (*William Shakespeare,* I, 157).

Shakespearian Criticism," appropriately heads one section, "Disintegration and Re-Integration." [106] Yet the disintegrative impulse does not die easily, as we shall note. In the non-Shakespearean field, study of individual authors and plays has continued apace. On the whole, the articles and monographs of the last three decades show that, while older methods have persisted unchanged in some quarters, they have been refined in others, and they have been joined by new techniques. These years have also witnessed a healthy, if limited, upsurge of interest in general principles.

Unquestionably the most striking of the new investigative techniques is the application of imagistic criteria to authorship questions. Such a development proceeds naturally from the modern interest in plays as dramatic poems and the consequent formulation of methods of classifying and analyzing images. The great seminal work is, of course, Caroline F. E. Spurgeon's *Shakespeare's Imagery and What It Tells Us* (1935). E. A. Armstrong's *Shakespeare's Imagination* (1946) has also been influential, as have been to a lesser degree the writings of Wolfgang Clemen, G. Wilson Knight, Robert Heilman, and others.

The term *imagery* is often left undefined, and some critics employ it very broadly indeed. In addition to metaphors and similes, it has been interpreted as including image-clusters (recurrent groupings of related figures and ideas) and primary patterns of words and symbols (e.g., gold in *Timon*). Even the non-verbal has been drawn into the net. Maurice Charney analyzed, in *Shakespeare's Roman Plays* (1961), "the large body of images that is not part of the spoken words of the text, but directly presented in the theater"; thus the "presentational"

---

106. "Fifty Years of Shakespearian Criticism: 1900–1950," *Shakespeare Survey 4* (Cambridge, 1951), p. 7.

image of Cleopatra's suicide by the asp climaxes the serpent theme expressed verbally through iterative imagery.[107] Heilman goes so far as to speak of "the large metaphor which is the play itself." [108]

Miss Spurgeon herself pointed the way in the use of imagery as an authorship test. In her British Academy lecture of 1931 she suggested, as regards *Henry VIII,* that figurative language is "a factor which should be taken into account in any investigation of the [authorial] problem." [109] Actually she had taken this factor into account the year before in dealing with another play. Although published before her famous book, "Imagery in the *Sir Thomas More* Fragment" was written after she had completed her investigation of Shakespeare's imagery. "My examination," she writes, "of dramatists contemporary with Shakespeare which I have made for purposes of comparison, shows me that, quite apart from style and method of forming them, each writer has a certain range of images which are characteristic of him, and that he has a marked and constant tendency to use a larger number of one or two kinds." [110] In the *More* Addition the images, "when classified, under headings such as ani-

107. Pp. 8, 98–101. "The poisonous asp as the means of death becomes the baby nursing at the breast, a potent symbol of life. The serpent theme culminates in a brilliant union of the fruitful and the lethal powers of the Nile" (p. 101). Charney's orientation towards imagistic studies resembles (as he acknowledges) that advocated by R. A. Foakes in an important article, "Suggestions for a New Approach to Shakespeare's Imagery," *Shakespeare Survey 5* (Cambridge, 1952), pp. 81–92. Foakes too focuses illuminatingly on the scene of Cleopatra putting the serpent to her breast (p. 91n.4).

108. R. B. Heilman, *This Great Stage: Image and Structure in King Lear* (Louisiana, 1948), p. 12. Similarly, Clifford Lyons thinks in terms of "that total 'image' which is the play" ("Stage Imagery in Shakespeare's Plays," *Essays on Shakespeare and Elizabethan Drama in Honour of Hardin Craig,* ed. Richard Hosley [London, 1963], p. 274).

109. "Shakespeare's Iterative Imagery," reprinted in *Aspects of Shakespeare,* p. 275n.

110. *Rev. of Eng. Stud.,* VI (1930), 258.

mals, nature, sickness, clothes, sport, etc., fall into exactly the same familiar categories that the Shakespearean images do." [111] Miss Spurgeon's article quickly drew an appreciative response from R. W. Chambers, who acknowledged a large debt to her in the first reworking of his early essay on *More*.[112]

It was not long before Miss Spurgeon's methods inspired a doctoral dissertation, Marion Bodwell Smith's *Marlowe's Imagery and the Marlowe Canon* (1940). Miss Smith classifies the images of the canonical writings along Spurgeon lines (the categories are Learning, the Body, Domestic Life, Nature, the Arts, etc.). Then, in a second half of the study dealing with the disputed passages and plays, she rejects the comic scenes of the 1604 and 1616 *Faustus,* finds Heywood or another in *The Jew of Malta,* and detects Marlowe's presence in *Arden of Feversham* (along with Shakespeare and possibly Kyd), *A Larum for London, 1* and *3 Henry VI,* and the *True Tragedy.* Systematic analysis of an author's imagery, Miss Smith asserts in her preface, "can be evolved into a powerful weapon for the determination of authorship." Conceivably; but in this case the weapon appears to have backfired. The subtle complexities of image collecting are much more fully appreciated by Muir in a later study, *Shakespeare as Collaborator* (1960), dealing with *Edward III, Pericles, The Two Noble Kinsmen,* and *Cardenio.*[113] The merits of this whole line of investigation are considered in Part Three.

In "Latin Title-Page Mottoes as a Clue to Dramatic

111. *Ibid.*

112. Chambers, "Some Sequences of Thought in Shakespeare and in the 147 Lines of 'Sir Thomas More,'" *Mod. Lang. Rev.,* XXVI (1931), 255.

113. Because Muir's book incorporates, in revised form, five articles published during the decade which preceded, I have not thought it necessary to cite those articles separately in this survey.

Authorship," in *The Library* (1945), James G. McManaway noted that some Elizabethan dramatists habitually supplied their plays with mottoes; the printed copies of Heywood's plays, for example, almost always carry some variant of *"Et prodesse solent et delectare."* A different Latin motto appears on the title-page of the anonymous *Dick of Devonshire,* and McManaway uses this clue to question A. M. Clark's ascription of the play to Heywood. A weightier, if not so novel, contribution to authorship study is made by those investigators—most notably Hart, Partridge, and Hoy—who extend and improve already existing verbal and linguistic tests.

Alongside the elaborate statistics and arguments of Alfred Hart, the unanalyzed word-lists or casual reflections on vocabulary offered by earlier students seem unsophisticated indeed. His papers on "The Vocabulary of *Edward III*" and "Shakespeare and the Vocabulary of *The Two Noble Kinsmen,*" in *Shakespeare and the Homilies* (1934), represents a conscious effort to suggest new methods of using the diction of Shakespeare's plays for purposes of comparative criticism." [114]

In studying *Edward III,* Hart counted the total vocabulary, compound words, and words beginning with certain prefixes (*be-, con-, de-,* etc.) or ending with certain suffixes (*-able, -tion, -ly,* etc.). He also made similar arithmetical calculations for plays of Shakespeare, Marlowe, Kyd, and others. Totals and averages are furnished in a series of tables. The data show that the author of *Edward III* has in common with Shakespeare a remarkably rich vocabulary—much richer, for instance, than Marlowe's. Hart believes that the evidence also points to single rather than multiple authorship, and to Shakespeare as sole author. Wisely Hart refrains from

114. *Shakespeare and the Homilies,* Preface, p. 5.

pressing too hard. "The other possibility," he recognizes, "is to accept the facts, confess our ignorance, and permit the play to remain authorless." [115] On the *Henry VI* trilogy, included in the tables, he takes a firmer line. The length of these plays, their large vocabularies, and the interrelations of their word-stock with that of canonical pieces—all these factors support the view "that Shakespeare wrote the plays on *Henry VI* and that the lines contributed by Marlowe are as many as the snakes in Ireland." [116]

When he turned to *The Two Noble Kinsmen,* Hart found 188 words not in Schmidt's *Shakespeare Lexicon.* He went on to classify the "rare" words in *Kinsmen* and five canonical plays from the period 1608–11. In all these works he counted words not previously employed by Shakespeare, and from these sorted out the first-used words (106 in all in *Kinsmen*) recorded as new to the language in the *Oxford English Dictionary.* Several of the nonce words (e.g., *disroot* and *disseat*) have, Hart suggests, a Shakespearean expressiveness. He also investigated, somewhat anticlimactically, the distribution of words with the prefix *un-* in *Kinsmen* and nine unquestioned pieces. His methods, as he explains in his conclusion, differ from those in general use:

. . . I may appear to be following the practice of critics who, by marshalling a medley of miscellaneous words and an array of parallel passages common to play X and to play Y, deduce from such points of resemblance that the two plays are by the one pen. My method of investigation rests not on sameness but on differences in vocabulary, and requires rather the absence than the presence of identical phrases and parallel passages. . . . The diction of Part A [scenes assigned to Shakespeare] I take to be his

115. *Ibid.,* p. 241.
116. *Ibid.*

because nearly every line bears the stamp of the essential qualities of his vocabulary, simplicity, directness, originality and copiousness, the whole shot through with imagination and alive with metaphor.[117]

Thus Hart admits *The Two Noble Kinsmen* to the Shakespeare canon. His interpretation of the objective evidence involves, as can be seen, subjective value judgments. Moreover, the Oxford Dictionary on which he relied does not always provide trustworthy information about first uses; in many instances, nonce words credited to Shakespeare can be traced to his reading. Still Hart makes an interesting case that has contributed to the increasing disposition on the part of responsible critics to see Shakespeare's presence in the play.

If Hart's vocabulary studies have greater refinement than earlier efforts, a similar advance may be noted in A. C. Partridge's application of linguistic critera to another great Shakespeare puzzle. *The Problem of Henry VIII Reopened* (1949) is the work of an accomplished grammarian. Partridge's evidence is satisfyingly concrete: the use of expletive *do* in affirmative statements (favored by Shakespeare), of *-th* inflectional endings in the third person singular present indicative of notional and auxiliary verbs (also favored by Shakespeare), and of colloquial clippings of personal pronouns (a Fletcher preference). These "grammatical peculiarities . . . seem to establish the presence of two hands, and they substantiate broadly the divisions of the play, made upon other grounds, by Spedding and Hickson." [118] Partridge is not

117. *Ibid.*, p. 256.
118. Partridge, p. 23. A revised and enlarged version of the essay, taking into account work done since 1949, is included under the title, *"Henry VIII:* Linguistic Criteria for the Two Styles Apparent in the Play,"* in Partridge's *Orthography in Shakespeare and Elizabethan Drama* (London, 1964), pp. 141–163.

concerned solely with such minute particulars, although he rests his case primarily upon them. In a brief, insightful discussion, he describes and illustrates the entangled syntactical constructs with which Shakespeare characteristically develops his ideas in verse—his tendency "to lose track of his relative clauses, especially in continuative function and in proximity to participial phrases, or adverbial clauses, of time." [119] Fletcher comes much closer to modern ideas of syntactical correctness.

Partridge's evidence, while compelling, is not so statistically impressive as to sweep all before it. Foakes observed that the 72 instances of *ye* in the portion given to Fletcher do not compare with the 349 occurrences of the same form in the 1647 Folio of *Bonduca*.[120] Furthermore, Partridge's theory of composition (Shakespeare left an unfinished play which Fletcher completed with modification of the original design) is by its very nature incapable of demonstration. Yet one can scarcely quarrel with Allardyce Nicoll's judicious estimate of Partridge's objective evidence: "[it] is valid and in all future discussions of the play must be taken into account. Here, as elsewhere in the field of scholarship, we need not be afraid of facts, although at the same time we may recognise that facts in themselves form merely the foundation for critical interpretation." [121]

The problem of *Henry VIII* is reopened once again by Cyrus Hoy in the concluding installment of "The Shares of Fletcher and His Collaborators in the Beaumont and Fletcher Canon," published serially in *Studies*

---

119. *Problem,* pp. 29–30.
120. [New] Arden *Henry VIII,* Introduction, pp. xx–xxi. The 1964 reprinting of Foakes's edition contains, as an addition to the Introduction, a "Postscript, 1962" (pp. xxvi–xxvii), in which he clarifies his stand, which is less strenuously anticollaboration than readers had inferred.
121. Partridge, *Problem,* Foreword, p. 6.

in Bibliography.[122] Hoy introduces no fresh evidence of his own, but he makes shrewd use of Charlton Hinman's discovery that the play was set in part by compositor B. That compositor tended to alter *ye* to *you,* and so Hoy is able to discount the relative infrequency of the former in the Fletcherian scenes of *Henry VIII.* Foakes's point thus loses some of its sting, but it is not rendered irrelevant; the play remains a great puzzle. Hoy may be justified, however, in feeling that the burden of proof has shifted to the proponents of single authorship.[123]

The inquiry of which his discussion of *Henry VIII* forms a part is the most ambitious effort in recent years to identify shares in a canon on the basis of internal evidence. Hoy's purpose, announced in the initial installment, is first to isolate Fletcher's unaided plays, and secondly, to show how their linguistic pattern may be used to distinguish between the work of Fletcher and Massinger. Hoy's linguistic criteria are the familiar pronominal, verbal, and contractional forms (*ye; hath, doth; 'em, i'th',* and the like). The novelty of the enterprise lies in its scale; Hoy delivers rather more than he promises. In addition to Fletcher and Massinger, he considers the roles of Beaumont, Field, Shirley, and others in the huge corpus; fifty-four plays are studied in all. Hoy thus covers almost precisely the same ground that Oliphant had traversed thirty years earlier. But unlike Oliphant's work, Hoy's is admirably lucid and well organized, and

122. The various segments appeared as follows: *Stud. in Bibl.,* VIII (1956), 129–146; IX (1957), 143–162; XI (1958), 85–106; XII (1959), 91–116; XIII (1960), 77–108; XIV (1961), 45–67; XV (1962), 71–90.

123. The dual-authorship theory has also received recent support from Ants Oras, "'Extra Monosyllables' in *Henry VIII* and the Problem of Authorship," *Jour. of Eng. and Germ. Phil.,* LII (1953), 198–213; R. A. Law, "Holinshed and *Henry the Eighth,*" *Texas Stud. in Eng.,* XXXVI (1957), 3–11; and Marco Mincoff, "*Henry VIII* and Fletcher," *Shakespeare Quar.,* XII (1961), 239–260.

it displays throughout a refreshing sanity. He has, moreover, absorbed the bibliographical discipline and can
face the specter of scribal or compositorial intervention.

But to be conscious of a problem is not necessarily to
solve it, and the possibility exists that Hoy's findings
may one day be challenged in consequence of fuller understanding of the transmission of the Beaumont and
Fletcher texts; compositor B stirs uneasy thoughts.
Furthermore, Hoy's linguistic criteria, which work well
enough for Fletcher and Massinger, yield less rewarding
data when applied to dramatists whose preferences are
not so distinctive. The tests are of no use at all when the
several writers have pooled their talents in intimate collaboration. The key, in other words, does not fit all the
locks it is called upon to open. The linguistic evidence
for Middleton's hand in *The Nice Valor* (for example)
is pathetically slight, and no external evidence links his
name with the play; "one turns perforce to such internal
evidence as is supplied by the play's thematic material
and the treatment thereof." [124] In *The Laws of Candy,*
assigned to Ford, Hoy records 37 instances of *ye,* but
the playwright uses the pronoun only 11 times in *The
Broken Heart* and as many as 65 times in *The Fancies
Chaste and Noble.* The other linguistic evidence is similarly inconclusive, and the *'ee* contractions (*d'ee, t'ee,*
etc.), found in all of Ford's accepted plays, do not once
occur. A passage from *Candy,* however, "seems cast
in the same verbal mould" as another from *The Lover's
Melancholy.* And so on; Ford inherits the entire play
on grounds no more relative than these. Hoy then goes
on to assign the same dramatist a share in Act II, scene i,
of *The Fair Maid of the Inn* because "one passage
therein echoes fairly closely a passage of similar import

124. "Shares," *Stud. in Bibl.,* XIII, 93.

from III, 2 of *The Laws of Candy*. . . ." [125] Thus, as
so often in the work of Hoy's predecessors, one inference
leads to another, supposition is erected upon supposition.

"With linguistic evidence," Hoy grants, "it is all,
finally, a matter of more or less, as this essay in evaluating it, and applying it to the authorial problem which
the Beaumont and Fletcher canon poses, will have abun-
dantly indicated." [126] For the heart of Hoy's concern
—Fletcher and Massinger—it is fortunately a matter
of more rather than less; here the evidence is solid. One
is hardly inclined to disallow the triumphant note on
which Hoy concludes his arduous labors:

It remained for linguistic evidence to show what metrical evidence
never showed: that it is possible to distinguish the work of Fletcher
and Massinger on the basis of fundamentally different language
practices. To demonstrate just how fundamental this difference
is, and how decisively it will serve to differentiate their work in
collaboration, has been the most signal achievement of this study.
On the basis of it, I will venture to make a large claim. There is
no longer any mystery about Massinger's share in the plays of the
Beaumont and Fletcher canon. [127]

The immediate impact of Hoy's work is evident from the
fact that his criteria have already been applied to a different set of problems by another investigator. [128]

In miscellaneous articles, scholars have examined criti-
cally several other popular tests: verbal, metrical, and

125. *Ibid.*, p. 102.
126. *Ibid.*, XV, 87.
127. *Ibid.*
128. See Peter B. Murray, "The Authorship of *The Revenger's Tragedy*," *Papers of the Bibl. Soc. of Amer.*, LVI (1962), 195–218, "The
Collaboration of Dekker and Webster in 'Northward Ho' and 'Westward
Ho'" (*ibid.*, pp. 482–486), and *A Study of Cyril Tourneur* (Philadelphia,
1964). Murray modifies slightly and supplements Hoy's tests; see below,
Part Three, pp. 214–215.

imagistic.[129] Much broader in scope and interest is the debate conducted in the pages of the *Bulletin of the New York Public Library* under the heading, "The Case for Internal Evidence." [130] The participants are concerned, more often than not, with Marvell or Johnson or Coleridge rather than with the Elizabethans, but their discussion of principles and procedures bears a high degree of relevance to the present inquiry.

It remains now to glance at the large mass of articles, monographs, and editions treating the authorship problem in individual plays and playwrights.

» XI «

THE PAST THREE DECADES of Shakespeare study have yielded a plentiful crop of work on familiar topics; rather too plentiful, one sometimes feels, in view of the slender nourishment provided. Yet there have been achievements as well as confusions and repetitions. On the evidence of language and thought, J. M. Nosworthy makes an impressive case for Shakespeare's authorship of the

129. See Arthur M. Sampley, "'Verbal Tests' for Peele's Plays," *Stud. in Phil.*, XXX (1933), 473–496; J. Swart, "Shakespeare without Tears," *Neophil.*, XXXVIII (1954), 221–224; Moody E. Prior, "Imagery as a Test of Authorship," *Shakespeare Quar.*, VI (1955), 381–386.

130. The following papers in the series are concerned with authorship attribution: Arthur Sherbo, "Can *Mother Midnight's Comical Pocket-Book* Be Attributed to Christopher Smart?" LXI (1957), 373–382; S. F. Johnson, "An Uncollected Early Poem by Coleridge," LXI (1957), 505–507; David V. Erdman, "Newspaper Sonnets Put to the Concordance Test: Can They Be Attributed to Coleridge?" LXI (1957), 508–516, 611–620, and LXII (1958), 46–49; George de F. Lord, "Two New Poems by Marvell?" LXII (1958), 551–570; Sherbo, "The Uses and Abuses of Internal Evidence," LXIII (1959), 5–20; Erdman, "The Signature of Style," LXIII (1959), 88–109; Ephim G. Fogel, "Salmons in Both, or Some Caveats for Canonical Scholars," LXIII (1959), 223–236, 292–308; Lord, "Comments on the Canonical Caveat," LXIII (1959), 355–366; Sherbo, "A Reply to Professor Fogel," LXIII (1959), 367–371.

twenty-one lines of Addition III of *Sir Thomas More*.[131] William T. Hastings and—very powerfully—Hereward T. Price defend the authenticity and homogeneity of *Titus Andronicus;* [132] but Dover Wilson in the Cambridge New Shakespeare (1948) and J. C. Maxwell in the new Arden (1953) urge Peele's authorship of Act I. In important articles, Price and Leo Kirschbaum insist upon the structural unity of *1 Henry VI*.[133] Charles Tyler Prouty argues weakly that the *Contention* is not a memorial reconstruction but an independent play by an earlier dramatist which Shakespeare revised as *2 Henry VI*.[134]

In his edition of the *Henry VI* plays (1952), Dover Wilson disintegrates them anew. He restates the collaboration-revision theory, points to internal contradictions in the plays, and uses the evidence of parallels to identify the hands of Nashe, Greene, and possibly Peele. If the methods are familiar, so too is the motive. "They [the verbal parallels]," Wilson asserts at one point, "should . . . clear Shakespeare of all responsibility for the dull, miserably commonplace, and often unmetrical verse found in these and a number of other scenes of the play." [135] He calls one part of his introduction "Back

131. "Shakespeare and *Sir Thomas More*," *Rev. of Eng. Stud.*, N.S., VI (1955), 12–25.

132. Hastings, "The Hardboiled Shakspere," *Shakespeare Assoc. Bull.*, XVII (1942), 114–125; Price, "The Authorship of 'Titus Andronicus,'" *Jour. of Eng. and Germ. Phil.*, XLII (1943), 55–81. See also Price's paper, "The First Quarto of Titus Andronicus," which, although not overtly concerned with the authorship question, adduces evidence of Shakespearean spelling idiosyncrasies from Q1 of *Titus* (*English Institute Essays 1947* [New York, 1948], pp. 137–168).

133. Price, "Construction in Shakespeare," *Univ. of Mich. Contributions in Mod. Phil.*, XVII (1951), 1–42; Kirschbaum, "The Authorship of *1 Henry VI*," *PMLA*, LXVII (1952), 809–822.

134. *"The Contention" and Shakespeare's "2 Henry VI": A Comparative Study* (New Haven, 1954). Some of Prouty's arguments are astonishing; see Price's devastating review, *Mod. Lang. Notes*, LXX (1955), 527–529.

135. New Shakespeare *1 Henry VI*, Introduction, p. xxvii.

to Malone," but no stampede has followed. Wilson's arguments are cogently rebutted by Andrew S. Cairncross in the new Arden editions of the three plays (1957–64). Further refutation has come from C. G. Harlow, who has shown the unlikelihood of Nashe's participation in Act I of *1 Henry VI*.[136]

The integrity of *The Taming of the Shrew* and its relation to *The Taming of a Shrew* (regarded by Alexander and his followers as a Bad Quarto of the same play) have provided matter for seemingly endless debate.[137] In contrast, the view that *Timon of Athens* is

136. "A Source for Nashe's *Terrors of the Night,* and the Authorship of *1 Henry VI,*" *Stud. in Eng. Lit.,* V (1965), 31–47, 269–281.

137. See Raymond A. Houk, "The Integrity of Shakespeare's *The Taming of the Shrew,*" *Jour. of Eng. and Germ. Phil.,* XXXIX (1940), 222–229; "Strata in *The Taming of the Shrew,*" *Stud. in Phil.,* XXXIX (1942), 291–302; "The Evolution of *The Taming of the Shrew,*" *PMLA,* LVII (1942), 1009–1038; "Shakespeare's *Shrew* and Greene's *Orlando,*" *PMLA,* LXII (1947), 657–671; Henry David Gray, "*The Taming of a Shrew,*" *Renaissance Studies in Honor of Hardin Craig,* ed. B. Maxwell *et al.* (Palo Alto, 1941), pp. 133–141; also *Phil. Quar.,* XX (1941), 325–333; G. I. Duthie, "*The Taming of a Shrew* and *The Taming of the Shrew,*" *Rev. of Eng. Stud.,* XIX (1943), 337–356; Hardin Craig, "The Shrew and A Shrew: Possible Settlement of an Old Debate," *Elizabethan Studies and Other Essays: In Honor of George F. Reynolds* (Univ. of Colorado Stud.; Boulder, 1945), pp. 150–154; Parrott, "The Taming of a Shrew—A New Study of an Old Play," *Elizabethan Studies and Other Essays,* pp. 155–165; Sidney Thomas, "A Note on *The Taming of the Shrew,*" *Mod. Lang. Notes,* LXIV (1949), 94–96; E. A. J. Honigmann, "Shakespeare's 'Lost Source Plays,'" *Mod. Lang. Rev.,* XLIX (1954), 302–304; K. Wentersdorf, "The Authenticity of *The Taming of the Shrew,*" *Shakespeare Quar.,* V (1954), 11–32; K. B. Danks, "'A Shrew' & 'The Shrew,'" *Notes and Queries,* CC (1955), 331–332; John W. Shroeder, "*The Taming of a Shrew* and *The Taming of the Shrew:* A Case Reopened," *Jour. of Eng. and Germ. Phil.,* LVII (1958), 424–443; Tommy Ruth Waldo and T. W. Herbert, "Musical Terms in *The Taming of the Shrew:* Evidence of Single Authorship," *Shakespeare Quar.,* X (1959), 185–199; Richard Hosley, "Sources and Analogues of *The Taming of the Shrew,*" *Huntington Lib. Quar.,* XXVII (1963–64), 289–308. Peter Alexander first suggested that *A Shrew* is a Bad Quarto of *The Shrew* forty years ago, in the correspondence columns of *The Times Literary Supplement* ("'The Taming of a Shrew,'" September 16, 1926, p. 614). His most recent restatement of his theory appears in the same periodical; Alexander writes, ". . . the structural features in which *a*

Shakespeare's unfinished work has steadily gained ground; here Una Ellis-Fermor has made the most notable single contribution.[138] J. C. Maxwell, editing *Pericles* for the New Shakespeare, finds it "best to leave the non-Shakespearian hand anonymous," but the Arden editor cautiously proposes, on the basis of stylistic parallels, that John Day wrote two or possibly three scenes.[139] Another case for Shakespeare's part-authorship of *The Two Noble Kinsmen* is made by Marco Mincoff, while the ultimate step of claiming the entire play for him is taken by Paul Bertram, who has not yet published his evidence.[140] In "Shakespeare's Bad Poetry," Hardin Craig discusses certain frequently rejected passages—the Hymen verses in *As You Like It,* the vision in *Cymbeline,* and the masque in *The Tempest*—and makes the intriguing suggestion that "in some . . . at least, Shakespeare consciously adapted a style in common use for masques and musical entertainments in his age." [141] If these heterogeneous expeditions into contested territory

Shrew differs from *the Shrew* can be explained by treating the quarto version as derived from that given in the First Folio; regarded however as independent creations these features defy rational or artistic justification" ("A Case of Three Sisters," *Times Lit. Supp.,* July 8, 1965, p. 588).

138. "*Timon of Athens:* An Unfinished Play," *Rev. of Eng. Stud.,* XVIII (1942), 270–283; reprinted, with annotations by the author, in *Shakespeare the Dramatist,* ed. Muir (London, 1961), pp. 158–176.

139. *Pericles,* ed. Maxwell (Cambridge, 1956), Introduction, p. xxv; *Pericles,* ed. F. D. Hoeniger (London, 1963), Introduction, pp. lxii–lxiii, and Appendix B, pp. 171–180.

140. Mincoff, "The Authorship of *The Two Noble Kinsmen,*" *English Studies,* XXXIII (1952), 97–115; Bertram, "The Date of *The Two Noble Kinsmen,*" *Shakespeare Quar.,* XII (1961), 32. Frederick O. Waller, in "Printer's Copy for *The Two Noble Kinsmen,*" *Stud. in Bibl.,* XI (1958), 61–84, also supports the dual-authorship hypothesis. For a denial of Shakespeare's part-authorship, see Ellis-Fermor's paper for the 1949 Shakespeare Survey Conference, "*The Two Noble Kinsmen,*" printed in *Shakespeare the Dramatist,* pp. 177–186.

141. "Shakespeare's Bad Poetry," *Shakespeare Survey 1* (Cambridge, 1948), p. 55.

reveal any trend, it is, not unexpectedly, the retreat (with occasional counterattacks) of the disintegrators. But the triumph of the fundamentalists is by no means total, and we must reckon on some at least of the great problems of the Shakespeare canon being with us for some time to come.

Work on the non-Shakespearean drama reflects a clearer trend: a movement towards concentration on the Jacobean and Caroline periods rather than on the plays of the nineties. The conjecturists appear to have given up on *Arden of Feversham*. This shift may be due in part to changes in sensibility, in part to recognition of the law of diminishing returns. A listing of representative articles will furnish a rough idea of recent lines of investigation: W. D. Dunkel, "Did Not Rowley Merely Revise Middleton?" *PMLA* (1933) [Dunkel replies to his own question in the affirmative; it is the wrong answer]; W. J. Lawrence, "Dekker's Theatrical Allusiveness," *Times Literary Supplement* (January 30, 1937) [Dekker is part-author of *Blurt, Master Constable*]; M. E. Borish, "John Day's *Law Tricks* and George Wilkins," *Modern Philology* (1937); J. H. Walter, *"Revenge for Honour:* Date, Authorship and Sources," *Review of English Studies* (1937); W. L. Halstead, "Collaboration on *The Patient Grissill,*" *Philological Quarterly* (1939); Paul H. Kocher, "Nashe's Authorship of the Prose Scenes in *Faustus,*" *Modern Language Quarterly* (1942); G. F. Sensabaugh, "Another Play by John Ford," *Modern Language Quarterly* (1942) [*The Great Favorite*]; Percy Simpson, "The Problem of Authorship of *Eastward Ho,*" *PMLA* (1944); Bertram Lloyd, "The Authorship of *The Welsh Embassador,*" *Review of English Studies* (1945); Gerald J. Eberle, "Dekker's Part in *The Familie of Love,*"

Adams Memorial Studies (1948); Waldo F. McNeir, "Robert Greene and *John of Bordeaux*," *PMLA* (1949); Dewar M. Robb, "The Canon of William Rowley's Plays," *Modern Language Review* (1950); George R. Price, "The Authorship and Manuscript of *The Old Law*," *Huntington Library Quarterly* (1953); C. L. Barber, "A Rare Use of 'Honour' as a Criterion of Middleton's Authorship," *English Studies* (1957) [*Second Maiden's Tragedy, The Puritan,* and *The Revenger's Tragedy*]; Gustav Cross, "The Authorship of 'Lust's Dominion,' " *Studies in Philology* (1958); Alfred Harbage, "The Mystery of *Perkin Warbeck*," *Holzknecht Memorial Volume* (1959); Arthur Freeman, "The Authorship of *The Tell-Tale*," *Journal of English and Germanic Philology* (1963). Of these the articles by Walter, Simpson, McNeir, Robb, and Harbage are perhaps of greatest interest. The exchanges between the Tourneur and Middleton claimants in the great struggle over *The Revenger's Tragedy* are described and evaluated in Part Three.

Problems of authorship are discussed, sometimes briefly and sometimes at length, in critical studies of individual playwrights. These include: Harold Jenkins, *The Life and Work of Henry Chettle* (1934); M. Joan Sargeaunt, *John Ford* (1935); John Bakeless, *The Tragical History of Christopher Marlowe* (1942); Lawrence B. Wallis, *Fletcher, Beaumont & Company: Entertainers to the Jacobean Gentry* (1947); H. J. Oliver, *The Problem of John Ford* (1955); S. Schoenbaum, *Middleton's Tragedies: A Critical Study* (1955); R. H. Barker, *Thomas Middleton* (1958); Clifford Leech, *John Ford and the Drama of His Time* (1957) and *The John Fletcher Plays* (1962). To these titles may be added

138

the recent series of notably detailed French dissertations: Jean Jacquot, *George Chapman (1559–1634): sa vie, sa poésie, son théâtre, sa pensée* (1951); Felix Carrère, *Le Théâtre de Thomas Kyd: contribution à l'étude du drame élizabethain* (1952); Robert Davril, *Le Drame de John Ford* (1954); A. José Axelrad, *Un Malcontent élizabethain: John Marston (1576–1634)* (1955); Michel Grivelet, *Thomas Heywood et le drame domestique élizabethain* (1957); and M. T. Jones-Davies, *Un Peintre de la vie londonienne: Thomas Dekker* (1958).

Canonical questions figure, although not very prominently, in the most important collected editions brought to completion during this period, the Herford and Simpson *Jonson* (1925–52) and the Bowers *Dekker* (1953–61). In editions of single works, attributions have sometimes been most elaborately argued. I give the proposed authors in square brackets: *The Fairy Knight*, ed. Fredson Bowers (1942) [Randolph]; *The Merry Devil of Edmonton*, ed. W. A. Abrams (1942) [Dekker]; *Rollo, Duke of Normandy*, ed. J. D. Jump (1948) [Fletcher, Chapman, Jonson, and Massinger]; *The Honest Man's Fortune*, ed. J. Gerritsen (1952) [Field, Fletcher, Tourneur, and possibly Massinger]; and *Queen Elizabeth's Entertainment at Mitcham*, ed. Leslie Hotson (1953) [Lyly]. The authorship question also enters into two extraordinary editions of familiar pieces: *The Three Parnassus Plays, 1598–1601*, ed. J. B. Leishman (1949), and *Marlowe's "Doctor Faustus," 1604–1616. Parallel Texts*, ed. Greg (1950). One may mention, lastly, the useful reviews of evidence in the Revels Plays *The Changeling*, ed. N. W. Bawcutt (1958), and *Dr. Faustus*, ed. Jump (1962).

139

» XII «

LOOKING BACK at the Golden Age over the gulf of three decades, we see it as already belonging to a somewhat remote past. Sykes and Oliphant, Robertson and Wells, are today fairly obscure figures, their writings seldom consulted and less often trusted. Licenses for the favorite Golden Age sport of parallel-hunting have long since expired. The journals no longer abandon their pages to the more exotic rites of speculation; even *Notes and Queries,* that last playground for the amateur, has effected an admissions policy under the firm editorial hand of J. C. Maxwell. One cannot, then, say of attribution studies, as one can regarding so much else, *plus ça change, plus c'est la même chose.* On the other hand, to believe in the inevitability of scholarly progress is to cherish an illusion. A few members of the older generation of investigators, their attitudes towards evidence fatally fixed before the Great Reaction, have carried on as though it never took place. Others, mainly of the middle generation, are conscious of shifting currents but cling tenaciously to old ways. Occasionally one detects a defensive note: the investigator may say, "Parallel passages [or metrical tests] are no longer the fashion, but . . ." then plunge ahead. The young, happily unaware of battles fought and lost, fight and lose them again; Sykes has had more than one reincarnation.

Sometimes the seemingly inexplicable will happen. Albert Feuillerat's *The Composition of Shakespeare's Plays* (1953), completed just before his death, was translated and ushered through the press with affectionate care by friends, colleagues, and pupils. This large book (the first installment of a projected trilogy) deals with the supposed authorship problem in six early plays, commencing with *2 Henry VI* and terminating with *Romeo and Juliet*. "The present volume," Feuillerat announces ominously in his preface, "is simply an unimaginative, minute analysis, verse by verse, line by line, of the text of Shakespeare's plays, a steadfast search of facts, facts turned into percentages leading to inevitable deductions which are still facts. . . ." [142] It is more imaginative than he realizes. For a standard by which to measure the authentic, Feuillerat turns to Shakespeare's non-dramatic poetry, the only writings (he feels) which are wholly Shakespearean. Elaborate verse analyses follow. The chief clues are the percentages of trochees and spondees ("as good as a signature of Shakespeare"). Theories discredited by years of patient research are resurrected. Shakespeare, we are told, began his professional career as a reviser of other men's work: "The plays of the company were still usable if only rejuvenated and improved according to the custom of the time: he felt that he could do this sort of work. And so it happened that Shakespeare set himself the task of recasting the repertoire of his company." [143] Feuillerat rejects the findings of modern textual scholarship; the *Contention* and *True Tragedy* are not Bad Quartos but composite plays which Shakespeare refurbished as *2* and *3 Henry VI*. Old apparitions once more stalk the scene. "The ghosts of three authors," Feuillerat writes, "whom I have called A, B, and C have throughout haunted the analysis of the plays." [144] One wistfully hoped that Alexander had exorcised these spirits. *The Composition of Shakespeare's Plays* marks a sad ending to the career of a scholar who,

142. *Composition,* p. vii.
143. *Ibid.,* p. 330.
144. *Ibid.,* p. 331.

almost half a century earlier, made a distinguished contribution to Elizabethan studies. That it should have been published by a great university press constitutes one of the more removed mysteries.

Still more recent is Seymour Pitcher's *The Case for Shakespeare's Authorship of the Famous Victories* (1961), also sponsored by a well-known university. Pitcher maintains, at great length, the fantastic thesis that Shakespeare wrote unaided the old play of *Henry V*. Denying the generally accepted view that the text of this crude, truncated drama of some 1,500 lines is debased, he finds much merit in the play; another critic, writing at about the same time, describes *The Famous Victories,* not unjustly, as "almost imbecile." [145] Although Pitcher cites external facts of doubtful significance, he relies mainly on internal evidence. He points to what he regards as Shakespearean characterization. He sees reflections of the dramatist's personal experiences ("The Prince as Mask" is the title of one chapter). In his longest section, Pitcher devotes forty pages to the testimony of language ("paired words," "fixed phrases," etc.). Never does he concede the necessity of negative checks on evidence; [146] needless to say, Miss Byrne's name does not appear in the extensive list of authorities consulted.

The last two studies I have described are admittedly extreme cases. Yet they represent the efforts neither of cranks nor of amateurs, but of professional scholars, men of learning and good will. Nor can they be dis-

145. A. R. Humphreys, Introduction, [New] Arden *1 Henry IV* (London, 1960), p. xxxiv.

146. "Persons better read in Elizabethan literature than I," Pitcher grants, "may be able to show that some of the alleged Shakespeareanisms are not in fact such"; but the admission of fallibility is immediately followed by an unwarranted show of confidence: "I do not expect my case to suffer much from such discoveries" (p. 162).

counted as mere diversions from their authors' weightier literary preoccupations; Feuillerat boasts that his opus was thirty years in the maturing. More important, the follies which show so baldly in the work of Feuillerat and Pitcher appear in less blatant form in a host of attribution studies, early and late.[147] If learning has so often gone fearfully astray, it must be owing in large measure to the investigator's ignorance or abuse of just method. To this aspect of our inquiry we now turn.

147. One may here lastly take note of E. B. Everitt's *The Young Shakespeare: Studies in Documentary Evidence* (Copenhagen, 1954). Everitt uses a wide variety of authorial criteria—handwriting, dramatic technique, thought, diction, etc.—to support his view that Shakespeare wrote the anonymous manuscript play *Edmund Ironside*. The thesis, argued with much zeal in almost impenetrable prose, is perhaps no more implausible than Everitt's other theories: that Shakespeare was a professional scribe, that he wrote *King Leir* and the *Troublesome Reign,* that the *Contention* and *True Tragedy* are not Bad Quartos, etc.; but those theories are eccentric enough.

III

Avoiding Disaster

» I «

No DOUBT it would be an understatement to suggest that the history of attribution study in the Elizabethan field is on the whole unexhilarating. Triumphs have been few and scattered, failures numerous and sometimes of appalling magnitude; one can take small comfort from the interludes of unpremeditated comic relief. "[It] is extraordinarily difficult," observed Miss Byrne in 1932, "to persuade most people to examine seriously the so-called 'stylistic' attributions of anonymous or acknowledged collaborate plays." [1] Her remark has lost none of its relevance. It is no easier—perhaps, indeed, it is more difficult—to persuade Bentley than it was to convince Chambers.

The errors and excesses of early pioneers, who must necessarily work in the dark, are understandable enough, but why did Oliphant, Sykes, and so many others in our own century come to grief? These men knew and loved the old plays, and were fertile of ideas and intuitions. Most of them were not, like Fleay, fantastics unwilling to support their theories with argument, prone to dizzying improvisations and changes of mind, possessed by demons of inaccuracy. They were in a position to profit from the adventures recorded in the *Transactions* of the

1. "Bibliographical Clues," p. 23.

New Shakspere Society and to build upon the great advances made by the nineteenth century in knowledge of Elizabethan stage history.

Yet they failed, and their great limitation was revealed inadvertently more than fifty years ago by Oliphant. Having raised the fundamental question of *how* the identification of unknown writers was to be accomplished, he offhandedly replied that this was "a matter which every investigator must settle for himself." [2] It is, I believe, this astonishing indifference to method that is the fatal weakness of the conjecturists of the Golden Age and the source of the anarchy still prevalent in attribution work.

These enthusiasts set vigorously to work without troubling about the essential preliminaries. They established no basic principles of procedure. They made no attempt to define the nature of evidence. They applied the various tests indiscriminately. They often ignored relevant external information about the plays they scrutinized so minutely. They failed to grasp the significance of the bibliographical revolution taking place under their noses: they were indifferent to the fortunes of copy in the printing house; they did not discuss compositors. Oliphant and his co-workers and followers were essentially literary amateurs unprepared by training or temperament to subject their investigations to the tedious rigor of scholarly discipline. Their approach—subjective, intuitive, ardent—differs little from that of the impressionist critics with whom they were contemporaneous.[3]

2. "Problems of Authorship," p. 459.
3. In fairness to Oliphant it is necessary to add that when, late in his career, he was stirred by the excesses of the parallelographic school, he showed an interest in methodology absent from his earlier work; see below, p. 192. In his own treatment of individual authorship problems, however, Oliphant remained to the end impressionistic.

But the canonical impressionists were mischievous in a way that the critics were not. For in rationalizing their intuitions and presenting them as evidence, they bequeathed a legacy of confusion and error. Little is to be gained by a belated resurrection of Oliphant's reputation, as R. H. Barker has attempted, on grounds that the strictures of our most distinguished authorities merely reflect the vagaries of scholarly fashion.[4] The gesture in the direction of Oliphant's memory may have sentimental appeal, but the strictures themselves are not easily dismissed, and indeed Barker makes no effort to refute them. If a case is to be made for the legitimacy of employing internal evidence to determine authorship, it must be with a full awareness of past failures and present limitations.

Those limitations are considerable. The investigator's task, as I see it, is to isolate and describe the special character of a literary work of unknown or doubtful authorship, to show the extent to which a known writer's work partakes of that special character, and from this evidence to arrive at an appropriate conclusion. The enterprise is hazardous, for an author's individuality never exists as pure essence, but is subtly alloyed by many interrelated factors: literary conventions and traditions; personal, professional, social, and religious influences. Of all writers the dramatist is most elusive, as he appears not in his own persona but in the manifold guises of the personages that are his imaginative creations. All plays, furthermore, are in a sense collaborations, shaped from conception to performance by the author's awareness of the resources of actors and theater, the wishes of

4. Barker, *Thomas Middleton*, p. 166. On attribution procedures I very much regret having to differ with Professor Barker, the virtues of whose stimulating book I have elsewhere highly commended.

impresario or shareholders, and the tastes and capacities of the audience.

The investigator working with the Elizabethan drama faces additional difficulties. Far removed in time from his materials, he may be easily misled into fancying as original what a contemporary would have instantly recognized as imitation. His task is not simplified by the fact that a great many plays of the period have perished or by the related fact that plays generally were not held in very high literary esteem, especially before the appearance of the great Jonson folio in 1616. Artistic individuality is scarcely to be expected in artifacts manufactured for a commercial market. That individuality nevertheless blossomed—that the age produced not only Shakespeare, Marlowe, and Jonson, but also Chapman, Marston, Webster, and a number of other distinctive voices—is a remarkable assertion of the creative principle. But it should not blind the investigator to the parlous conditions of his labor, conditions that favor not the establishment of facts but the proliferation of conjecture.

I cannot, then, accept Arthur Sherbo's "basic premise" that, in questions of authorship, "internal evidence deals with essentials while external evidence deals with accidentals," and that "short of an unequivocal acknowledgment by the author himself, the value of internal evidence outweighs any other." [5] External evidence may and often does provide incontestable proof; internal evidence can only support hypotheses or corroborate external evidence. So far as the Elizabethan drama is concerned, the justification for the use of internal evidence in determining a canon lies primarily in the inadequacy of the available outward evidence. The principal sources of such informa-

5. Sherbo, "Uses and Abuses of Internal Evidence," p. 6.

tion are the title-pages and dedications of plays, the Stationers' Register, the Office-Book of the Master of the Revels, the early play catalogues, and references by sixteenth- and seventeenth-century commentators and anthologists. About each of these types of evidence and its limitations something must be said.

» II «

TITLE-PAGES. These furnish invaluable data about authorship, and about theatrical auspices, which may be a clue to authorship. But many Elizabethan plays were published anonymously, or merely with the writer's initials, or with erroneous or incomplete attributions.

We know from other sources that some title-pages do not tell the full story. The 1604 and 1605 quartos of *1 The Honest Whore* give the play exclusively to Dekker, but an entry made by Henslowe in his *Diary* on March 14, 1604, reveals that Middleton also had a hand in it. A more striking example of incomplete title-page information is furnished by the 1647 and 1679 folios of *Comedies and Tragedies* "Written by Francis Beavmont and Iohn Fletcher Gentlemen." There is elsewhere ample external evidence of Fletcher's collaboration with Massinger, Field, and Rowley on plays included in these volumes.

The Shakespeare Apocrypha provides the most blatant examples of false title-page ascriptions. *1 Sir John Oldcastle, The London Prodigal, A Yorkshire Tragedy,* and *1* and *2 The Troublesome Reign of King John* were all printed as Shakespeare's during his lifetime, and afterwards included in the Third Folio of 1664. But Shakespeare's was not the only celebrated name to suffer unscrupulous exploitation. *The Coronation* appeared in

1640 as "Written by *John Fletcher,* Gent." and was admitted to the 1679 Beaumont and Fletcher folio. The play belongs rightfully to James Shirley, and in the catalogue of the dramatist's writings inserted in his *Six New Plays* (1653), it is listed with the comment, "Falsely ascribed to Jo. Fletcher." Needless to say, Fletcher was a much more popular playwright than Shirley in the second quarter of the seventeenth century; a commercial motive for deception is not far to seek.[6] Other plays with title-page misattributions include *Alphonsus, Emperor of Germany* (1654), given to Chapman; *The Thracian Wonder* (1661), assigned to Webster and Rowley; and *Lust's Dominion* (1657), printed as Marlowe's. None of the more considerable modern authorities has been taken in by these claims, but in the past the ascriptions have misled able critics and scholars: Malone assumed *Lust's Dominion* to be by Marlowe, and Hazlitt, in the second of his *Lectures on the Dramatic Literature of the Age of Elizabeth* (1820), quoted generously from the same play in order to illustrate Marlowe's mighty line. For some pieces the title-pages supply the only information we have concerning authorship, and although the information may be wrong, we are not in a position to tell. *Two Lamentable Tragedies,* assigned to the mysterious Robert Yarington, is a case in point.

Misleading initials can be more pernicious than full names as encouragement to fruitless speculation. *Locrine* (1595), *Thomas Lord Cromwell* (1602), and *The Puritan* (1607) all appeared with "W. S." on their title-pages and duly found their way into the Shakespeare

---

6. An odd aspect of the affair is that William Cooke, one of the publishers of the 1640 quarto of *The Coronation,* was then Shirley's principal publisher, having already brought out a dozen of his plays; the dramatist, moreover, was alive and still productive. These facts are noted by Bentley, "Authenticity and Attribution," pp. 110–111.

Apocrypha; some critics have guessed, idly, that the initials stand for Wentworth Smith or William Sly. *Selimus,* published anonymously in 1594, was reissued in 1638 with a title-page assignment to "T. G.," no doubt to suggest the name of Thomas Goffe, author of several Caroline plays on Turkish history. The fact that Goffe was born in 1591 makes the ascription somewhat less than plausible.

Even where no deception is intended, the mere presence of initials on a title-page is by itself not often very helpful, and the conjectures of distinguished scholars have sometimes had unfortunate aftermaths. A striking instance concerns not a print but a manuscript play, *The Launching of the Mary,* "written by. W: M. gent. in his returne from East India. āo. 1632." The initials and subject matter led Joseph Quincy Adams to identify the author as William Methold, who entered the service of the East India Company in 1613. At first Adams presented his identification as a hypothesis, but afterwards he referred to it as an established fact.[7] ("One of the brain's most efficient departments," the delightful Archie Underwood once said in a reflective moment, "is the one that turns possibilities into probabilities, and probabilities into facts.") In actuality *The Launching of the Mary,* the manuscript of which is holograph, was written by a different employee of the East India Company, Walter Mountfort, as Boas demonstrated on the evidence of handwriting.[8] Adams' embarrassment neatly illustrates the danger of using inadequate internal evidence to bolster an argument based on inadequate external evidence.

7. Adams, "The Authorship of Two Seventeenth Century Plays," *Mod. Lang. Notes,* XXII (1907), 137; *Dramatic Records of Sir Henry Herbert,* ed. Adams, p. 34.
8. Frederick S. Boas, *Shakespeare & the Universities* (Oxford, 1923), pp. 167–182.

STATIONERS' REGISTER. These records offer less help than do the title-pages. Although the ordinances of the Stationers' Company required the registration of every book published in London and environs, many titles escaped entry. Of extant printed plays subject to licensing, 123 (between one-quarter and one-third of the total) do not appear in the Hall Book kept by the Clerk of the Company.[9] At one point in the detailed accounts there is a lacuna of five years, from July 22, 1571, to July 17, 1576.

Of plays entered in the Register a large number—many more than appeared in print anonymously—are listed without mention of authors. Other entries furnish the same misinformation as the title-pages of the editions which followed, although the occasional discrepancy between license and print may be suggestive (e.g., *Alphonsus* is ascribed to John Peele in the Register, and *The Noble Soldier,* printed as by "S. R.," is twice given to Dekker). Careless or fraudulent entries account for other peculiarities. Thus the Register for 1566–67 records a license "for the pryntinge of a boke intituled the ix[th] and x[th] tragide of lucious Anneus oute of the laten into englesshe by T W fellowe of pembrek hall in chambryge." [10] Seneca's ninth tragedy, the *Octavia,* was translated by Thomas Nuce, whose name appears in the table of contents of the 1581 collection, *Seneca His Ten Tragedies;* the tenth tragedy, *Hercules Oetaeus,* was rendered into English by John Studley, who is also cited correctly in the 1581 collection. These errors of omission and commission have resulted from mere inadvertence.

9. The figures were compiled by Greg, and are given in fuller detail in his *Bibliography of the English Printed Drama to the Restoration* (London, 1939–51), IV, clxiv–clxvi.
10. Records of the Stationers' Company, ed. Greg, in *Bibliography,* I, 3.

Not so those in the large block of titles (forty-two in all) entered by Humphrey Moseley in 1653. In order to smuggle through two plays for a single fee, Moseley in some cases gave double titles for what are in fact independent pieces; as many as seventeen items in his list may be affected. Not surprisingly these entries have given rise to much confusion.

THE REVELS OFFICE-BOOK. Each of the successive holders of the mastership of the Revels—Edmund Tilney (1578–1610), Sir George Buc (1610–22), Sir John Astley (1622–23), and Sir Henry Herbert (1623–42)— customarily maintained a book in which he or his deputy recorded licensing fees, court performances, and other business related to the Office. Because the Master of the Revels by virtue of his position had access to facts about every phase of the theatrical life of his day, the records of this agency assume an authority unmatched by any other source of external evidence.

The original documents, however, have perished, except for a single scrap of waste paper containing a list of plays. The Office-Books kept by Tilney and Buc have vanished without trace. That begun by Astley and continued by Herbert was available to Chalmers and Malone, whose extracts were printed in, respectively, the *Supplemental Apology for the Believers in the Shakspeare-Papers* (1799) and the third volume of the *Variorum Shakespeare* (1821).[11] Thus only a small fragment of this material, of priceless value to the historian, has come down to us in any form. From Herbert's Office-Book

11. Also extant is an independent transcript of Herbert's Office-Book in a nineteenth-century hand, possibly that of Craven Ord. The various entries have been cut up and pasted into appropriate places in J. O. Halliwell-Phillipps' scrapbooks, now in the possession of the Folger Shakespeare Library.

we learn (among other significant facts) that *The Duchess of Suffolk* was written by Thomas Drue, that Fletcher's *Night Walker* was "corrected" by Shirley, and that *The Maid in the Mill* was the joint work of Fletcher and Rowley. (The less reliable Stationers' Register entry gives the last title to Beaumont and Fletcher.)

Yet, however superior the Office-Book is to other contemporary records, it cannot be regarded as beyond reproach. Herbert's licenses include one for "A new Tragedy called, *A Late Murther of the Sonn upon the Mother:* Written by Forde, and Webster." [12] The researches of C. J. Sisson in the Public Record Office have revealed that this lost work was written not by two but four authors: Dekker, Ford, Webster, and Rowley. Dekker, whom Herbert neglects even to mention, had the principal share.[13]

CATALOGUES. Three compilations require notice as embodying pre-Restoration tradition. The earliest was published by Richard Rogers and William Ley as an appendix to *The Careless Shepherdess* (1656). The second was included by Edward Archer in his edition of *The Old Law,* printed later in the same year. The third playlist, by Francis Kirkman, appeared in his 1661 reprint of the old interlude, *Tom Tyler and His Wife;* a decade later he attached a revised and enlarged edition of the catalogue to Dancer's translation of Corneille's *Nicomède.* We are not obliged to regard these compilations, except for Kirkman's, as the work of the publishers under whose names they were issued. All have been edited by Greg in volume three of *A Bibliography of the English Printed Drama to the Restoration* (1957). The pub-

12. *Dramatic Records of Sir Henry Herbert,* ed. Adams, p. 29.
13. Sisson, *Lost Plays of Shakespeare's Age* (London, 1936), pp. 80–124. I owe this illustration to Bentley, "Authenticity and Attribution," pp. 108–109.

lishers of the first two catalogues describe them as "exact and perfect"; Kirkman declared his to be "True, perfect, and exact." These claims are grossly exaggerated, and not least with respect to authorship attributions.

The Rogers and Ley list is a very casual performance, with authors cited for only a third of the plays.[14] Whoever is responsible for it must be credited with the invention of no less than five mythical playwrights. Dekker's *Shoemakers' Holiday, or The Gentle Craft* becomes Holiday's *Gentle Craft; The Revenge of Bussy* is assigned to the (in both senses) ghostly Damboise; Cooke's *Greene's Tu Quoque* emerges charmingly as "Greens tu quoque cookt"; and so on. For the great majority of assignments the cataloguer took his information from printed editions of the plays. When he deviates from the prints, he is invariably wrong; when he attaches playwrights to anonymous pieces he is wrong at least half the time. Thus he gives Lewis Wager's *Repentance of Mary Magdalene* to "B. H." (another ghost), Marlowe's *Edward II* to Shakespeare, and Rowley's *All's Lost by Lust* to Massinger. On the other hand, he correctly ascribes *The Jovial Crew* to Samuel Sheppard and *Imperiale* to Sir Ralph Freeman.

Archer's catalogue improves upon "Rogers and Ley," from which it derives. Archer finds authors for many more plays than did his predecessor. Blunders remain numerous, however: Chettle's *Hoffman* and Fletcher's *Chances* are given to Shakespeare; Heywood's *Iron Age* is assigned to Dekker, and Drue's *Duchess of Suffolk* to Heywood. More than half of Archer's attributions of anonymous printed plays are demonstrably incorrect, and others are questionable.

14. For this analysis of the playlists I owe a large debt to Greg's masterly paper, "Authorship Attribution in the Early Play-lists, 1656–1671," *Edinburgh Bibl. Soc. Trans.*, II (1938–45), 305–329.

His playlist, in turn, provides the basis for Kirkman's. Again there is improvement, and again the final results leave much to be desired. Kirkman rightly gives *If You Know Not Me You Know Nobody* to Heywood, *The Varieties* to Newcastle, and *The Queen of Aragon* to Habington. His attribution of *Alphonsus* to Peele has considerable interest, and he is the first authority expressly to ascribe *Tamburlaine* to Marlowe. So far so good. But Kirkman leaves anonymous some plays published with their authors' names or initials, and he perpetuates such false ascriptions as those of Peele's *Arraignment of Paris* and the anonymous *Merry Devil of Edmonton* to Shakespeare. Errors for which he cannot share discredit include the assignment of "T. B."'s *Country Girl* to Anthony Brewer, Chettle and Munday's *Downfall* and *Death of Robert, Earl of Huntingdon* to Heywood, and the anonymous *Two Wise Men and All the Rest Fools* to Chapman.

Because the information given in the early catalogues is sometimes right, it cannot safely be ignored. Nevertheless, Greg's verdict seems inescapable: *"In this respect* [the attribution of anonymous plays] *far too much reliance has been placed on them, and many of the blunders of bibliographers can be traced to this source."* [15]

MISCELLANEOUS ALLUSIONS AND CITATIONS. The reliability of these varies enormously and is directly dependent upon the knowledge, care, and *bona fides* of the individual writer or anthologist.

Only the most unwary student could possibly cite as his authority Edward Phillips' *Theatrum Poetarum* (1675). Phillips, whose chief distinction is that he was nephew to John Milton, makes some remarkable author-

15. *Bibliography,* III, 1320. Italics Greg's.

ship assignments. He gives *The Old Wives Tale* to Thomas May, *1* and *2 Tamburlaine* to Thomas Newton, *A Warning for Fair Women* to John Lyly, *See Me and See Me Not* to Thomas Nashe, *The Faithful Shepherd* (by John Dymock?) to John Marston, and *Cupid's Whirligig* to Thomas Goffe. Thomas Forde's *Love's Labyrinth* goes to John Ford. Phillips just misses a perfect score on Robert Greene, who could not possibly have written four of the five plays unhesitatingly ascribed to him; indeed, Greene had himself heaped scorn on the anonymous author of one, *Fair Em*.[16] Phillips is admittedly an extreme case, but his inspired performance has excellent competition.

» III «

PARTICULARLY COMPLEX PROBLEMS arise when the external evidence is contradictory, as with *Fedele and Fortunio* (or *Two Italian Gentlemen*). This play, a translation of Pasqualigo's *Il Fedele* (1576), was entered in the Stationers' Register on November 12, 1584, without mention of author, and printed anonymously the next year. An extract of eighteen lines from the play was included in *England's Helicon* (1600) over the signature "*Shep. Tonie.*" Shepherd Tony appears to have been a pseudonym for Anthony Munday. In *England's Parnassus*, another anthology published in the same year as *England's Helicon*, two lines from the already quoted passage were given by the compiler, Robert Allot, to "S. G." (Stephen Gosson?). Elsewhere in Allot's

16. *Greenes Farewell to Folly* (London, 1591). In his preface Greene admits the playwright responsible for *Fair Em* to the company of "witlesse cockescombes." One of those, Greene sneers, who "can not write true Englishe without the helpe of Clearkes of parish Churches, will needes make him selfe the father of interludes" (sig. A4ᵛ).

miscellany two brief quotations from *Fedele and Fortunio* are signed *"G. Chapman."* Confusion is worse confounded by the testimony of the only early edition of the play. Of this quarto three copies survive, only one of which is perfect. The dedicatory epistle of the complete (Folger) copy is signed "M. A.," and the same initials follow the epilogue. But in the Huntington copy, which wants the epilogue, the dedication is signed "A. M." The third copy lacks epistle and epilogue. It is not entirely clear that the author of the dedication is the author of the play, and the initials at the end may conceivably apply to the epilogue alone. Under the circumstances it is hardly surprising that different scholars reviewing the same evidence have arrived at different conclusions. Crawford, the editor of *England's Parnassus,* favors Chapman; Chambers, who classifies *Fedele and Fortunio* as anonymous, regards Gosson as the most promising claimant; Miss Turner casts her vote for Munday.[17] The situation thus appears hopeless.

In fact it is not. The play is surely too early for Chapman, who first appears as a writer with publication of *The Shadow of Night* in 1594. The self-contradictory ascriptions of *England's Parnassus* need not be taken too seriously; Crawford himself counts 130 misassigned quotations in that anthology. The incidence of error in *England's Helicon* is much lower, but it would obviously be imprudent to rest a whole case on a pseudonymous attribution in a not unimpeachable source. The argument cannot, therefore, be settled on external grounds; inevitably one turns to the internal evidence. That evidence

17. Crawford, "Belvedere, or The Garden of the Muses," *Englische Studien,* XLIII (1910–11), 203; E. K. Chambers, *Elizabethan Stage,* IV, 14; Celeste Turner, *Anthony Mundy: An Elizabethan Man of Letters* (Berkeley, 1928), pp. 65, 192–193.

strongly favors Munday.[18] It reinforces and is reinforced by the testimony of *England's Helicon* and the variant dedication.

Fedele and Fortunio, a mere translation, might seem hardly worth all the fuss, were it not for the fact that the historian must by occupational necessity concern himself with minor as well as with major works. But even famous "standard" attributions sometimes rest on remarkably fragile foundations of external fact. No record, for example, survives from Kyd's lifetime to connect his name with *The Spanish Tragedy.* The only external evidence that he wrote the age's most sensationally popular melodrama is Heywood's statement in his *Apology for Actors,* which appeared eighteen years after Kyd's death. Yet *The Spanish Tragedy* is linked inseparably with Kyd's name, and justly so. For we recognize, with the play's most recent editor, that it stands in "a peculiarly intimate relation" to the closet drama *Cornelia,* translated by Kyd from Garnier, and that "the only reasonable way of accounting for the relationship is to say that the same man was responsible for both works." [19] In this case, as in others, the external evidence, by itself hardly overwhelming, is buttressed by the evidence of style.

Internal evidence used in fruitful conjunction with the meager external facts stirs no controversy but provides, rather, welcome illumination of the obscurity in which we must too often work. But it is another matter to

18. See Parrott, "The Authorship of *Two Italian Gentlemen,*" *Mod. Phil.,* XIII (1915–16), 241–251; M. St. Clare Byrne, " 'The Shepherd Tony'—A Recapitulation," *Mod. Lang. Rev.,* XV (1920), 364–373, and "Anthony Munday's Spelling as a Literary Clue," pp. 9–23. See also above, Part Two, p. 98.

19. *The Spanish Tragedy,* ed. Philip Edwards (Revels Plays [London, 1959]), Introduction, p. xvii.

suggest authors where the external evidence is pathetically insufficient, as in the case of *The Bloody Banquet,* with its 1639 title-page ascription to "T. D."; or nonexistent, as with *The Fairy Knight, Dick of Devonshire,* and many other plays. It is risky to attempt the allocation of scenes in collaborations, even when all the partners are known—Middleton, Rowley, and Massinger's *The Old Law,* for example, which has come down in a wretched text; riskier still when not all the collaborators are specified, as in the Beaumont and Fletcher corpus, amply dissected by the disintegrators. Fraught with even greater perils are the investigator's efforts to transform into collaborations plays for which the outward evidence points to single jurisdiction: Lucas and others seeing Webster in *Anything for a Quiet Life,* the Shakespeare disintegrators finding Peele in *Titus Andronicus* or Middleton in *Timon of Athens.* But most hazardous of all is the endeavor to overthrow by the weight of internal evidence alone an attribution for which some external support exists, and here we have the interminable struggle over *The Revenger's Tragedy.*

» IV «

THE INVESTIGATOR who works without external evidence to bolster his conclusions assumes the full burden of proof; he must anticipate that his assumptions, methods, and claims will undergo the severest scrutiny. It is a measure of the amateurism of Boyle and Sykes and the rest that they did so little to fortify themselves against this inspection. But even today, when there is less excuse, attribution studies frequently offer little or nothing in the way of description or defense of the methods employed. In some cases apparently no thought *has* been given to methodology, or so one would conclude from the cavalier violations of ordinary principles of logical procedure. In recent years one investigator has even, by implication, expressed impatience with the rigors of methodological discipline; but the vague standard of doing "the best one can," offered instead (although attractively modest), may seem inadequate to the conscientious student faced with the frustrating complexities of a canon.[20] I cannot, therefore, really apologize for the elementary character of the procedures that I now recommend to canonical investigators. Such interest as these principles may have will lie primarily in the fact that they have to be stated at all. That they do need stating, the illustrations (as well as some of the cautionary tales in Parts One and Two of this study) will, I trust, demonstrate.

1. *External evidence cannot be ignored, no matter how inconvenient such evidence may be for the theories of the investigator.*

The Spanish Gypsy, claimed wholly or in part for Ford

20. Barker writes:

I have avoided enumerating Middleton's "characteristics," partly because this has often been done before, and partly because I feel that to do so here would be to misrepresent the process of determining authorship, which is anything but deductive. One just does the best one can. One reads and forms, or tries to form, impressions; finally a play or a scene or a passage gets to "sound like" Middleton or Dekker or Rowley. Then one looks for somewhat more objective evidence that can be used to convince other readers (*Thomas Middleton,* p. 155).

Oliphant, on the other hand, thus describes the same process:

However strong the internal evidence may be, it is after all only a matter of deduction: because the style of a play, the literary form, the vocabulary, the phraseology, the dramatic technique, the characterization, the philosophy, the outlook on life, are characteristic of a certain writer, we assume his authorship (*Plays of Beaumont and Fletcher,* p. 13).

Yet Barker, as noted, pays generous tribute to Oliphant, and both men approach attribution study in ways not too dissimilar. That they should disagree on so fundamental a matter as whether the method they employ is inductive or deductive would seem to indicate that they have not fully considered the nature of their own assumptions and procedures.

by Sykes, Sargeaunt, and others,[21] is credited to Middleton and Rowley on the title-pages of the 1653 and 1661
quartos. The *bona fides* of the publisher, Richard Marriott, is not beyond reproach. He must be held responsible
for the assignment of *Revenge for Honor* to George
Chapman on the title-page of the 1654 quarto—although
he had previously entered the play on the Stationers'
Register as the work of Henry Glapthorne. Marriott was
almost certainly right the first time. The most plausible
explanation *is,* in this instance, a dishonest commercial
intention on the publisher's part; the name of the famous
translator of Homer, thus displayed, might well have
been expected to spur the play's sales. But Middleton and
Rowley are another matter. The flaunting of their names
on a title-page would scarcely have stimulated buying,
if one can judge from their unspectacular contemporary
reputations. The attribution, moreover, is in keeping with
the fact that the play was licensed for acting by the Lady
Elizabeth's men (July 9, 1623). In the previous year the
same company had performed the same authors' *Changeling,* which indeed is advertised by an allusion in the
second act of *The Spanish Gypsy.*[22] The outward evidence of authorship is then fairly strong—certainly too
strong to be ignored—and the play cannot be dislodged
from the Middleton canon on the basis of subjective critical impressions, especially since some Middletonians have

21. Sykes, *Sidelights on Elizabethan Drama,* pp. 183–199; Oliphant,
Shakespeare and His Fellow Dramatists (New York, 1929), II, 18;
Sargeaunt, *John Ford* (Oxford, 1935), pp. 41–57; Barker, *Thomas Middleton,* pp. 208–209 (but Barker is surely justified in expressing aston-
ishment at Oliver's view, *Problem of John Ford,* p. 34, "that Middleton,
the chameleon dramatist if ever there was one, is always likely to imitate
someone else's style perfectly"). I have myself in the past accepted too
easily the arguments for Ford (*Middleton's Tragedies,* pp. 202, 247).

22. This point is made by Bentley, who finds "no persuasive evidence
to contradict the normal assumption that the play was an ordinary collaboration between Middleton and Rowley" (*Jacobean and Caroline
Stage,* IV, 894, 895).

no difficulty in reconciling the play on critical grounds with the dramatist's acknowledged later work.

Other instances may easily be cited of the too casual treatment of relevant external facts. There is Lucas' work on *The Fair Maid of the Inn,* licensed by Herbert in 1626 as Fletcher's composition and printed in the 1647 Beaumont and Fletcher folio. Lucas includes the play in his standard edition of Webster, and divides it among Webster, Ford, and Massinger, thus eliminating Fletcher entirely.[23] It is Bentley's painful duty to point out that, contrary to Lucas' suppositions, the Master of the Revels was not an advertising agent, and the King's men, who produced the play and took a direct part in the preparation of the 1647 folio, knew their business.

The Shakespeare canon, regarded as a whole, affords the most awesome example of the waste and folly that result from the disregard, misrepresentation, or misinterpretation of external evidence. The First Folio contains thirty-six plays gathered together by Shakespeare's friends and fellow actors, men uniquely qualified for their task. That Heminges and Condell took a responsible view of their undertaking is evident from their Preface "To the great Variety of Readers." "It had bene a thing, we confesse," they wrote in a famous passage,

worthie to haue bene wished, that the Author himselfe had liu'd to haue set forth, and ouerseen his owne writings; But since it hath bin ordain'd otherwise, and he by death departed from that right, we pray you do not envie his Friends, the office of their care, and paine, to haue collected & publish'd them; and so to haue publish'd them, as where (before) you were abus'd with diuerse stolne, and surreptitious copies, maimed, and deformed by the frauds and stealthes of iniurious imposters, that expos'd them: euen those, are now offer'd to your view cur'd, and perfect of their

23. Webster, *Works,* IV, 148–152.

limbes; and all the rest, absolute in their numbers, as he conceiued them.[24]

Moreover, Good and Bad Quartos of fifteen Folio plays bear Shakespeare's name on their title-pages. Other quartos assign him *Pericles* and a share in *The Two Noble Kinsmen,* neither of which appears in the Heminges and Condell volume. Further external evidence in the form of contemporary allusions has corroborative value; in this category Meres's list of a dozen plays in *Palladis Tamia* (1598) is most important. "This evidence," Chambers reasonably observes of the sum of external data, "is of a kind which is ordinarily accepted as determining the authorship of early literature." [25]

Even after allowance is made for the fact that Heminges and Condell do not speak with the precision expected of a modern editor concerned with a classic text, their testimony offers cold comfort to the doubters, disintegrators, and revisionists. For over two centuries those inclined to tinker with the Folio contents have either ignored these early witnesses or sought to undermine their credit. Today *Pericles* is universally regarded as canonical if not homogeneous. Almost certainly Shakespeare had a hand in *Sir Thomas More.* Most, but not all, authorities believe that he collaborated with Fletcher on *Henry VIII.* These special cases, unaccounted for in the prefatory matter of the Folio, do not necessarily call into question the good judgment of the first editors. The fact remains that no satisfactory evidence has ever been adduced to dislodge a single one of the plays they printed.

Yet almost in the same breath with his defense of Shakespeare's friends, Chambers can remark that

24. *Mr. William Shakespeares Comedies, Histories, & Tragedies* (London, 1623), sig. A3ʳ.
25. E. K. Chambers, *William Shakespeare,* I, 206,

. . . the inclusion of an individual play under the comprehensive title of that collection must not be pressed too far. . . . It is quite possible that they [Heminges and Condell] saw no harm in including without comment a play which Shakespeare had only revised, one or two for which he had a collaborator, and one to which he had contributed little, but which had long been linked to other 'parts' of an historical series. It follows, of course, that alien matter may be present in other plays than *Titus Andronicus, Taming of the Shrew, Henry VIII,* and *1 Henry VI.*[26]

Thus the scholar who more than any other was responsible for the discrediting of the disintegrators lets disintegration in again (as it were) through the back door; Chambers ends by himself undervaluing the testimony of the most crucial single document in the annals of authorship attribution.

One may state as a corollary to this first principle that *appropriate weight must be given to the absence of relevant external evidence.* Thomas Creed, who printed *The Famous Victories* as an anonymous play in 1598, also printed *Richard III* in the same year with Shakespeare's name on the title-page. In arguing the preposterous thesis that *The Famous Victories* is by Shakespeare, Pitcher faces a number of difficulties, not least of which is the publisher's strange failure to advertise the name of an extraordinarily popular dramatist whose authorship of the play he would be in a position to know. It is perhaps unnecessary to note that Pitcher fails to clear this hurdle.[27]

2. *If stylistic criteria are to have any meaning, the play must be written in a style.*

26. *Ibid.,* p. 207.
27. For Pitcher's speculations, which lack conviction, see *Authorship of The Famous Victories,* pp. 168–171. His assertion that Creed was "early confident of the salability of plays rightly or wrongly associated with Shakespeare" (p. 171) is of doubtful service to Pitcher's cause.

"Very few writers," remarks Miss Byrne, "are capable of anything so distinguished as a recognizable style, and the minor Elizabethan dramatists are definitely not among that happy band. Men like Munday and Chettle used blank verse as quickly, as slickly, and in as unremarkable a manner as the modern journalist uses his so-called prose." [28] The editors of the Oxford *Jonson* make much the same point about Jacobean prose dialogue: "From the beginning of the seventeenth century there was a tendency for individual dramatic styles in prose dialogue to converge on one more or less established type; somewhat as a modern journal acquires a distinctive style to which all who write for it tend to conform." [29] The point is well taken in connection with both verse and prose.

Collaborations (which prompted the foregoing observations) and revisions are less likely to manifest stylistic individuality than the unrevised work of a single author. The partners may adjust their styles to one another; the reviser may imitate his predecessor. In *Eastward Ho,* Jonson, Marston, and Chapman—three of the age's most individualistic writers—pooled their talents to produce a play with remarkable consistency of texture. Whoever added to *The Spanish Tragedy* acquired, as Prior points out, mannerisms and characteristic images of the original author.[30] I do not envy the future investigator who attempts, on the basis of style, to discriminate between the work of William Faulkner and his collaborators on the screenplay of *Land of the Pharaohs*.[31]

Yet a recognizable style, and hence one that may be

28. "Bibliographical Clues," pp. 22–23.
29. Jonson, *Works,* ed. Herford and P. and E. Simpson, IX, 637.
30. "Imagery as a Test of Authorship," p. 383.
31. For further discussion of the special questions raised by collaborate plays, see the Appendix, below, pp. 223–230.

described, is perhaps rather less rare than Miss Byrne would have us believe. Even hacks like Chettle and Munday, with whom she is concerned, may have occasional strange quirks of individuality. And when she suggests that style is likely to answer our question only when we are dealing with genius, Miss Byrne overlooks the startling distinctiveness that really bad writing can have. Marston at his worst, for example.

The principle holds, however: no style, no stylistic evidence. A collection of stylistic commonplaces isolates nothing and persuades only the gullible or those already convinced. Such collections—Sykes's stock in trade—have unfortunately been the rule rather than the exception (*vide* Bentley). As preposterous as any are the last attribution studies of the incredible Wells, who, after expressing learned disagreement with Sykes, goes on to use similar "evidence" to assign *King Leir, Alphonsus Emperor of Germany, The Troublesome Reign of King John, Edward II*, and other plays to Thomas Kyd. The number of strange additions to the Kyd canon is, Wells allows, "large enough to evoke hilarious incredulity among leading authorities with a too conservative bent." [32] With this point I hesitate to quarrel.

3. *The investigator must always work with the most reliable texts, preferably directly with the early prints or manuscripts.*

There can be few branches of humanistic or scientific inquiry where this principle fails to apply. A classic illustration of the unhappy consequences which may follow from its violation is provided by Sigmund Freud in his *Leonardo da Vinci and a Memory of His Childhood* (*Eine Kindheitserinnerung des Leonardo da Vinci*).

32. "Thomas Kyd and the Chronicle-History," p. 219.

Leonardo's reminiscence—the only childhood recollection set down in the voluminous Notebooks—concerns a vulture that thrust its tail into his mouth as he lay in his cradle. "Where does this vulture come from," Freud asks, "and how does it happen to be found in its present place?"[33] For his answer he goes back to the vulture-headed mother goddess *Mut* (surely connected somehow with *Mutter?*) worshipped by the Egyptians and represented in their hieroglyphics. He explores the vulture's fabled monosexuality and her curious mode of impregnation by the wind. In tracing the origin of Leonardo's fantasy, Freud is reconstructing the psycho-sexual development of a genius; the importance of that vulture can hardly be overestimated. It is therefore especially regrettable that Freud trusted to Marie Herzfeld's translation (1906) of the Notebooks. Leonardo's *nibio* becomes *Geier* (vulture); but *nibio* (or, in modern Italian, *nibbio*) plainly signifies a different bird, the kite, and should have been translated as *Milan*. Textual study gives a hint as to why Leonardo chose this particular creature. The childhood memory appears on the verso of a sheet with notations on the flight of birds, and of all birds the kite was most useful to Leonardo in his observations on the mechanics of flight.[34]

In attributional investigations, which require the closest and most scrupulous study of texts, the importance of the principle should be self-evident. Apparently it has not

33. Freud, "Leonardo da Vinci," *Complete Psychological Works,* ed. James Strachey (London, 1953—), XI (1957), 88.

34. Strachey remarks on the "strange fact" that "until very recently" Freud's error went undetected (Freud, *Works,* XI, 60–61). Actually the mistake was noticed over forty years ago by Eric Maclagen, in "Leonardo in the Consulting Room," *Burlington Magazine,* XLII (1923), 54–57. The multiple significances attached to the kite (apart from possible psychoanalytic symbolism) are too complex to be dealt with here; the curious reader may be referred to Meyer Schapiro's admirable paper, "Leonardo and Freud: An Art-Historical Study," *Jour. of the Hist. of Ideas,* XVII (1956), 147–178.

been. At the beginning of the present century Ashley
Thorndike, in his *Influence of Beaumont and Fletcher on
Shakspere,* courted and won disaster. Applying his *'em-
them* test to the Beaumont and Fletcher plays, he discovered that Fletcher used *'em* sparingly, that Beaumont
employed the two forms indiscriminately, and that Massinger invariably chose *them.* Thorndike prided himself
on having discovered an objective test that yielded such
satisfactory results, and he did not question the reliability of the editions which supplied him with his data.
"Modern texts follow the first quartos or folios carefully," he declared; "and the uniformity of the results,
compared with the diversity of editions, shows that printers' errors may be disregarded." [35] But Thorndike's com-
placence was unwarranted, as he shortly discovered. In a
spasm of belated prudence he checked the Massinger
quartos while his book was in press and found that Gifford,
whose fidelity to the old prints he had assumed, had
changed *'em* to *them* throughout his collected edition
of the playwright. Thorndike had a correction slip bound
into the *Influence* with an admission of his error and a
withdrawal of arguments based upon it. His embarrassment should have served to forewarn others, but did not.

Sykes too learned from experience the unwisdom of
relying on modernized texts. In *Sidelights on Elizabethan
Drama* he tells how an old-spelling edition of *The Spanish Gypsy* sent him scurrying to the British Museum,
where he consulted the Ford quartos and discovered the
dramatist's fondness for *d'ee* and *t'ee* contractions—
linguistic evidence by which Sykes sets great store. In his
nineteenth-century editions the forms had been silently
altered to *d'ye* and *t'ye.*[36] Wisdom came but knowledge
lingered: for other papers (including those in the same

35. *Influence,* p. 27.
36. *Sidelights on Elizabethan Drama,* pp. 188–189.

volume) Sykes trusted to whichever edition came first to hand. He used Hazlitt's *Webster* for *Appius and Virginia* and *The Fair Maid of the Inn,* and the same editor's *Dodsley* for *The Second Maiden's Tragedy, Lust's Dominion,* and other plays. He depended on Dyce's *Middleton* for *Anything for a Quiet Life,* Pearson's reprint of *Chapman* for *Alphonsus,* and (not without amply justified misgivings) the Mermaid *Webster and Tourneur* for *The Revenger's Tragedy.* Nevertheless T. S. Eliot defers to Sykes "as perhaps our greatest authority on the texts of Tourneur and Middleton." [37] So much for our greatest.

"It is time," wrote Greg in 1925,

to recognise that an edited text—perhaps legitimate as an aid to aesthetic enjoyment—is from the point of view of every sort of critical investigation merely a text from which most of the relevant evidence has been carefully removed. To rely on it is like trying to solve an archaeological problem, not by the study of the finds *in situ,* but from neatly ticketed specimens in a museum.[38]

Investigators continue, however, to work with unsuitable texts. In two recent books concerned with the Dekker canon, the data—often involving small details of style— were taken from the miserable Shepherd reprint of Dekker's plays. If for any reason the original quartos were unavailable (unlikely in these days of microfilm), the authors could have consulted the first volumes of the superb Bowers *Dekker,* which for several years had been readily accessible.[39]

4. *Textual analysis logically precedes stylistic analysis.* The wise investigator knows his own text and what

37. Eliot, "Cyril Tourneur," *Selected Essays,* p. 186.
38. Greg, review of Sykes's *Sidelights on Elizabethan Drama,* in *Mod. Lang. Rev.,* XX (1925), 199.
39. Jones-Davies, *Un Peintre de la vie londonienne;* Barker, *Thomas Middleton.*

evidence it may afford of authorship, revision, or corruption. In his edition of the anonymous *Charlemagne,* Schoell furnishes a mass of parallel passages as well as other internal evidence in support of Chapman's claim to the tragedy. Schoell assumes, probably correctly, that the manuscript is holograph; he refers to "le scribe auteur." But the hand is not Chapman's. This information, which it apparently did not occur to Schoell to seek, may be said to diminish the force of his argument. A similar consideration must be reckoned with in the manuscript of *The Second Maiden's Tragedy,* which, although scribal, has corrections that (in Greg's words) "imply a knowledge of the author's own preference or intention." [40] Most investigators concerned with the play's parentage have overlooked the possible evidential significance of these revisions. While not ignoring them in my discussion of Middleton's claim to *The Second Maiden's Tragedy,* [41] I have (I now feel) attached insufficient weight to their presence. The hand responsible for these corrections does not belong to Middleton. Or, to cite a textual consideration of another kind: apparently Lawrence did not know the quarto of *Eastward Ho* when he proposed that before publication the play underwent authorial revision, presumably by Jonson, so that offensive passages might be deleted and the gaps "neatly" closed. [42] The editors of the Oxford *Jonson* have since shown that the cuts were almost certainly the publisher's work and that, with the exception of the notorious passage on the Scots in Act III, no gaps were in fact closed. [43]

40. *Second Maiden's Tragedy,* ed. Greg (Oxford: Malone Soc., 1909), pp. vi–vii.
41. *Middleton's Tragedies,* p. 184.
42. Lawrence, *Pre-Restoration Stage Studies* (Cambridge, Mass., 1927), pp. 363–364.
43. Jonson, *Works,* ed. Herford and P. and E. Simpson, IV, 495–498; IX, 637.

Thus the canonical question bears an intimate relation to the textual question. Further, an apparent matter of style may conceivably be an actual matter of text. Scholars since Malone's time have prodigally expended ink and energy in debating the rival claims of Greene, Kyd, Lodge, Marlowe, Peele, and Shakespeare to *The Contention of York and Lancaster* and *The True Tragedy of Richard, Duke of York*. Since these plays are Bad Quartos of *2* and *3 Henry VI,* the authorities have analyzed the style of what are, in effect, nonexistent plays. Because (to give another illustration) the only extant early edition of Shakespeare's *Pericles* falls into sections of unequal merit, most modern authorities have assumed the romance to be a collaboration. The second author, according to this view, took over with the third act, when the style suddenly improves. But if Edwards is correct in suggesting that the 1609 quarto represents a memorial reconstruction by a pair of reporters—the first responsible for the first two acts; the second, better skilled, for the last three—then we need not regard the original play of *Pericles* as the work of more than one dramatist.[44] Edwards' suggestion is of course only one hypothesis of many that have been offered to explain an especially difficult problem, and there are difficulties in the way of accepting it.[45] But it illustrates a possibility that other canonical investigators have failed even to consider.

In dealing with the minute features of a dramatic text —spelling, linguistic forms, punctuation, and the like— the investigator has a specal problem. He must recognize

44. Edwards, "An Approach to the Problem of *Pericles,*" in *Shakespeare Survey 5* (Cambridge, 1952), pp. 25–49.
45. See the New Shakespeare edition of *Pericles,* in which Maxwell considers and rejects the arguments in Edwards' "important article" (Introduction, pp. xvi–xviii); also Hoeniger's introduction to the new Arden edition, pp. xxxv–xxxvi.

the possibility of scribal intervention in the case of manuscripts, and both scribal and compositorial intervention in the case of printed texts. We know that compositors and scribes were capable of exercising considerable autonomy over certain features of the manuscripts they reproduced. The impressionists do not often trouble themselves with considerations so hostile to romance, and it is not surprising that the skeptical reader should trouble himself as little with data gathered in a vacuum. As noted in Part Two, one reason why Hoy's monograph on the Beaumont and Fletcher plays has commanded respect from the first is that he does not ignore textual considerations.

This principle relates to the next.

5. *Plays of which all the early printed or manuscript texts are continuously defective offer no fit quarries for evidence and are no fit subjects for canonical investigation.* Corruption is a matter of degree, but very little value can attach to stylistic and linguistic minutiae gathered from a quarto representing not the author's written transcript but a memorial reconstruction of that transcript.

In his census of twenty-two Bad Quartos, Kirschbaum includes *Edward I, Fair Em, The Famous Victories, George a Greene, A Knack to Know a Knave, Orlando Furioso, Pericles,* and *Sir Thomas Wyatt.*[46] None of the anonymous or collaborate plays in this grouping has escaped attributional speculation, and several have been the subject of elaborate study. Peele's *Edward I* and Greene's *Orlando* have been used again and again as

46. Kirschbaum, *Shakespeare and the Stationers* (Columbus, 1955), Appendix A, pp. 257–279. Kirschbaum subsequently added *Mucedorus* to his list ("The Texts of 'Mucedorus,'" *Mod. Lang. Rev.,* L [1955], 1–5).

sources of verbal, phraseological, and metrical data. To Kirschbaum's catalogue may be added *John of Bordeaux,* apparently a manuscript "Bad Quarto" that never reached print.[47] There no doubt are other severely defective Elizabethan dramatic texts as yet unclassified. *Jack Straw,* the single surviving contemporary edition of which has only four acts and twelve hundred lines, looks highly suspicious; yet several conjecturists have not hesitated to thrust it on the hapless Peele. Few enthusiasts have shown the resolute forbearance of Bowers in declining to allocate scenes of *Sir Thomas Wyatt* between Dekker and Webster.

6. For any author proposed, a reasonable amount of unchallenged dramatic writing, apart from collaborations, must be extant. The more plays the better; better yet if some precede and others follow the work under consideration, as a theory of imitation is then with more difficulty maintained.

Concerning *The Honest Lawyer,* the 1616 quarto of which was published as "Written by S. S.," Chambers writes: "A conceivable author is Samuel Sheppard . . . , but the absence of extant early work by him makes a definite attribution hazardous."[48] Hazardous indeed! *The Honest Lawyer* appeared in print before Sheppard was born (in *c.* 1624).

In claiming all or parts of four plays for Samuel Rowley, Sykes has only one unquestioned work, *When You See Me You Know Me,* to serve as a quarry for evidence.[49] This play on the reign of Henry VIII is of

47. H. R. Hoppe, *"John of Bordeaux:* A Bad Quarto That Never Reached Print," in *Studies in Honor of A. H. R. Fairchild* (Univ. of Missouri Stud., XXI [1946]), 121–132.
48. *Elizabethan Stage,* IV, 19.
49. Sykes, "The Authorship of 'The Taming of a Shrew,' 'The Famous Victories of Henry V,' and the Additions to Marlowe's 'Faustus,'" *Side-*

uncertain date, undistinguished style, and possibly derivative character (Rowley, we know, was acquainted with two earlier plays on Cardinal Wolsey acted by the Admiral's men).[50] Not surprisingly, Sykes's evidence consists almost entirely of such trivial commonplaces as the expressions "souns," "O brave," and "I warrant thee," or such grand commonplaces as the manifestation of a "fiercely anti-papal spirit." Sykes simply has not enough to go by, and in squeezing dry his material he manages simultaneously to violate the second as well as the sixth of my principles.

Oliphant carries disregard for this principle a step further. He suggests the possibility that Thomas Watson had a hand in *Thorney Abbey* (printed in 1662 as by "T. W."), and he goes on to advise that "Anyone who wants a quite new field of Elizabethan study might first steep himself in a knowledge of Watson's poetry and then read the dramas (and especially the unattached dramas) of the period prior to the middle of 1592, with an eye to determining his presence." [51] The value of the advice is lessened by the fact that not a single play survives that is known to be the work, in whole or in part, of Thomas Watson. Thus a whole new field of study remains unexplored.[52]

The next—and ultimate—step is to attribute plays to persons for whom we have no literary remains whatever, and that step has been taken more than once. Several

lights on Elizabethan Drama, pp. 49–78. The fourth play is *Wily Beguiled.*

50. See F. P. Wilson's introduction to the Malone Society Reprint (Oxford, 1952), p. ix.

51. Oliphant, "Problems of Authorship," p. 439.

52. This happy neglect now unfortunately shows signs of being remedied. L. L. Schücking has recently suggested that *The Spanish Tragedy* was written jointly by Kyd and Watson ("Zur Verfasserschaft der 'Spanish Tragedy,'" *Bayerische Akademie der Wissenschaften. Philosophisch-Historische Klasse* [Munich, 1963]).

students have proposed Sebastian Westcott as the author of various surviving and lost Tudor plays.[53] As Arthur Brown points out, however, "there is neither music nor literature extant which can with certainty be attributed to him," and "until we know a good deal more about Master Sebastian, we must continue to treat his claim to any of these plays as *not proved.*" [54] Miss Marjorie L. Reyburn has recently suggested that Owen Gwyn—for whom, similarly, no surviving writings of any kind have been preserved—collaborated in the Parnassus trilogy.[55]

7. *Intuitions, convictions, and subjective judgments generally, carry no weight as evidence.* This no matter how learned, respected, or confident the authority.

In every branch of scientific inquiry the creative role of intuition is well recognized. "It is the highest degree astonishing," Helmholtz said of Michael Faraday in his 1881 memorial lecture, "to see what a large number of general theorems, the methodical deduction of which requires the highest powers of mathematical analysis, he found by a kind of intuition, with the security of instinct, without the help of a single mathematical formula." [56] Other scientists have possessed similar gifts, if not often to the same degree. In the lesser sphere of attribution

53. See H. N. Hillebrand, "Sebastian Westcote, Dramatist and Master of the Children of Paul's," *Jour. of Eng. and Germ. Phil.,* XIV (1915), 568–584; C. W. Roberts, "The Authorship of *Gammer Gurton's Needle," Phil. Quar.,* XIX (1940), 97–113; and James Paul Brawner, "Early Classical Narrative Plays by Sebastian Westcott and Richard Mulcaster," *Mod. Lang. Quar.,* IV (1943), 455–464.

54. "A Note on Sebastian Westcott and the Plays Presented by the Children of Paul's," *Mod. Lang. Quar.,* XII (1951), 134–136.

55. "New Facts and Theories about the Parnassus Plays," *PMLA,* LXXIV (1959), 325–335.

56. Quoted by James Kendall, *Michael Faraday: Man of Simplicity* (London, 1955), p. 138. Kendall makes the frequently stressed point that Faraday was "ignorant of all but the merest elements of arithmetic" (*ibid.*).

study, too, the investigator's intuitions may have inestimable value. But their value can be known only after he has presented his case; the evidence alone counts.

Yet responsible scholars pay to the pronouncements of experts a respect that reasoned demonstration alone can legitimately claim. In dealing with Heywood's possible involvement in *Pericles,* J. C. Maxwell refers to "the leading authority on that author, Dr. A. Melville Clark" and, while taking mild issue with him, concedes that "Even his [Clark's] unargued verdict carries considerable weight." [57] But how can any unargued verdict carry any weight at all? After making his own case for Shakespeare's part-authorship of three scenes of *The Two Noble Kinsmen,* Muir declares that "the evidence of other tests, together with the convictions of Coleridge, Bradley, Theodore Spencer, and Middleton Murry, make it reasonably certain that Shakespeare wrote also [four additional scenes]." [58] But how can anyone's convictions resolve any controversial question? As I trust my earlier sections have shown, great scholars have made great mistakes.

The poets have erred no less. If the sensibility that is the poet's glory and torment can subtly transform the consciousness of the age which produced him, so too is it molded by the age. On questions of authorship involving the literature of the past, the poet's sensibility is foredoomed to be an anachronistic guide. As likely as not, moreover, he will be dependent upon a superficial acquaintance with the historical scholarship of his own day, and not necessarily the best scholarship. The aberrations of Pope I have mentioned earlier. As striking a lapse as any is Robert Browning's uncritical endorsement of

57. *Pericles,* Introduction, p. xxv.
58. *Shakespeare as Collaborator,* p. 122.

Boyle's preposterous division of *Henry VIII* between Fletcher and Massinger. "The versification," Browning solemnly asserted, "is nowhere Shakspere's." [59]

Despite all the lessons that experience reputedly teaches, the pattern of blind trust in the judgment of the critic or the sensibility of the poet persists. Such deference surfaces exquisitely in an anonymous review in *The Times Literary Supplement:*

> Tourneur's case [for *The Revenger's Tragedy*] has rested partly on historical evidence (admittedly flimsy), but far more upon the judgment of critics such as Mr. Eliot or Professor Ellis-Fermor or Professor Nicoll, who write with a special sensibility for such matters as the poetic style of the two authors [Tourneur and Middleton], their range of characterization and their dramatic idiom and texture. 'Middleton,' says Mr. Eliot, 'has a different feel of the relation of the tragic and the comic.' This is of course the kind of view which a critic may hold with an instinct bordering on certainty, but which is quite unsusceptible of proof.[60]

But a case cannot rest upon "judgment," and a view "unsusceptible of proof" has no binding force. There is a special piquance to the reviewer's citation of Eliot. To show that Middleton is on occasion "a great master of versification," the most highly esteemed man of letters of our time singles out the passage beginning, "I am that of your blood was taken from you/For your better health. . . ." [61] The speech occurs in the last scene of *The Changeling*—a scene which, according to all the evidence and all the reputable authorities, is the unaided work of William Rowley.

---

59. *New Shakspere Society Transactions,* 1880–86, p. 119*.

60. Review of Schoenbaum's *Middleton's Tragedies,* in *Times Lit. Supp.,* February 17, 1956, p. 102.

61. Eliot, "Thomas Middleton," *Selected Essays,* p. 169. Eliot misquotes the passage, presumably because he trusts to the silently emended Mermaid text, which reads, "I that am of your blood. . . ."

The principle applies with equal strength to conclusions based on evidence where that evidence is not produced. In his article on "The Canon of William Rowley's Plays," Robb provides a brief, somewhat impressionistic but nevertheless reasonable account of Rowley's style and subject matter. He then proceeds to give his findings in "most summary fashion" with regard to nineteen extant works associated with the dramatist. But a *general* description will not suffice to validate a judgment with regard to any *specific* play. Hoy, by giving the linguistic evidence, is able to cast doubt on the integrity of at least one of the plays, *A Match at Midnight,* accepted by Robb as the unaided work of Rowley.[62] Quite possibly the journal that carried Robb's paper had very limited space to offer him; if so, he should have published it elsewhere. John D. Jump, in the introduction to his edition of *Rollo, Duke of Normandy,* assures readers that he has assembled much "detailed evidence" to justify his division of the play among four writers. This evidence—parallel passages and metrical statistics—Jump has placed on deposit in the University Library of Liverpool.[63] There it can be of little service to students confronted with one of the most notoriously difficult works of the Fletcher canon. Small wonder that Bentley treats Jump's unsupported findings with barely concealed impatience![64] The *Rollo* episode reveals, as effectively as any, the difficulties that even a very competent scholar may experience when he fails to set forth his evidence in full.

8. *Wherever possible, stylistic evidence should be supplemented by bibliographical evidence.*

62. Hoy, "Shares," *Stud. in Bibl.,* XIII, 82–83, 104.
63. Fletcher *et al., Rollo,* ed. Jump, Introduction, p. xxvii.
64. Bentley, *Jacobean and Caroline Stage,* III, 405.

A playwright's individuality may find expression in a number of accidentals: his idiosyncrasies with regard to speech prefixes, stage directions, act divisions, the recording of entrances, etc.; his peculiarities of spelling, punctuation, and abbreviation. As with linguistic preferences, the usefulness of the data depends entirely upon the fidelity with which scribe or compositors have followed the author's manuscript—provided they worked from authorial copy. Because so little autograph dramatic manuscript has survived from the Elizabethan period, it is often impossible to do more than theorize about a playwright's habits with regard to these minutiae. Yet bibliographical evidence may at times provide a valuable corroboration of an attribution already probable on critical grounds. This is demonstrated in Bowers' textual introduction to Dekker and Massinger's *The Virgin Martyr*.[65] For Massinger there survives the holograph of *Believe as You List;* for Dekker the only dramatic writing available in manuscript is a single scene of *Sir Thomas More,* but valid inferences can be made from Dekker's printed texts. The 1642 quarto of *The Virgin Martyr* was set by a single compositor, probably from the holograph papers of the two authors. Guided by such minute features of the text as the spellings *Cesarea* and *Cæsarea* and the use of hyphens in compounds, Bowers effectively supplements the stylistic evidence for scene allocation.

I have already mentioned the exceptional interest attached to the spelling *scilens* in the *More* fragment.[66] Evidence of this kind has not often enough been brought to bear on attribution problems. *The Puritan,* to cite but one example, has for long puzzled scholars. Printed in 1607 as by "W. S.," it is certainly not by Shakespeare. A number of authorities feel it may be a Middleton work. The

65. Dekker, *Dramatic Works,* ed. Bowers, III, 368–374.
66. See above, Part Two, p. 105.

play is a comedy of London life acted by the Children of Paul's about 1606; at that time Middleton was the chief dramatist of Paul's, and he was writing city comedies. There is some stylistic evidence for Middleton. No other plausible candidate for authorship has been proposed. But the case, as it stands, is inconclusive; further evidence is badly needed if the play is to be given even a conjectural place in the Middleton canon. Yet, although a number of investigators have made pronouncements about *The Puritan,* and although we have a sufficient quantity of dramatic manuscript in Middleton's hand, the 1607 quarto has never been gone over for spelling, punctuation, and other textual clues to authorship. Nor, for that matter, has it been studied for the related evidence of linguistic preferences.

The eight principles I have outlined do not exhaust the possibilities for cautionary advice to canonical investigators. Other strictures, at least equally wholesome, will no doubt occur to readers who have concerned themselves with authorship problems. The principles I have suggested derive from my own experience with particular questions as well as with the literature of attribution. All eight reflect my dissatisfaction with the casual methodlessness of stylistic impressionism, the dominant mode of investigation since Langbaine commented on "the Stile, or Oeconomy" of *The Fair Maid of the Exchange* in his *Account* in 1691. That methodlessness is, I feel, largely responsible for the Great Reaction of the 1920's and 1930's and for the disesteem in which authorship studies in the field of Elizabethan drama are now held.

» V «

IT IS NOT POSSIBLE here to deal with all of the tests by means of which investigators in their wisdom or folly have sought to prove authorship by style. Some of the criteria that have been employed are, in any case, too feeble even to require citation; a few minor tests have already been discussed briefly in previous parts. But several widely used and abused techniques—tests of verse and imagery, parallels of phraseology and thought—call for more extended comment.

VERSE TESTS. As long ago as 1874, in the discussion following Fleay's first paper for the New Shakspere Society, Alexander Ellis pointed to some of the limitations of an investigative technique that seemed to hold great promise. On the rhyme test he commented: "The actual rhymes relied upon must be each seen and passed, for what looks like rhyme to modern eyes was not always rhyme to Shakspere's ears, and conversely." [67] He discerned (without fully appreciating its strength) a subjective element in verse tests; a change in the reader's intonation, he observed, could produce a rhythm where at first none was felt. In generalizing about verse techniques, one must, Ellis further noted, take into account that a poet's usual metrical habit may be diverted by the exigencies of creation or the pressures of momentary inspiration. The calculation of proportions raised methodological problems. Even the ostensibly straightforward job of counting syllables and accents was not so simple a matter: "The resolution of syllables, as, *pu-is-sance, le-o-pard, cre-a-ture,* &c., and the difference of accent, as *ad-vér-tise;* the syllabic *r,* as *Hen-r-y, fi-re;* and *l,* as, *crad-l-es,* &c., threw also much difficulty into the way of merely statistical inquiry." [68]

67. *New Shakspere Society Transactions,* 1874, p. 19.
68. *Ibid.,* pp. 19-20. Furnivall early rejected outright Fleay's more extravagant claims. "In no sense," the former declared, "'can metrical tests be calld 'scientific'. They get their value from the coincidence of their results with those of aesthetic criticism and external data. They

Ellis' remarks, voiced as part of the give and take of informal debate, are not profound. But they are nonetheless pertinent, and in touching upon the subjective factor in the appreciation of verse technique, he put his finger on a basic difficulty. To Ellis' premonitory admonitions may be added others yielded by hindsight. Overall metrical tabulations for a play tend to mislead by obscuring wide fluctuations between scenes. Verse peculiarities, which as a rule the investigator artificially isolates for analysis, can actually be understood only in relation to content. The cadences of the council chamber may be expected to differ from those of the boudoir; were abstract metrical characteristics the sole considerations, one might have to regard the play put on by the comedians in Elsinore as debris from the primitive ur-*Hamlet*. The danger of scribal, compositorial, or modern editorial interference casts a shadow over verse as over other tests; such interference may affect both rhythm and lineation. The list of hazards could be extended.

"The danger of metrical evidence is that it is too often believed." So wrote Lucas some years back in his edition of Webster.[69] After giving entirely persuasive reasons for regarding the tests with profound distrust, he goes on to apply them himself to *Anything for a Quiet Life* and *The Fair Maid of the Inn,* with results no happier than those of his predecessors. Today little danger exists of metrical statistics being too easily believed, except perhaps by their compilers. If the use of such evidence can be justified at all, it is only as corroboration for the assignment of scenes of collaborate plays in which the partners have been identified and are known to have widely differing metrical habits (e.g., Middleton and

are merely empirical; and though they yield the right result on twenty-five applications, there is no reason why they should do so on the twenty-sixth" (*ibid.,* p. 32).

69. Webster, *Works,* ed. Lucas, IV, 250.

Rowley's *Fair Quarrel* and *Changeling*). But even in such cases previous results testify to the need for extreme caution.

IMAGISTIC TESTS. In her 1931 British Academy lecture, Caroline Spurgeon voiced her faith in the value of the revelations her method would produce. "[It] seems to me," she said, "to serve as an absolute beacon in the skies with regard to the vexed question of authorship." [70] That beacon has since guided a number of investigators, and it is a cause for regret that they have so often suffered shipwreck. The perils are nicely illustrated in the work of Marco Mincoff and Una Ellis-Fermor. Each made, unaware of the other, a detailed study of the imagery of *The Revenger's Tragedy*.[71] Mincoff identified the author as a townsman, Middleton; Ellis-Fermor inferred, from similar evidence, that he must be a countryman, Tourneur. Mincoff avoids certain pitfalls; he is much less prone to use imagery as the basis for pseudo-biographical reconstructions (e.g., the playwright's boyhood), which must be reckoned as evidentially worthless. But skeptical readers will hardly be persuaded by his data, and the conflicting results achieved by two well-known scholars working on the same play and concerned with the narrowest possible field of author-candidates do not inspire confidence in the method.

The strictures (discussed below) relevant to the test for parallels may be held to apply to imagistic tests as well, and may provide some discipline. But the image-

70. Spurgeon, "Shakespeare's Iterative Imagery," p. 257.
71. Ellis-Fermor, "The Imagery of 'The Revengers Tragedie' and 'The Atheists Tragedie,'" *Mod. Lang. Rev.*, XXX (1935), 289–301; Mincoff, "The Authorship of the Revenger's Tragedy," *Studia Historico-Philologica Serdicensia*, II (1939), 1–87.

hunter faces special difficulties. The need for selection—
few words do not convey an image of some kind—and
classification inevitably enlarges the subjective factor in
attribution work. The investigator is, moreover, ham-
pered by our very limited knowledge of the images and
image-patterns favored by the various minor Elizabethan
dramatists. Detailed study of imagery is a relatively recent critical preoccupation, and misgivings about applying
its techniques prematurely to authorship problems would
seem to be fully warranted.[72]

A novel and especially interesting imagistic test has
recently attracted notice as a result of its employment by
Kenneth Muir in a sympathetically received study.[73] Muir
is concerned less with metaphors and similes as such than
with groupings of unconsciously associated words, ideas,
and figures that recur from one work to another by the
same author. The term for these groupings—image clusters—we owe to Edward A. Armstrong who, in his seminal work on *Shakespeare's Imagination,* divined their
relevance to attribution problems. "As no two poets employ the same image clusters," Armstrong asserted,
"therefore work of doubtful provenance can be assigned
to a poet with certainty if it contains clusters, or exhibits
principles of cluster formation, characteristic of writings known to be authentic." [74] In a later passage Armstrong judiciously modified this substantial claim. He got
down to cases only to the extent of suggesting that

72. Certain of the pitfalls are usefully discussed by Prior in "Imagery
as a Test of Authorship," pp. 381–386. The complexities of definition and
classification are ably surveyed by Edward B. Partridge in *The Broken
Compass: A Study of the Major Comedies of Ben Jonson* (London, 1958),
pp. 19–36. Partridge believes that "imagery cannot be safely used to
settle questions about the canon of an author" (p. 14).

73. *Shakespeare as Collaborator.* See, for example, Clifford Leech's
review, *Notes and Queries,* CCVI (1961), 156–157.

74. *Shakespeare's Imagination,* Appendix, p. 184.

Shakespeare's share was small in *Henry VIII* and non-existent in *Two Noble Kinsmen*. Muir, in his inquiry into the authorship of the latter play, dwells on image clusters which eluded his predecessor. Shakespeare, Armstrong had noted, associates the kite with bed—death—spirits —birds—food. At least three of these associations surround all fourteen kite references in canonical plays. In Act I, scene i, of *Two Noble Kinsmen,* the kite appears at the center of the entire cluster. The presence of the whole cluster, which Armstrong astonishingly missed, is arresting, and some of the other syndromes which Muir points to in *Two Noble Kinsmen* and also in *Edward III* have equal interest. As an investigative technique, cluster criticism has the merit of exploiting the psychology of unconscious associative patterns, a factor generally left out of account in stylistic analyses.

But troublesome second thoughts arise. What role does accident play in the formation and repetition of the clusters? To what extent are the known clusters tissues of commonplaces? How influential are literary models, which after all are grist to the unconscious as well as source materials for the shaping imagination? Clearly we should know more than at present we do about the nature and frequency of image clusters in Elizabethan literature. The *blot*-cluster that Muir cites as evidence for Shakespeare's hand in *Edward III* has recently been discovered in the anonymous *Edmund Ironside,* which (*pace* Everitt) Shakespeare is most unlikely to have written.[75] Confidence is further shaken by Jackson's discovery of the *beetle*-cluster (which enters into *Lear* and ten other Shakespearean plays) in a poem by Shelley. "The possibility that Shakespeare wrote *The Boat on the Ser-*

75. MacD. P. Jackson, "Shakespeare and 'Edmund Ironside,'" *Notes and Queries,* CCVIII (1963), 331–332.

chio," Jackson drily concludes, "can presumably be discounted." [76] The moral is simple but nonetheless worth drawing: no matter how promising a new test may seem, it behooves the investigator to proceed with extreme caution.

PARALLEL PASSAGES. The foundation of most stylistic attributions during the past fifty years has been neither metrical nor imagistic data but the testimony of parallels: unusual correspondences of language and thought, generally in brief passages, between the doubtful play and the acknowledged works of the suggested dramatist. This test too has occasioned doubts and skeptical protests. "There is nothing more dangerous," Chambers declared, "than the attempt to determine authorship by the citation of parallels." [77] More recently, the editors of the Oxford *Jonson* have remarked upon "the illusory test of parallel passages," and Bentley has deprecated, with customary vigor, the "parallel-passage 'evidence' of modern enthusiasts." [78] But in this instance the difficulties are, I feel, different in character and significance from those presented by the tests I have already touched upon. Most conservative editors, the Simpsons included, are able to use the evidence of parallels, and most conservative historians, Chambers and Bentley included, can take seriously attributions based chiefly on such evidence.

In his account of the disintegration of Middleton's *Anything for a Quiet Life* by the impressionist quartet of Sykes, Oliphant, Lucas, and Dunkel, Bentley provides an at times almost farcical but essentially sad chronicle of the misuse of stylistic evidence. That evidence consists mainly of parallel passages. Bentley's chief complaint is

76. *Ibid.,* p. 332.
77. *William Shakespeare,* I, 222.
78. Jonson, *Works,* ed. Herford and P. and E. Simpson, IX, 636; Bentley, *Jacobean and Caroline Stage,* IV, 860.

that "Most of the passages are not parallel, and the words and phrases are by no means peculiar to Webster [Middleton's proposed collaborator]." [79] The objection to commonplace or unparallel parallels occurs often in *The Jacobean and Caroline Stage*. It is a legitimate objection but applies less to a method than to its abuses. For if the parallels are not parallel and the words and phrases are commonplace, the test, in a very real sense, has not been employed.

The abuses that Bentley properly deplores did not pass with the impressionists of the freewheeling twenties. In 1948 G. J. Eberle published a study of *The Family of Love*, a comedy printed anonymously in 1608 and assigned to Middleton in Archer's 1656 playlist. The aim of the study is to demonstrate that the play "is a revision by Dekker and Middleton of an early play written by Middleton with considerable help from Dekker." [80] A thesis as complicated as this is difficult either to prove or to disprove; unfortunately for Eberle the onus of proof rests with him. To support his argument he assembles a number of parallels, or "touchstones," as he calls them. "Even distant echoes in Middleton" are cited. "Commonplaces and proverbial expressions" are "included as confirmatory evidence if Dekker uses them often and Middleton never." [81] Thus Middleton's collaborator—if he had one—is from the outset presumed to be Dekker. Eberle assumes also that *The Puritan* and *The Revenger's Tragedy* are Middleton's, and he gives to Dekker all or part of *Blurt, Master Constable; The Weakest Goeth to the Wall; The Bloody Banquet; The Merry Devil of Edmonton;* and *The Black Book.* All these

79. *Jacobean and Caroline Stage*, IV, 860.
80. Eberle, "Dekker's Part in *The Familie of Love*," p. 726.
81. *Ibid.*, p. 725.

ascriptions are the proposals of modern critics, and all are controversial. To parallels from these works Eberle adds others from composite plays: *The Changeling; 1 The Honest Whore* (a Dekker-Middleton collaboration!); *The Roaring Girl* (also by Dekker and Middleton); *The Old Law* (where the authorities disagree on the assignment of some scenes); and *A Fair Quarrel* (where an episode almost certainly by Rowley is cited as evidence for Middleton). Despite the catholic variety of sources Eberle has to draw upon, many of his parallels are not parallel. The entire essay is, indeed, a fine illustration of the inadequacy of good intentions alone. "This study," Eberle had assured his readers at the beginning, "attempts to approach the ideal set down by Bentley for studies in attribution." [82]

If Eberle's study falls short of his own ideal, it is because he has set up no *a priori* rules of procedure for his own guidance in collecting data and has made no effort to classify and evaluate the evidence once gathered. Rather he has amassed ungraded parallels. The amassing of ungraded parallels proves nothing. This truth was stated three decades ago by Miss Byrne. At the same time she offered five Golden Rules, as she reasonably described them, for the improvement of parallel-hunting. They deserve quotation:

(1) Parallels may be susceptible of at least three explanations: (*a*) unsuspected identity of authorship, (*b*) plagiarism, either deliberate or unconscious, (*c*) coincidence;
(2) *Quality* is all-important, and parallels demand very careful grading—e.g. mere verbal parallelism is of almost no value in comparison with parallelism of thought coupled with some verbal parallelism;

82. *Ibid.*

(3) mere accumulation of ungraded parallels does not prove anything;

(4) in accumulating parallels for the sake of cumulative effect we may logically proceed from the known to the collaborate, or from the known to the anonymous play, but not from the collaborate to the anonymous;

(5) in order to express ourselves as certain of attributions we must prove exhaustively that we cannot parallel words, images, and phrases as a body from other acknowledged plays of the period; in other words, the negative check must always be applied.[83]

To these rules I would venture to add a sixth: parallels from plays of uncertain or contested authorship prove nothing.

In a spirited article, "How Not to Play the Game of Parallels," Oliphant anticipated several of Miss Byrne's strictures (e.g., "The only true parallel is one that duplicates both thought and the expression of the thought").[84] He offers, too, some shrewd clinical observations on the psychopathology of the more extreme practitioners: their passion to claim every play in sight for an author on whom they have obsessively fixed; their tendency to stress stylistic mannerisms helpful to their case when considering one play but to ignore, when considering another, the significant absence of the same mannerisms.

Oliphant's essay suffered almost total neglect, failing even to find its way into the *Year's Work* or the *Annual Bibliography*. Miss Byrne's paper has not fared very much better. The impressionists, unable to challenge the validity of any of her tenets, have either left the article severely alone or glanced at it approvingly and then ignored its implications. In the latter category belongs

83. Byrne, "Bibliographical Clues," p. 24.
84. *Jour. of Eng. and Germ. Phil.*, XXVIII (1929), 1-15.

Dover Wilson, who, in his edition of *2 Henry VI,* cites
Miss Byrne as an authority for the present-day view that
merely verbal parallels have little evidential value. Yet
he includes them as supplementary evidence. At the same
time he stresses other kinds of parallels: ". . . syntactical peculiarities, little mannerisms and tricks of style,
proverbial phrases (sometimes used incorrectly or with a
special twist), classical or other allusions, and clichés of
various types." [85] This is to fall back on data even more
vulnerable than those censured by Miss Byrne, data which
in any event do not lie outside the jurisdiction of her
rules. Of these Wilson violates at least four, and in addition my sixth. Eberle is in good company.

LITERARY CORRESPONDENCES. Allied to verbal parallels,
and subject to some of the same strictures governing the
admissibility of evidence, are the larger parallelisms of
thought and theme, characterization and dramatic technique. But parallels of this kind, for convenience desig-
nated as literary correspondences, also make special
demands of their own. Their usefulness depends closely
upon the investigator's capacities for literary analysis,
and the precision with which he can formulate critical
distinctions. In practice the canonical impressionists have
been, as we might expect, critical impressionists, and the
subjective element present in all criticism has been in
their work pervasive and detrimental. Their inclination,
insufficiently resisted, is to make oversimplified descrip-
tive pronouncements and pass oversimplified value judgments. A scene is by Jonson because it is "masterful," by
Middleton because "it has his irony" (but how, one may
ask, does his irony differ, say, from Jonson's?), by Peele

85. New Shakespeare *2 Henry VI,* ed. Wilson, Introduction, pp. xxvii–
xxviii.

or Greene or Heywood because it is not very good. As evidence for Dekker's authorship of *Blurt, Master Constable,* Lawrence suggests that two songs in the play ". . . have a good deal of that careless grace of style, what one might characterise artful artlessness, which marks Dekker's lyrics." [86] Apparently it did not occur to Lawrence that precisely the same observations might be made about any tolerable Elizabethan lyric, and the age produced a number of tolerable lyrics. The limited critical value of this kind of impressionism is obvious. As evidence for authorship its value is nil.

Yet verbal parallels and literary correspondences—defined correspondences, not mere impressions—may provide a basis for attributions acceptable to the responsible historian, critic, and editor. Such evidence (especially the larger stylistic resemblances) for the assignment of *The Queen* to Ford is most impressive.[87] Archer surely erred in assigning the play to Fletcher in his 1656 playlist, and the error is satisfactorily explained by Greg. The attribution has gone unchallenged since Bang proposed it over half a century ago. An equally successful argument for attribution was made by Cyrus Day, who pointed out striking parallelisms of phraseology, dramatic situation, and character portrayal between an anonymous seventeenth-century comedy, *The Drinking Academy,* and the known writings of Thomas Randolph, a distinctly minor dramatist who habitually pillaged his own works.[88] The literary correspondences are in this case satisfyingly concrete: the characters of Worldly, Knowlittle, and

86. Lawrence, "Dekker's Theatrical Allusiveness," *Speeding Up Shakespeare* (London, 1937), p. 118. The passage does not appear in the shorter version of Lawrence's article published in *The Times Literary Supplement* in the same year.
87. Discussed above, Part Two, p. 78.
88. "Thomas Randolph and *The Drinking Academy,*" pp. 800–809.

Cavaliero Whiffe in *The Drinking Academy* have their equivalents in Simo, Asotus, and Ballio in *The Jealous Lovers*. The verbal parallels with nine of Randolph's acknowledged pieces are numerous and often unusual. There are no external facts to contradict the evidence of style, and Randolph's authorship of the play has been accepted by (among others) Hyder Rollins, Fredson Bowers, and G. E. Bentley.

» VI «

THE RESULTS of any single test of authorship have to be viewed, of course, as part of a larger design. An investigator such as Hoy, applying a limited number of linguistic criteria to the Beaumont and Fletcher corpus, must at times supplement his findings with other kinds of evidence, and he recognizes fully that his own work depends in part upon the work of others before him. A case for attribution may well represent the patient efforts of a number of scholars over a long period of time. Each contributes his particular bits of evidence. The ultimate effect sought is a cumulative one, in which all the internal evidence—stylistic, bibliographical, and linguistic—converges inexorably upon a single possible author-identification, an identification compatible with the known external information.

This cumulative effect so often (and properly) stressed by internal evidence enthusiasts is no doubt, as Sherbo and others have urged, something apart from and greater than the individual pieces of testimony of which it is composed, just as a building transcends the material—the steel, concrete, wood, and plaster—that have gone into its making. But the architect of attributions must beware lest his materials be merely of the air, airy, the formulas of style and expression that are the common currency of an age. One recalls the recent unfortunate experience of the Rev. A. Q. Morton who, armed with the resources of the modern electronic computer, asserted the presence of no less than six hands in the fourteen Pauline epistles of the New Testament.[89] Mr. Morton maintained that the use of certain excessively familiar words (*in, but, and,* etc.) was so individually distinctive in any writer as to constitute, in effect, a fingerprint of the brain. The test came to the attention of the Rev. Dr. John W. Ellison who was able by the same means to prove that Joyce's *Ulysses* was written by five authors, none of whom had any part in the *Portrait of an Artist*.[90] Dr. Ellison arrived at the not unwarranted conclusion that Mr. Morton's method was "an abuse of both computers and scholarship."

Closer to home, examples of the unshamefaced citation of the most paltry stylistic "evidence" are not difficult to come by. One of the building stones used by Golding to construct his argument for Robert Wilson's authorship of *A Larum for London* is the phrase "ha, ha, ha!" favored by the facetious Wilson.[91] The episode deserves a place in attribution history as the Case of the Solemn Ha, Ha, Ha. The word *dilling,* as the Simpsons complain with understandable irritation, "is not 'a Mar-

89. Morton, "A Computer Challenges the Church," *The Observer,* November 3, 1963. See also Morton's paper, "Statistical Analysis and New Testament Problems," in *The Authorship and Integrity of the New Testament* (London, 1965), pp. 40–60. He makes the startling claim that, with the utilization of computing-laboratory resources, "most of the standard problems of the authorship of the New Testament epistles will be completely solved and much confused scholarship will have been swept away" (p. 55).

90. Reported in the *New York Times,* January 23, 1965.

91. Golding, "Robert Wilson and 'Sir Thomas More,'" *Notes and Queries,* CLIV (1928), 239. Another of Golding's parallels is, "It may be so." Then again, it may not.

ston word' because it occurs once in the text of Marston
. . . and 'well-parted' . . . is not exclusively a Jonson
phrase when it is found in Shakespeare, Webster and
Rowley, and Field." [92] On the possibility of Chapman's
part-authorship of *Rollo, Duke of Normandy,* Hoy declares: "Mr. Wells's evidence is of the sort which, viewed
piecemeal, seems worthless; when viewed in the aggregate, it amounts to convincing proof. I am personally
persuaded that he has established Chapman's presence in
the play. . . ." [93] But it is difficult to see why a great
heap of rubbish should possess any more value than a
small pile of the same rubbish. Zeros, Ephim Fogel
neatly puts it, no matter how numerous, add up to zero.[94]

Yet even proper methods, employed by disinterested
seekers after truth, may yield inconclusive results. Attribution proposals as firmly supported as those for *The
Queen* or *The Drinking Academy* are after all rare, and
the successful identification of the authors of collaborate
plays rarer still. The investigator may find himself, sooner
than he anticipated, at the frontiers of ignorance, which
after so much expenditure of sweat and ink, remains a
spacious domain. The words with which Baldwin Maxwell concludes his study of *A Yorkshire Tragedy* apply
equally well to a number of other plays of anonymous or
doubtful authorship. "A convincing identification of the
author or authors . . . ," Maxwell writes, "if it is ever
to be accomplished, must await our clearer knowledge of
what were the peculiar characteristics of the various
Jacobean dramatists." [95]

The trend away from simple impressionism to a more
analytical criticism (well exemplified by such recent work

92. Jonson, *Works,* IX, 636–637.
93. "Shares," *Stud. in Bibl.,* XIV, 61.
94. "Salmons in Both," p. 304.
95. *Studies in the Shakespeare Apocrypha,* p. 196.

as Jonas Barish's *Ben Jonson and the Language of Prose Comedy*) should help to provide that knowledge with regard to the larger aspects of dramatic art. So far as the small particulars of style—individual words, phrases, lines—are concerned, the electronic computers may in future be expected to play an essential role, although we must discount the more fantastic claims made in their behalf. These devices, after all, are not mechanical brains with magical potencies but serviceable tools of human intelligence.

Serviceable tools are rarely in oversupply, and I would not underestimate their importance even for such operations as simple numerical counts. Any investigator who has compiled word-lists (however carefully) and checked his results must be conscious of the disheartening tendency of repeated tabulations to yield different totals each time. In an early stage of their important work on the authorship of the contested *Federalist Papers,* Mosteller and Wallace arrived at "an important empirical principle: people can't count, at least not very high." [96] Moreover, people tire, but machines do not and are therefore capable of assuming greater quantitative burdens. The computers, then, will make possible on a wide scale the compilation of accurate statistical data on spelling, linguistic preferences, and other accidentals of style. They will also expedite work on lexicons and concordances, and even print out the results in a form that is economically if not aesthetically attractive. The few available older concordances of Elizabethan dramatists (Shakespeare, Kyd, Marlowe), although painfully inadequate by present-

96. Frederick Mosteller and David Wallace, "Notes on an Authorship Problem," *Annals of the Computation Laboratory of Harvard University,* XXX (1961), 164.

day standards, have shown how vulnerable is some of the vocabulary evidence advanced by the impressionists. Further shocks are certain to be felt as the stock of source materials for negative checks increases. Computer programming, finally, will facilitate use of less elementary statistical techniques (e.g., calculations of probability) than those now customarily employed. Significantly, Mosteller and Wallace are professional statisticians.

Cornell University has led the way in the pioneering application of electronic computers to literary research, and equally important work has gone on at Cambridge (Massachusetts), Los Angeles, and other centers. But these experiments have been concerned with Homer or Dryden or Jefferson or Arnold—worthy subjects all— rather than with the Elizabethans. The machines have yet to produce a concordance for any Tudor or Stuart dramatist, nor am I aware of one in preparation. This despite the exhortations of Fogel and others, and enlightened support on the part of International Business Machines for projects in the humanities. If there can be little real doubt that the day of the computer will shortly dawn in Elizabethan studies, candor requires the admission that thus far progress has been disappointingly slow.

It would be excessively hopeful to assume that, even with better tools and more refined methods, students will be able to find answers—plausible explanations, I should say—for the majority of our vexing attribution problems. The investigator may be halted by unbridgeable gaps in his evidence; he may find himself faced with the stubborn reluctance of facts to dispose themselves conveniently in support of hypotheses. Mention of these unwelcome but very real possibilities brings us to the extraordinary question of *The Revenger's Tragedy*. The most important

Elizabethan play of seriously disputed authorship, it may serve as an object lesson in the perplexities and frustrations of canonical research.

» VII «

THE FEW SPARE SEVENTEENTH-CENTURY RECORDS offer little foretaste of the interest that the play would excite three hundred years later. On October 7, 1607, George Eld entered *The Revenger's Tragedy,* along with Middleton's *A Trick to Catch the Old One,* on the Stationers' books. As so often with Register entries, there is no mention of an author. Later in the same year Eld published the only early quarto edition of *The Revenger's Tragedy.*[97] The title-page sheds no light on authorship but does state that the play is printed *"As it hath beene sundry times Acted, by the Kings Maiesties Seruants."* Although this extraordinary tour-de-force was mounted, apparently with some success, by the premier theatrical company of the age, and although it left a mark on subsequent drama, no allusion to play or playwright by a contemporary diarist or miscellanist has come to light. *The Revenger's Tragedy* remained anonymous in the 1656 Rogers and Ley catalogue, but in Archer's list of the same year "Revenger" was assigned to "Tournour." In his 1661 catalogue, and again in 1671, Kirkman, who sometimes corrects his predecessor's misattributions, retained the ascription; at the same time he expanded the play's title and added the dramatist's Christian name *"Cyrill."*

The seventeenth-century playlists, as we have seen, do not command respect for their meticulousness. Nevertheless, it is easier to account for the erroneous assign-

97. The title-pages of some copies bear the variant imprint 1608.

ment of (for example) *The Queen* to Fletcher or *The Merry Devil of Edmonton* to Shakespeare than it is to account for a mistake—if indeed a mistake occurred—in bequeathing a play to the obscure Tourneur. For Tourneur, whose biography remains largely a blank despite much diligent sleuthing, playwriting appears to have represented only a passing phase in the career of a courtier and soldier. One play known definitely to be his, *The Atheist's Tragedy* (published 1611), has survived; contemporary records credit him with only two others: *The Nobleman* (Stationers' Register, 1612) and, with Daborne, *The Arraignment of London* (1613). But possibly the likeness of title between *The Revenger's Tragedy* and *The Atheist's Tragedy,* rather than any special knowledge, led Archer to make an attribution which Kirkman in this instance uncritically followed.[98] Similar parallelisms of title are presumably responsible for the assignment, in the same catalogues, of *The Maid's Metamorphosis* to Lyly on the analogy of *Love's Metamorphosis,*[99] and of *Two Wise Men and All the Rest Fools* to Chapman on the analogy of *All Fools.* Apart from the early catalogues, no external evidence links Tourneur's name with *The Revenger's Tragedy.* For over two centuries their testimony went unquestioned.

That the play first became the object of controversy in the late nineteenth century is no chance event. By then *The Revenger's Tragedy* had been reprinted in Scott's *Ancient British Drama* (1810), the four editions of

98. This possibility was first suggested by Mincoff, "Authorship of the Revenger's Tragedy," p. 6.

99. The attribution of *The Maid's Metamorphosis* to Lyly is now generally rejected. See E. K. Chambers, *Elizabethan Stage,* IV, 29; also Golding, "Authorship of *The Maid's Metamorphosis,*" pp. 270–279. G. K. Hunter's *John Lyly: The Humanist as Courtier* (London, 1962), the most recent comprehensive study of the dramatist, contains no mention of the play.

Dodsley's *Select Collection of Old Plays* (1744–1876), Churton Collins' *Plays and Poems of Cyril Tourneur* (1878), and the Mermaid *Webster and Tourneur* (1888). Lamb had thrilled to the great encounter between Vindice and his fallen mother.[100] In *The Revenger's Tragedy* Hazlitt had found "those profound reaches of thought, which lay open the soul of feeling." [101] Swinburne was intoxicated with Tourneur's "savage and half-crazy genius" from the day when, as a twelve-year-old schoolboy at Eton, he had furtively encountered Vindice's quaint devices in his tutor's *Dodsley*. Never notable for restraint, Swinburne gave unbridled expression to his ardor in his essay on Tourneur. "There never was such a thunderstorm of a play," he wrote; "it quickens and exhilarates the sense of the reader as the sense of a healthy man or boy is quickened and exhilarated by the rolling music of a tempest and the leaping exultation of its flames." [102] By the last decade of the nineteenth century, then, *The Revenger's Tragedy* had achieved, at least for a limited circle of admirers, the status of a minor classic. Even minor classics—and their authors—rarely escape inquisitive scrutiny.

The first great critical problem to occupy the early Tourneur enthusiasts was that of reconciling his two plays with one another as aspects of a coherent artistic development. Collins and others found the plot of *The Atheist's Tragedy* "disconnected, outrageous, and im-

100. "The reality and life of this Dialogue passes any scenical illusion I ever felt. I never read it but my ears tingle and I feel a hot blush spread my cheeks" (Charles Lamb, *Specimens of English Dramatic Poets* [London, 1808], p. 193).

101. Hazlitt, *Lectures*, p. 135.

102. Algernon Charles Swinburne, "Cyril Tourneur," *The Age of Shakespeare*, in *Complete Works*, ed. Gosse and Wise (London, 1925–27), XI, 465. Swinburne mentions the play often in his correspondence; see *The Swinburne Letters*, ed. Cecil Lang (New Haven, 1959–62), I–VI, *passim*.

probable"; the character portrayal showed "a tendency to simple caricature"; there were other grievous shortcomings. *The Revenger's Tragedy*, on the other hand, was "the consummate work of consummate genius." [103] Therefore (it was reasoned) the play must have been written after *The Atheist's Tragedy*, although the latter was published several years later. Collins in his edition accordingly reversed the traditional sequence and printed *The Atheist's Tragedy* first. Other critics and historians —among them Swinburne, Symonds, and Schelling—followed suit, thus accounting to their own satisfaction for the aesthetic inequalities which disturbed them. Their solution is not really a very happy one, for *The Atheist's Tragedy* is almost certainly the later play.[104]

From this initial dissatisfaction with chronological sequence it was an easy step to question whether the same author could indeed have written the two works. That step was first taken, appropriately enough, by Fleay, who found *The Revenger's Tragedy* too good for Tourneur, and proposed Webster instead.[105] Fleay noted resemblances—all superficial—between *The Revenger's Tragedy* and *The White Devil*, and he confidently declared the meter of the former to be "purely Websterian." [106] Poor Fleay! His "scientific" method, like some computer gone berserk, was forever playing tricks on him. Deliberate and bookish Webster is the least plausible claimant for the intensely immediate *Revenger's Tragedy*, although, given his well-known assimilative tendencies, he may well have been influenced by it.

103. Tourneur, *Plays and Poems,* ed. Collins (London, 1878), I, xxxvi, xxxvii.
104. See Tourneur, *Works,* ed. Nicoll, Introduction, pp. 22–23; also *The Atheist's Tragedy,* ed. Irving Ribner (Revels Plays [London, 1964]), Introduction, pp. xxiii–xxv.
105. *Biographical Chronicle,* II, 264, 272.
106. *Ibid.,* p. 272.

These early efforts to reverse a traditional chronology and to disintegrate a traditional canon rest upon an assumption that must be regarded as one of the vulgar errors of criticism, an error that has persisted with remarkable tenacity in times of presumably greater sophistication. The critic presupposes the inability of an artist to produce a poor, or even relatively inferior, composition after he has demonstrated mastery of his medium; the offending work must therefore be either juvenile or spurious. A critic who rearranges a canon on this basis is, of course, acting upon subjective value judgments which subsequent criticism may either modify or (in some cases) reverse entirely. But, even granting the validity of the original evaluation, to *assume* priority or authenticity on aesthetic grounds alone is patent nonsense. Examples are legion of writers whose later works fall lamentably short of earlier triumphs. The author of *The Sun Also Rises* produced in his declining years the unintended self-parody of *Across the River and into the Trees;* the craftsman who provided the overrated but technically impressive *The Crucible* was able afterwards to descend to the banalities and ineptitudes of *After the Fall.* It may be objected that these are special cases which can be explained by circumstances in the lives of their creators. But all works of the imagination are special cases. If relevant personal documents are wanting for the Elizabethan dramatists, we cannot therefore assume that they were exempt from stresses which affected the character and quality of their plays. Nor, on the other hand, can we profitably speculate on what those stresses might have been.

Fleay's suggestion won support from no one, but in asking for the first time on what authority the traditional ascription of *The Revenger's Tragedy* rested, he stirred unease.[107] In 1919 Sykes, armed with his execrable Mermaid edition, attempted to restore the old harmony by citing minute stylistic resemblances between *The Revenger's Tragedy* and *The Atheist's Tragedy*.[108] His performance, however, was ineffective even by Sykes's accommodating standards, and (report holds) he deliberately excluded this essay from *Sidelights on Elizabethan Drama*.[109] Thus matters stood until 1926, when Oliphant published his now famous article urging Middleton's authorship of *The Revenger's Tragedy*.[110]

Oliphant's approach to the problem is typically Golden Age in its emphasis upon verse characteristics and parallels of expression and thought. Metrical evidence, always suspect, is in this instance pointless: the 1607/8 quarto of *The Revenger's Tragedy* is mislined, and modern editors have not agreed as to what the proper arrangement should be.[111] Oliphant himself regretfully admitted that impressionistic comments on the music of the verse—the factor that meant most to him—would not convince anybody. Accordingly he rested his case mainly on the parallel passages. A mixed batch, they violate most of Miss Byrne's Golden Rules. Several of the "Middletonian"

---

107. Thus C. E. Vaughan, in the *Cambridge History of English Literature* (VI, 166), observes that "nothing more than tradition" connects the play with Tourneur. Schelling speaks of the play as "attributed to Tourneur" (*Elizabethan Drama,* II, 413; see also I, 568), and Ashley H. Thorndike remarks that "his authorship is accepted rather than certain" (*Webster and Tourneur* [New York, 1912], p. 337).

108. Sykes, "Cyril Tourneur: 'The Revenger's Tragedy': 'The Second Maiden's Tragedy,'" *Notes and Queries,* 12th Ser., V (1919), 225–229.

109. Oliphant, "Tourneur and Mr. T. S. Eliot," *Stud. in Phil.,* XXXII (1935), 546. Oliphant further reports that he learned from a mutual friend that Sykes shortly before his death had switched from the Tourneur to the Middleton camp.

110. "The Authorship of *The Revenger's Tragedy,*" *Stud. in Phil.,* XXIII (1926), 157–168.

111. See Foakes, "On the Authorship of 'The Revenger's Tragedy,'" *Mod. Lang. Rev.,* XLVIII (1953), 130–134.

words are hardly rare (e.g., *shine, comfortable*), and some of the phraseological parallels and stylistic mannerisms (e.g., the presence of ironical asides) are similarly vulnerable. For his data Oliphant draws upon composite works (*A Fair Quarrel, The Old Law, The Roaring Girl*) and plays in which Middleton's share is, to say the least, doubtful (*The Bloody Banquet, The Second Maiden's Tragedy, Timon of Athens*). There remains a residue of admissible parallels, and Oliphant does cite some genuinely unusual words and usages.[112] This evidence, regarded in the aggregate, is not nearly sufficient to justify Oliphant's hope (touching in the event) that his paper would help to settle the authorship dispute. He did, however, succeed very nicely in reopening debate.

In the decades following, Oliphant's thesis received reinforcement from Dunkel, Mincoff, Barker, and others.[113] The most solid support came from Barker, whose masterfully organized essay supplemented Oliphant on a wide front. Barker pointed to larger correspondences of situation, dramatic irony, and manner of word-play between the contested piece and acknowledged Middleton works, especially *The Phoenix*. He noted the presence in *The Revenger's Tragedy* of the rare word *luxur,* possibly a Middleton coinage, and he drew attention to the author's preference (shared with Middleton) for the ejaculation

---

112. But they are less than extraordinary; examples are the idiom "give . . . due" (e.g., "giue Reuenge her due"), the use of *covetous* in such phrases as "Ime couetuous / To know . . . ," etc. Perhaps the most striking word cited by Oliphant is *sasarara* (a corruption of *certiorari*), variants of which appear in *The Phoenix:* but the form had already been noted by Bullen, although not in connection with the authorship problem (Middleton, *Works,* ed. Bullen, I, 122).

113. Dunkel, "The Authorship of *The Revenger's Tragedy,*" *PMLA,* XLVI (1931), 781–785; Mincoff, "Authorship of the Revenger's Tragedy"; Barker, "The Authorship of the *Second Maiden's Tragedy* and *The Revenger's Tragedy,*" *Shakespeare Assoc. Bull.,* XX (1945), 51–62, 121–133.

push, as distinguished from *tush*, employed in *The Atheist's Tragedy*. He provided metrical tables for a number of plays. Above all, Barker presented a number of new phraseological parallels, many of which meet Miss Byrne's criteria for acceptability. The case for Middleton was thus appreciably strengthened. At the same time, one must note that some of Barker's literary correspondences are too vague to have much significance, and that his verse statistics suffer from the same drawbacks as any others for a mislined text. For his data involving the small particulars of style, Barker apparently relies entirely upon modern editions. He does not include the results of negative checks. Also, in making his argument to some degree dependent upon acceptance of Middleton's claim to *The Second Maiden's Tragedy*, he has fallen into a tactical error. Although Barker cites Greg's observation that one of the revising hands in the manuscript is probably the author's, he has not gone on to investigate whether it belongs to Middleton. As we have seen, it does not. Despite these limitations, Barker's paper is one of the most important to appear on the subject.

While Oliphant and his adherents vigorously promulgated their heresy, the orthodox showed no slackness in defending the traditional faith. Eliot skirmished with the Middletonians in the correspondence columns of *The Times Literary Supplement*, where he was outnumbered; but Tourneur's advocates campaigned more ambitiously in the journals.[114] Of particular interest are

114. The letters in *The Times Literary Supplement* appeared as follows: Oliphant, "Tourneur and 'The Revenger's Tragedy,'" December 18, 1930, p. 1087, and February 5, 1931, p. 99; Eliot, "Tourneur and 'The Revenger's Tragedy,'" January 1, 1931, p. 12; B. M. Wagner, "Cyril Tourneur," April 23, 1931, p. 327; F. L. Jones, "Cyril Tourneur," June 18, 1931, p. 487. Eliot's essay on Tourneur has already been cited, as have the papers on *The Revenger's Tragedy* by Ellis-Fermor and Foakes.

the contributions of Jenkins and Foakes. Jenkins' essay represents the first significant attempt to demonstrate in *The Atheist's Tragedy* an advance upon *The Revenger's Tragedy,* and thus to reconcile the two plays with one another without an arbitrary juggling of chronology. Foakes reveals the shakiness of some of the evidence adduced in behalf of Middleton.

By 1955 the literature on the question was so extensive that the time seemed ripe for a summing up and evaluation of all the evidence. To this end I devoted a chapter of my book on Middleton's tragedies, supplementing where I could the available information.[115] While presenting the evidence for Middleton fully and (I believe) accurately, I can now see, after the lapse of over a decade, that unconsciously I tended to undervalue the counterarguments of the opposition.

One example must suffice. In my book I upheld the view, first advanced by Dunkel, that *The Revenger's Tragedy* is possibly to be identified with a lost Middleton tragedy, *The Viper and Her Brood,* mentioned in a lawsuit in 1609.[116] The action brought by Robert Keysar, manager of the Queen's Revels at Blackfriars in 1605–6, concerned a debt which the dramatist claimed to have satisfied by delivering to him the *Viper* on May 7, 1606. This date suits *The Revenger's Tragedy,* which was written about 1604–6; the title aptly decribes the Duchess

To these may be added "Cyril Tourneur," by Harold Jenkins (*Rev. of Eng. Stud.,* XVII [1941], 21–36) and "Cyril Tourneur on Revenge," by Henry Hitch Adams (*Jour. of Eng. and Germ. Phil.,* XLVIII [1949], 72–87).

115. Schoenbaum, pp. 153–182.

116. *Ibid.,* pp. 166–167. The suit was discovered by H. N. Hillebrand ("Thomas Middleton's *The Viper's Brood," Mod. Lang. Notes,* XLII [1927], 35–38). The contest was left undecided in the document discovered by Hillebrand. Although some years ago I searched diligently through the *Coram Rege* Rolls, I was unable to track down any sequel record; presumably the case was settled out of court.

and her three sons and two stepsons. But although several plays of the period take their names from the underplot, it seems unlikely that the author himself would devise a title of this kind—especially if his work had already reached print under another, more fitting designation. It is not absolutely certain that Middleton actually delivered the play mentioned in the suit. The title-page of *The Revenger's Tragedy,* moreover, unequivocally states that the King's men acted the piece. There is no evidence to contradict this information, which as Miss Ekeblad has shown, is supported by the use in Act V of a blazing star, a stage effect for which the Globe Theatre was noted.[117] Nor is there any evidence that Middleton had a connection with the King's men at this time. He was then the leading playwright for Paul's boys, providing them almost singlehandedly with a comic repertory. Stranger things have happened, but it does not on the face of it seem plausible that he would have undermined his own efforts by contributing plays to the powerful company with whom his own troupe was waging an increasingly desperate competitive struggle. A conceivable explanation —if Middleton wrote the play—is that *The Revenger's Tragedy* was originally performed by the children, and somehow afterwards passed, like Marston's *The Malcontent,* into the repertory of the adult company; but this is mere speculation. It is a fact that in 1610 the King's men denied ever having received playbooks from Keysar.[118]

A decade ago the identification of *The Viper and Her Brood* with *The Revenger's Tragedy* seemed less

117. Ekeblad, "A Note on 'The Revenger's Tragedy,'" *Notes and Queries,* CC (1955), 98. Miss Ekeblad now writes under her married name, Ewbank.

118. C. W. Wallace, *Shakespeare and His London Associates* (Univ. of Nebraska Stud., X, No. 4 [Lincoln, 1910]), 93–94.

improbable. If the weight of the internal evidence so skill-fully assembled by Oliphant and Barker did not, even then, appear overwhelming, it did impress me as sufficient to warrant assigning *The Revenger's Tragedy* provision-ally to Middleton and discussing it along with canonical plays. This conclusion and this procedure received a mixed reception. Those persuaded beforehand of the rightness of the cause applauded. The Tourneur adherents felt no obligation to defect. Several of the uncommitted inclined towards Middleton; others remained on the fence. It was, in short, pretty much the *status quo ante.*

Indeed, whatever I was able to say in support of Mid-dleton was balanced by what others were saying, at around the same time, in behalf of Tourneur. Miss Eke-blad pointed to the Globe's burning star; John Peter, in an important study, showed the common indebtedness of *The Revenger's Tragedy* and *The Atheist's Tragedy* to the medieval tradition of satirical complaint.[119] On the basis of intimate familiarity with the plays and their prob-lems, Henri Fluchère, the most recent editor of *The Re-venger's Tragedy,* supported the traditional position.[120]

Against this background of wearying and inconclusive debate, Barker's announcement, in 1958, in the Preface to his *Thomas Middleton,* stirred expectation: ". . . I have given new evidence," he wrote, "that will, I think, settle the controversy about authorship once and for all." The new evidence consists of a literary correspondence, supported by a phraseological parallel, between *The Re-venger's Tragedy* and Middleton's *A Mad World, My Masters.* Barker suggests that the two plays are com-panion pieces: Vindice and Follywit, their protagonists,

119. Peter, *Complaint and Satire in Early English Literature* (Oxford, 1956), pp. 255–287.
120. *La Tragédie du vengeur,* ed. Fluchère (Collection bilingue des classiques étrangers [Paris, 1958]), Introduction, pp. 35–44.

are examples of "the clever man who is blinded by his own cleverness, the self-satisfied hero who turns out to be anything but a hero in the end." When the cycle has run its course, the ostensible hero—actually a sinner—"suddenly becomes his own victim." [121] This is so, but the idea, far from being uniquely Middletonian, belongs to the permanent wisdom of the race and goes back at least as far as the Book of Proverbs: "His own iniquities shall take the wicked himself, and he shall be holden with the cords of his sins. He shall die without instruction; and in the greatness of his folly he shall go astray" (5:22–23).[122] Such a reversal provides the classic peripeteia of drama, tragedy and comedy alike. The fate that overtakes Vindice and Follywit, as one reviewer was quick to note, also overtakes the clever and self-satisfied Volpone, and the list of complacent protagonists thus undone might be indefinitely extended. Barker's new verbal parallel, on the other hand, is remarkably exact. He compares Follywit's:

> Peace, tis mine owne yfaith, I haa'te. . . .
> Thankes, thankes to any spirit,
> That mingled it mongst my inuentions. . . .
> And thou shalt see't quickly yfaith; nay tis in graine,
> I warrant it hold colour.[123]

with Vindice's:

> But I haue found it;
> Twill hold, tis sure, thankes, thankes to any spirit,
> That mingled it mongst my inuentions. . . .
> Nay doubt not tis in graine, I warrant it hold collour.[124]

121. Barker, *Thomas Middleton*, pp. 70–71.
122. In this context *without* apparently has the sense, "for want of."
123. *A Mad World, My Masters* (London, 1608), sig. E4[r-v] (Bullen ed.: III, iii, 68–71, 81–82).
124. *The Revengers Tragædie* (London, 1607), sig. H1[r-v] (Nicoll ed.: IV, ii, 226–228, 255).

The parallel is a welcome addition to the stylistic evidence for Middleton. It weighs no more, however, than any other acceptable parallel. Nor does a verbal-cum-literary correspondence make companion pieces of the two plays, which are as notable for their disparity of tone as they are for their similarity of ironic method.

Controversy over the authorship of *The Revenger's Tragedy* has continued apace since Barker optimistically declared the issue settled. The Tourneur proponents have proceeded with their exploration of thematic and other links between the two plays associated with the dramatist's name.[125] While not going so far as to reject the verdict of earlier critics who unanimously preferred *The Revenger's Tragedy,* recent commentators have responded sympathetically to *The Atheist's Tragedy,* arguing that it must be judged by the standards of polemic rather than those of realistic drama. We should not expect psychological verisimilitude in the portrayal of D'Amville, who represents an intellectual stance; other conventional objections to characterization and plot design may be similarly irrelevant. Viewed in this light, *The Atheist's Tragedy* does not seem so odd a sequel to the earlier masterpiece. The new approach is certainly an improvement upon the florid impressionism of Tourneur's nineteenth-century admirers, and also upon those, more recent, who have set for themselves the impossible task of analyzing the playwright's psyche.

John Peter (as previously noted) has stressed Tourneur's medieval heritage, and I have myself called atten-

125. See Ekeblad, "An Approach to Tourneur's Imagery," *Mod. Lang. Rev.,* LIV (1959), 489–498, and "On the Authorship of *The Revenger's Tragedy,*" *English Studies,* XLI (1960), 225–240; Robert Ornstein, *The Moral Vision of Jacobean Tragedy* (Madison, 1960), pp. 105–127; Ribner, *Jacobean Tragedy: The Quest for Moral Order* (London, 1962), pp. 72–96, and *The Atheist's Tragedy,* ed. Ribner, Introduction, pp. xxxii–lxvi.

tion to the indebtedness of *The Revenger's Tragedy* to the great themes of Death's Dance and *de contemptu mundi*.[126] An analogous medievalism, it is now argued, informs *The Atheist's Tragedy*. Ribner, Miss Ekeblad, and others see in the two plays the same traditional Christianity, the same emphasis on *vanitas*, the *memento mori*, and the *exemplum horrendum*. The futility of private vengeance and the certainty of heavenly retribution are shown implicitly in *The Revenger's Tragedy* by the ultimate failure of Vindice and the triumphant survival of the pious and passive Antonio, and overtly in *The Atheist's Tragedy* by the ultimate failure of D'Amville and the vindication of the pious and passive Charlemont. Both plays, furthermore, are marked by a similar moral passion. Both make the same association between the sexual and the macabre, between lechery and the skull. That moral passion and that association do not appear in Middleton plays of the same period.[127]

These observations are pertinent. They do not, however, prove that Tourneur wrote both plays. After all, many writers of the period upheld the traditional faith and traditional moral values (indeed, one sometimes feels in reading Ribner that a single pious dramatist produced the whole corpus of Jacobean tragedy). But after recent work on Tourneur, one can no longer complacently maintain that *The Revenger's Tragedy* and *The Atheist's Tragedy* are so dissimilar in fundamental respects of theme, thought, and intention as not possibly to represent the achievement of the same man.

126. "*The Revenger's Tragedy*: Jacobean Dance of Death," *Mod. Lang. Quar.*, XV (1954), 201–207.

127. I have maintained, not without company, that Middleton and the author of *The Revenger's Tragedy* hold similar views on sin and retribution ("'The Revenger's Tragedy' and Middleton's Moral Outlook," *Notes and Queries*, CXCVI [1951], 8–10). This is, I still believe, the

Yet the Tourneur supporters have not been allowed the last word. While they have dwelt on the plays as (in Miss Ekeblad's phrase) "total entities," the Middletonians have been assembling technical data in keeping with the new directions in attribution study. In 1960 George R. Price published the results of his bibliographical study of *The Revenger's Tragedy*.[128] Behind the 1607/8 quarto, he maintains, lies a fair copy of the play in the author's own hand. The printed text, he goes on to suggest, preserves such features of the manuscript as stage directions and speech-prefixes, and also (to a large extent) punctuation and spelling. In respect of all these textual features *The Revenger's Tragedy* is consistent with Middleton's preferences but not with those revealed in the 1611 quarto of *The Atheist's Tragedy*. The force of Price's argument is weakened somewhat by his prior assumption that *The Revenger's Tragedy* is Middleton's —an assumption that occasionally influences his evaluation of the evidence. Moreover, the total absence of Tourneur holograph presents an inescapable difficulty. There can be no question, however, that Price has produced a substantial quantity of worthwhile evidence for Middleton. Additional support came in 1961 from Peter B. Murray, who found a significant correlation between the frequency of occurrence of certain spellings and colloquial contractions in *The Revenger's Tragedy* and in accepted Middleton plays; again *The Atheist's Tragedy* offers a contrasting pattern.[129] Murray's essay is carefully reasoned, and he supplies comparative tables illustrating the spelling and linguistic habits of other contem-

case, but a distinction between moral outlook and moral passion is worth preserving.

128. "The Authorship and the Bibliography of *The Revenger's Tragedy*," *The Library*, 5th Ser., XV (1960), 262–277.

129. "The Authorship of *The Revenger's Tragedy*," pp. 195–207.

porary dramatists. Of all the scholars who have taken part in the long-drawn-out controversy, Murray alone makes use of a mathematical yardstick of probability (the chi-square test). Yet much of his evidence is of a type which may be susceptible of alternative explanation. The possibility of printing-house interference is, too, always a danger, but Murray is conscious of the problem and deals with it efficiently if not definitively.[130] A further bit of linguistic evidence for Middleton has most recently been adduced by MacD. P. Jackson, who notes that *ay* (the affirmative particle favored by Middleton) predominates over *yes* in *The Revenger's Tragedy,* whereas Tourneur almost invariably chooses *yes* in *The Atheist's Tragedy.*[131]

The technical data brought forward so late in the day by Price, Murray, and Jackson considerably enhance the argument for Middleton. So, too, the controlled critical

130. Murray incorporates his essay (with other matter) in *A Study of Cyril Tourneur* (Philadelphia, 1964) which came to hand too late to be taken into account in my text. "My study of *The Revenger's Tragedy,*" Murray announces in his Preface, "has turned up new and I think conclusive internal evidence that Thomas Middleton is the author . . ." (p. 7). This large and familiar claim, based essentially on the evidence already published in his article, is substantially qualified in his chapter on the play, entitled "The Anonymous Revenger's Tragedy." Murray writes:

So long as we study this problem from a text at least one remove from the author's papers, we can never do more than establish a *probability* of authorship by means of linguistic and spelling tests, and that probability is only as good as the inferences about scribes and compositors on which it is based. Moreover, other statistical analyses than those I have made will yield different degrees of certainty for assignment of the play to Middleton, some of them no doubt less than I have shown (p. 173).

Then, admitting a "slight chance" of Tourneur's authorship, he includes a literary analysis of the play in his study of the dramatist. Although no doubt is left in the reader's mind concerning Murray's preference from among the possible options—that the play is Middleton's, that it is Tourneur's, that it is best left anonymous—he gives rather the impression of taking three incompatible positions simultaneously.

131. "Affirmative Particles in 'Henry VIII,'" *Notes and Queries,* CCVII (1962), 374.

analyses of Miss Ekeblad and others help Tourneur. Each side may take legitimate pride in its accomplishment, but neither can very well draw comfort from the achievement of the other. By this point the bewildered student may be tempted to ask Pilate's question and, like him, not stay for an answer. Yet a rational position with respect to the whole problem is not only desirable but, I believe, also possible.

The chief issues may be briefly recapitulated. Our external evidence of authorship is not very satisfactory— if it were, the controversy would probably not have arisen —but such information as we have favors Tourneur. The internal evidence is more complicated. In some ways *The Revenger's Tragedy* is a unique product of the Jacobean stage, and hence unlike either Tourneur or Middleton. It bears, however, enough general resemblance of theme and dramatic method to *The Atheist's Tragedy* for the attribution to Tourneur to be acceptable to many. But on the basis of other considerations, involving minute particulars of style and linguistic preference, it is difficult to accommodate the two works with one another as the creations of a single author. Indeed, our severest authorities have expressed their qualms. Chambers, as we have seen, was skeptical enough about Tourneur's claim to *The Revenger's Tragedy* to classify the play as an anonymous work in *The Elizabethan Stage;* Greg doubted that it would have been assigned to Tourneur at all were it not for the seventeenth-century catalogues.[132] On the other hand, the stylistic and substylistic evidence for Middleton is extensive and varied.

Still the internal evidence does not sweep all before it, and the situation, as it stands, is that neither Middleton's nor Tourneur's advocates have been able to bring

132. "Authorship Attributions in the Early Play-Lists," pp. 317–318.

forward the kind of proof to which one party or the other must submit. Indeed, no conclusive proof for Tourneur is possible because his unquestioned dramatic writing is quantitatively inadequate for testing (see Principle 6, *supra*) ; at the same time, precisely because the sampling is so small, it is impossible definitely to rule out his claim to *The Revenger's Tragedy*. Hence the seemingly endless exchanges of replies and counterreplies in the journals. Whatever his own personal *feeling* about the attribution may be, the task of the historian is, as I see it, to record the fact of uncertainty, which is in this case the only certainty. For this reason, in the "Authors" column of my revised edition of Harbage's *Annals of English Drama,* the entry for *The Revenger's Tragedy* reads: Anonymous (Tourneur, C.?   Middleton, T.?).

» VIII «

DOES THIS INCONCLUSIVE CONCLUSION mean that the extraordinary efforts of a number of scholars over the past thirty years represent so much wasted labor? I think not. By focusing intensively on so many manifestations of style, the work on *The Revenger's Tragedy* has fostered a more sensitive awareness of the distinctive characteristics of two dramatists, one of whom is a major dramatist. It has raised questions that needed raising. Less than a century ago Churton Collins could edit Tourneur without any sense of the limitations of the evidence for the authenticity of the play upon which the poet's fame chiefly rests. This uncritical certainty has been superseded by a reasonable doubt, and a serious hypothesis of alternative attribution has been proposed—a hypothesis that the responsible historian cannot safely ignore. Our understanding of the nature of a particular problem has been to some extent modified.[133] That is a legitimate achievement of scholarship. However much we may yearn for certainties, and for grander and more romantic accomplishment, we recognize—or should recognize—that the scholarly process usually proceeds by the slight modification of already existing knowledge.

There is a place for hypothesis as well as for demonstration, and in the field of Elizabethan drama, where the factual records are far from satisfactory, hypothesis assumes an especially important role. We want to know; something there is that doesn't love an anonymous play. And so scholars use internal evidence as a basis for attribution. Some of the hypotheses are much better supported than others; some are almost certainly correct. But all of them remain hypotheses. Despite the safeguards devised, a subjective element resides in all attribution work, and even the utilization of electronic computers will not eliminate the need for the exercise of scholarly judgment. Bentley, in including *The Queen* in his section on Ford, judiciously adds the proviso that the play "may be accepted as his until evidence of its composition by a very clever imitator is forthcoming." [134] The proviso is justified. Still, we would be the poorer without Bang's hypothesis, as indeed we would without a number of others.

But if hypothesis is to be accorded its full value it must be recognized and presented as such. Not only in authorship inquiries but in almost every specialty, we have encountered studies in which the evidence does not support the claims which the advocate's enthusiasm has led him to make. No doubt many a worthwhile speculation has

133. Thus R. A. Foakes's forthcoming edition of *The Revenger's Tragedy* is advertised (*Times Literary Supplement,* July 29, 1965) as "Attributed to Cyril Tourneur" rather than as "By Cyril Tourneur."
134. *Jacobean and Caroline Stage,* III, 457.

been too easily dismissed because of the impatience that excessive partisanship arouses. In scholarship, fortunately, it is rarely too late, and as time goes by, these potentially useful hypotheses may well be resurrected and reconsidered by more prudent investigators.

It is good, I believe, that now and then we pay tribute to the virtue of recognizing our limitations. "Several things dovetailed in my mind," wrote John Keats in perhaps the most famous passage of his correspondence, "& at once it struck me, what quality went to form a Man of Achievement, especially in Literature & which Shakespeare posessed so enormously—I mean *Negative Capability,* that is when man is capable of being in uncertainties, Mysteries, doubts, without any irritable reaching after fact & reason. . . ." [135] The scholar no less than the poet must have his own kind of negative capability. He must know and accept the often frustrating limitations of the methods available to him if, in his quest to dispel illusions and errors, he is not to create new ones in their place.

135. Keats, *Letters,* ed. Hyder Edward Rollins (Cambridge, Mass., 1958), I, 193.

Appendix

A Note on Dramatic Collaboration

No DEFINITION of *collaboration* is needed, but it should be remembered that the term, as ordinarily employed, fails to accommodate certain varieties of composite writing. I am thinking of such plays as *The Spanish Tragedy* and *Dr. Faustus,* whose popularity inspired the commissioning of additional scenes years after Marlowe and Kyd were dead; also, works begun by one dramatist, only to be abandoned and resumed by another (e.g., *The Insatiate Countess,* which Marston apparently left unfinished when he abruptly deserted the stage in 1608, and which William Barksted afterwards completed for production). These instances may fairly be described as collaboration after the fact. Although there is much uncertainty about how often and how extensively plays were revised for revival, we know that the practice existed. Indeed, the role of the reviser may be extremely important—outweighing in some instances that of the original author. A decade after Fletcher's *The Wandering Lovers* was first produced in 1623, Massinger so thoroughly revamped the play, now called *The Lover's Progress,* that he could reasonably demand and receive *"the pay / For a new Poem."* [1] Although the canonical investigator cannot very

1. *The Lover's Progress* is almost certainly to be identified with *The*

well afford to ignore these categories of mixed writing, I am not here primarily concerned to extend the boundaries of definition. The more orthodox types of collaboration present enough problems in their own right.

Before considering the nature of Elizabethan dramatic collaboration, one may reasonably ask how widespread was joint-authorship, which must be regarded as on the whole inimical to the interests of stage art. With Henslowe's *Diary* as his source, W. J. Lawrence tabulated the number of productions by the Admiral's men at the Rose and the Fortune from 1597 to 1603, and found that of the 128 new plays put on during that period, 70 were composite, with two, three, four, or as many as five dramatists working in association.[2] It is, however, significant that almost half the plays represented in the sampling were *not* collaborations, despite the fact that Henslowe's mode of operation, to a larger degree than that of any other theatrical management of the day, fostered such writing arrangements. At the other extreme from Henslowe utilitarianism we have the Caroline phenomenon of the influx of amateurs into the commercial theater: Literary gentlemen like Lodowick Carlell and Thomas Killigrew were not subject to the same pressures of economic necessity or professional commitment as those who wrote for their bread, and so were less likely to enter into temporary partnerships in order to meet producers' deadlines. Between the journeymen of the nineties, on the one hand, and the Cavalier dilettantes, on the other, lies much theatrical history and a wide spectrum of playhouse custom. But all the major dramatists of the period —if we accept Shakespeare's share in the revised *More*

Wandering Lovers, and Massinger is almost certainly the reviser; see Bentley, *Jacobean and Caroline Stage,* III, 360–362.

2. Lawrence, "Early Dramatic Collaboration: A Theory," in *Pre-Restoration Stage Studies,* pp. 349–350.

—wrote in collaboration at one time or another. Even the magnificently independent Jonson was contributing rather than sole playwright at least nine times in his career. Henslowe records Jonson's participation in four lost plays: *Hot Anger Soon Cold,* with Porter and Chettle; *Page of Plymouth,* with Dekker; *The Scot's Tragedy,* with Chettle, Dekker, and Marston; and an unnamed tragedy, with Chapman. He had some share in Nashe's scandalous *Isle of Dogs.* On September 25, 1601, and June 22, 1602, he was paid (altogether) a substantial sum by Henslowe for "new adicyons for Jeronymo." [3] In the stage version of *Sejanus,* Jonson tells us in his epistle "To the Readers" prefixed to the quarto edition, "a second Pen had good share"—a share (Chapman's?) that Jonson excised and replaced with his own work when he revised the tragedy for publication. He joined forces with Chapman and Marston on *Eastward Ho;* finally, *The Widow* was published as written by Jonson, Fletcher, and Middleton. Still, the sum total of this work, while by no means negligible, constitutes a small portion of Jonson's total output. Shakespeare wrote still less in collaboration, even if we add *Henry VIII, Pericles,* and *Two Noble Kinsmen* to the list with *More.* While recognizing joint-authorship as a fact of Elizabethan theatrical life, we must guard against exaggerating its importance; many dramatists preferred to work singly as much as possible, and increasingly they had the opportunity to do so.

The canonical investigator who relies on internal evidence to divide up a play between dramatists is, whether he realizes it or not, proceeding according to certain assumptions as to how Elizabethan writers worked together. It is well to bear in mind that composite works

3. Henslowe, *Diary,* ed. Greg, I, 149, 168. These additions, which are lost, should not be confused with those first printed in the 1602 quarto of *The Spanish Tragedy;* see Edwards' edition, Introduction, pp. lxi–lxvi.

may evolve in a wide variety of ways. Even for a simple division of labor—the participants working separately —a number of different arrangements are possible: (1) allocation of scenes may be entirely mechanical, e.g., when there are five dramatists, each takes one act; (2) one author may supply the plot, the other(s) being responsible for the execution; (3) one writer may take the main action, another the underplot; (4) or the division may be worked out with reference to the character of the material, one playwright undertaking farcical scenes while another assumes responsibility for tragic or satiric episodes. But was the distribution invariably simple? Or did some dramatists prefer to work in intimate association, going over one another's drafts, revising, deleting, and interpolating, so that the special character of any given scene would be the result of the merging of individual identities? And then we must reckon with the possibility of the final product, however it was achieved, being revised by one of the original authors—or by someone not previously associated with the play—because of censorship requirements or playhouse exigencies, or for publication or revival. The hypothetical patterns I have enumerated do not exhaust the possible combinations. It must, furthermore, be borne in mind that my categories are not mutually exclusive; conceivably when three playwrights undertook a joint assignment, two might have worked closely together while the third wrote independently.

These questions—indeed, all the ramifications of Elizabethan dramatic collaboration—have received relatively little systematic attention, despite their intrinsic interest, which transcends the limited scope of the present inquiry. An early study by Elbert N. S. Thompson has shortcomings characteristic of the scholarship of its day.[4] Thomp-

4. Thompson, "Elizabethan Dramatic Collaboration," *Englische Studien,* XL (1909), 30–46.

son's point of departure is not the documentary evidence but a highly questionable set of assumptions which he inclines to regard as fact. "Shakespeare," we are told, "had undoubtedly his helper on *Henry VI,* and perhaps received due reward for taking full credit to himself there when publishers of the next generation, to bolster up their hazardous literary ventures, wedded his name to the immortal verse of a Rowley or his like." [5] Following Fleay on the authorship of *The Spanish Gypsy,* Thompson asserts that Rowley "doubtless added only the comic gipsy scenes of the second act after Middleton, its author, had preceded Rowley to the King's Company." [6] He suggests that one of the conditions of the Beaumont-Fletcher partnership was that Fletcher was relieved of responsibility for first acts; when collaborating with Massinger, he was excused from writing the last act as well, and thus contributed only the three blocks of action that constitute the emotional center of the play.[7] These interesting speculations, which are offered with some confidence, are based on the stylistic analyses of the metrical critics and parallelographers (Fleay, Boyle, Oliphant, and company) or, rather, on those analyses purportedly accorded general acceptance. The argument is thus circular. Moreover, as Hatcher was quick to observe in a reply to Thompson's article, the learned authorities cited by the latter disagree in their conclusions.[8] Yet Thompson's

5. *Ibid.,* p. 31.
6. *Ibid.,* p. 32.
7. *Ibid.,* pp. 36–37.
8. O. L. Hatcher, "Fletcher's Habits of Dramatic Collaboration," *Anglia,* XXXIII (1910), 219–231. Hatcher found that:

the chosen critics frequently differed not only from others but among themselves, as to the plays cited by him [Thompson]; and that they often differed not only as to what part should be assigned to Fletcher and what to Beaumont in the Fletcher-Beaumont plays, or what to Fletcher and what to Massinger in the Fletcher-Massinger group, but as to the actual authors involved at all in the plays in question; and thus reduced the problem of collaboration to its first stage of uncertainty . . . (p. 221).

ineffective and dated study is one of the few which Chambers can recommend in his *William Shakespeare*.[9]

The same problem is approached differently by Lawrence, who expresses impatience with conjectures based on stylistic evidence. His own engagingly simple view is that the division of labor was always by acts. In plays of dual authorship he declares flatly that "one writer supplied the first three acts, and the other the remainder."[10] Unfortunately, Lawrence's evidence is insufficient to sustain the weight of hypothesis, and for this inadequacy he compensates, not very satisfactorily, by positiveness of assertion. It is true that the title-page of the first quarto of *Gorboduc* states that "*three Actes were wrytten by Thomas Nortone, and the two laste by Thomas Sackuyle*"; also that, according to the 1573 edition of *Jocasta*, the first and fourth acts were "Done by F. Kinwelmarshe," and the second by Gascoigne (Acts III and V are not subscribed). The manuscripts of *Gismonde of Salerne*, furthermore, show that each of the first four acts was taken by a different author; the last, which is unassigned, may be by a fifth. But these instances (as Lawrence realizes) all come from the Inns-of-Court drama and do not necessarily constitute a pattern for the commercial theater. With respect to the latter, Lawrence can only support his argument with the following Henslowe entry: "Lent vnto Robart shawe & Jewbey the 23 of octob[er] 1598 to lend vnto m^r Chapmane one his playe boocke & ij ectes of a tragedie of bengemens plotte the some of. . . . iij^li."[11] But a single record does not, as Lawrence claims, establish that "the act unit was in force at the close of the sixteenth century."[12] If such were the

9. Vol. I, p. 204.
10. Lawrence, "Early Dramatic Collaboration," p. 353.
11. Henslowe, *Diary*, ed. Greg, I, 98. The version of the entry supplied by Lawrence (p. 352) is remarkably inaccurate.
12. Lawrence, p. 352.

case, how should we account for the fact that of the £6 disbursed by Henslowe to Dekker, Drayton, Hathway, Munday, and Wilson for *Fair Constance of Rome*, Wilson received only 11 shillings? "My firm belief in the allotment by acts," Lawrence declares in a revealing sentence, "forces me to the conclusion that there was a hierarchy of the pen and that Wilson was at the foot of the ladder." [13] Thus are facts accommodated to speculation. The flimsiness of the whole edifice is ably shown by Oliphant, who has no difficulty also in disposing of Lawrence's subsidiary hypothesis that revisers were never given collaborative status on the title-pages of printed plays.[14]

Actually, Lawrence's supposedly all-binding central theory is disproved by the Star Chamber proceedings in connection with *Keep the Widow Waking*. Dekker, one of the four authors of that play and a defendant in the suit, described his share as consisting of "two sheetes of paper conteyning the first Act . . . and a speech in the last Act of the Boy who had killed his mother." [15] This testimony moreover suggests that Dekker contributed both to the tragic narrative of the murder of Joan Tindall in Whitechapel and to the comic action dealing with the enforced drunkenness of the Widow Anne Elsdon. The frequent assumption of impressionist critics that in collaborations the tragic material was parceled out to one writer and the comic to another is, as Sisson observes, not borne out by the facts of this case.[16]

---

13. *Ibid.*
14. Oliphant, "Collaboration in Elizabethan Drama: Mr. W. J. Lawrence's Theory," *Phil. Quar.*, VIII (1929), 1–10. Oliphant works himself up into a fine paroxysm, and ends by accusing Lawrence of "a mad disregard of facts and probabilities in the pursuit of his always interesting theories" (p. 10).
15. Sisson, *Lost Plays of Shakespeare's Age*, p. 110.
16. *Ibid.*, p. 113.

My remarks are not meant to imply that Elizabethan plays were not, in many instances, composed in the manner described by Lawrence, or that the division of labor was not sometimes determined by subject matter. Indeed, I suspect that all the combinations which I have mentioned, as well as others which I have not, were entered into at one time or another during three generations of prolific and astonishingly varied dramatic activity. But suspicions count for nothing as evidence. What remains needed is a proper investigation of all the available documents: the dramatic manuscripts themselves (e.g., *Sir Thomas More, The Faithful Friends*), Henslowe, the *Keep the Widow Waking* depositions, scattered allusions, biographical and autobiographical references, prologues and epilogues, etc. Such an investigation, the subject for a monograph rather than an appendix, cannot be undertaken here. The results of the inquiry might well be disappointing because of the vagueness or inconclusiveness of the data. As things stand, however, many popular assumptions and facile generalizations about the nature of Elizabethan dramatic collaboration have no secure foundation in external fact, but rest instead on undemonstrated theories or on internal evidence garnered in cheerful violation of the elementary methods I have outlined in Part Three of this study.

WORKS CITED

THIS LIST *is restricted to monographs, articles, editions, etc., concerned directly or indirectly with questions of authorship attribution in Elizabethan drama.*

ABERCROMBIE, LASCELLES. "A Plea for the Liberty of Interpreting," in *Aspects of Shakespeare* (Oxford, 1933), pp. 227–254.

ADAMS, HENRY H. "Cyril Tourneur on Revenge." *Journal of English and Germanic Philology,* XLVIII (1949), 72–87.

ADAMS, JOSEPH Q. "The Authorship of *A Warning for Fair Women.*" *PMLA,* XXVIII (1913), 594–620.

———. "The Authorship of Two Seventeenth Century Plays." *Modern Language Notes,* XXII (1907), 135–137.

———. "Captaine Thomas Stukeley." *Journal of English and Germanic Philology,* XV (1916), 107–129.

———. *"Every Woman in Her Humor* and *The Dumb Knight."* *Modern Philology,* X (1913), 413–432.

ALEXANDER, PETER. "A Case of Three Sisters." *The Times Literary Supplement,* July 8, 1965, p. 588.

———. "Conjectural History, or Shakespeare's *Henry VIII."* *Essays and Studies,* XVI (1930), 85–120.

———. *Shakespeare's Henry VI and Richard III.* Cambridge, 1929.

———. *Shakespeare's Life and Art.* London, 1939.

———. " 'The Taming of a Shrew.' " *The Times Literary Supplement,* Sept. 16, 1926, p. 614.

ANDREWS, C. E. "The Authorship of *The Late Lancashire Witches.*" *Modern Language Notes*, XXVIII (1913), 163–166.

ANON. *Arden of Feversham*, ed. A. H. BULLEN. London, 1887.

———. *Charlemagne*, ed. F. L. SCHOELL. Princeton, 1920.

———. *The Fary Knight; or Oberon the Second, a Manuscript Play Attributed to Thomas Randolph*, ed. FREDSON BOWERS. Univ. of Virginia Studies, 2. Chapel Hill, 1942.

———. *The Merry Devil of Edmonton*, ed. W. A. ABRAMS. Durham, N.C., 1942.

———. *Queen Elizabeth's Entertainment at Mitcham*, ed. LESLIE HOTSON. New Haven, 1953.

———. *The Queen, or The Excellency of Her Sex*, ed. W. BANG. *Materialien zur Kunde des älteren englischen Dramas*, Vol. XIII. Louvain, 1906.

———. Review of *Middleton's Tragedies* by S. SCHOENBAUM. *The Times Literary Supplement*, Feb. 17, 1956, p. 102.

———. *The Second Maiden's Tragedy*, ed. W. W. GREG. Oxford, 1909.

———. *The Shakespeare Apocrypha*, ed. C. F. TUCKER BROOKE. Oxford, 1908.

———. *Sir Thomas More*, ed. A. DYCE. Shakespeare Society Publications. London, 1844.

———. *The Three Parnassus Plays, 1598–1601*, ed. J. B. LEISHMAN. London, 1949.

———. *The Tragedy of Sir John Van Olden Barnavelt*, ed. WILHELMINA P. FRIJLINCK. Amsterdam, 1922.

ARMSTRONG, E. A. *Shakespeare's Imagination*. London, 1946.

AXELRAD, A. JOSÉ. *Un Malcontent élizabethain: John Marston (1576–1634)*. Paris, 1955.

BAKELESS, JOHN. *The Tragical History of Christopher Marlowe*. 2 vols. Cambridge, Mass., 1942.

BALD, R. C. *"The Booke of Sir Thomas More* and Its Problems," in *Shakespeare Survey 2* (Cambridge, 1949), pp. 44–61.

BARBER, C. L. "A Rare Use of 'Honour' as a Criterion of Middleton's Authorship." *English Studies*, XXXVIII (1957), 161–168.

Works Cited

BARKER, R. H. "The Authorship of the *Second Maiden's Tragedy* and *The Revenger's Tragedy.*" *Shakespeare Association Bulletin,* XX (1945), 51–62, 121–133.

————. *Thomas Middleton.* New York, 1958.

BEAUMONT, FRANCIS, and FLETCHER, JOHN. *A King and No King* and *The Knight of the Burning Pestle,* ed. R. M. ALDEN. 2 vols. in 1. Belles-Lettres Series. Boston, 1910.

————. *Works,* ed. A. DYCE. 11 vols. London, 1843–46.

————. *Works,* ed. A. H. BULLEN (gen. ed.). Variorum Edition. 4 vols. London, 1904–12.

BENTLEY, G. E. "Authenticity and Attribution in the Jacobean and Caroline Drama," in *English Institute Annual 1942* (New York, 1943), pp. 101–118.

————. *The Jacobean and Caroline Stage.* Oxford, 1941—. 5 vols.

BERTRAM, PAUL. "The Date of *The Two Noble Kinsmen.*" *Shakespeare Quarterly,* XII (1961), 21–32.

BOAS, F. S. *Shakespeare & the Universities.* Oxford, 1923.

BORISH, M. E. "John Day's *Law Tricks* and George Wilkins." *Modern Philology,* XXXIV (1937), 249–266.

BOYLE, ROBERT. "Beaumont, Fletcher, and Massinger," in *Transactions of the New Shakspere Society* (London, 1880–86), pp. 579–628.

————. "Beaumont, Fletcher and Massinger." *Englische Studien,* V (1882), 74–96; VII (1884), 66–87; VIII (1885), 39–61; IX (1886), 209–239; X (1887), 383–412.

————. "Daborne's Share in the Beaumont and Fletcher Plays." *Englische Studien,* XXVI (1899), 352–369.

————. *"Henry VIII.* An Investigation into the Origin and Authorship of the Play," in *Transactions of the New Shakspere Society* (London, 1880–86), pp. 443–487.

————. "Mr. E. H. Oliphant on Beaumont and Fletcher." *Englische Studien,* XVII (1892), 171–175; XVIII (1893), 292–296.

————. "On Massinger and *The Two Noble Kinsmen,*" in *Transactions of the New Shakspere Society* (London, 1880–86), pp. 371–399.

————. "On Wilkins's Share in the Play Called Shakspere's

Pericles." *Transactions of the New Shakspere Society* (London, 1880–86), pp. 323–340.

———. "*Pericles.*" *Englische Studien,* V (1882), 363–369.

———. Review of *An Inquiry into the Authorship of the Middle-ton-Rowley Plays* by PAULINE WIGGIN. *Englische Studien,* XXVI (1899), 63–64.

———. "Shakespeare und Die Beiden Edlen Vettern." *Englische Studien,* IV (1881), 34–68.

———. "Troilus and Cressida." *Englische Studien,* XXX (1901), 21–59.

BRAWNER, JAMES P. "Early Classical Narrative Plays by Sebastian Westcott and Richard Mulcaster." *Modern Language Quarterly,* IV (1943), 455–464.

BRIGGS, WILLIAM D. Review of *Sidelights on Elizabethan Drama* by H. DUGDALE SYKES. *Modern Language Notes,* XLII (1927), 545.

BROOKE, C. F. TUCKER. *The Authorship of the Second and Third Parts of "King Henry VI."* New Haven, 1912.

———. "The Marlowe Canon." *PMLA,* XXXVII (1922), 367–417.

BROOKE, RUPERT. *John Webster and the Elizabethan Drama.* London, 1916.

BROWN, ARTHUR. "A Note on Sebastian Westcott and the Plays Presented by the Children of Paul's." *Modern Language Quarterly,* XII (1951), 134–136.

BULLEN, A. H., ed. *A Collection of Old English Plays.* 4 vols. London, 1882–85.

BYRNE, M. ST. CLARE. "Anthony Munday's Spelling as a Literary Clue." *The Library,* 4th Ser., IV (1923), 9–23.

———. "Bibliographical Clues in Collaborate Plays." *The Library,* 4th Ser., XIII (1932), 21–48.

———. " 'The Shepherd Tony'—A Recapitulation." *Modern Language Review,* XV (1920), 364–373.

The Cambridge History of English Literature, ed. A. W. WARD and A. R. WALLER. "The Drama to 1642." Vols. V and VI. Cambridge, 1910. [Chapters in which authorial questions are discussed include G. GREGORY SMITH, "Marlowe and Kyd,"

V, 142–164; F. W. MOORMAN, "Plays of Uncertain Authorship Attributed to Shakespeare," V, 236–258; ARTHUR SYMONS, "Middleton and Rowley," VI, 58–80; and G. C. MACAULAY, "Beaumont and Fletcher," VI, 107–140.]

CAPELL, EDWARD, ed. *Prolusions: or, Select Pieces of Antient Poetry.* London, 1760.

CARRÈRE, FELIX. *Le Théâtre de Thomas Kyd: contribution à l'étude du drame élizabethain.* Toulouse, 1951.

CHALMERS, GEORGE. *A Supplemental Apology for the Believers in the Shakspeare-Papers.* London, 1799.

CHAMBERS, SIR EDMUND K. "The Disintegration of Shakespeare," in *Aspects of Shakespeare* (Oxford, 1933), pp. 23–48.

———. *The Elizabethan Stage.* 4 vols. Oxford, 1923.

———. "The Integrity of *The Tempest." Review of English Studies,* I (1925), 129–150.

———. *Shakespeare: A Survey.* London, 1925.

———. *William Shakespeare: A Study of Facts and Problems.* 2 vols. Oxford, 1930.

CHAMBERS, R. W. "The Expression of Ideas—Particularly Political Ideas—in the Three Pages, and in Shakespeare," in *Shakespeare's Hand in the Play of Sir Thomas More* (Cambridge, 1923), pp. 142–187.

———. "Shakespeare and the Play of *More,"* in *Man's Unconquerable Mind* (London, 1939), pp. 204–249.

———. "Some Sequences of Thought in Shakespeare and in the 147 lines of 'Sir Thomas More.' " *Modern Language Review,* XXVI (1931), 251–280.

CHAPMAN, GEORGE. *Plays and Poems,* ed. T. M. PARROTT. 2 vols. London, 1910–14. [*Tragedies* (1910) and *Comedies* (1914) only; *Poems* not published.]

CHELLI, MAURICE. *Étude sur la collaboration de Massinger avec Fletcher et son groupe.* Paris, 1926.

CLARK, ARTHUR M. "The Authorship of 'Appius and Virginia.' " *Modern Language Review,* XVI (1921), 1–17.

———. *Thomas Heywood, Playwright and Miscellanist.* Oxford, 1931.

COKAYNE, SIR ASTON. *Poems,* ed. A. E. COKAYNE. Congleton, 1877.

COLERIDGE, SAMUEL TAYLOR. *Notes and Lectures upon Shakespeare,* ed. MRS. H. N. COLERIDGE. 2 vols. London, 1849.

————. *Table Talk and Omniana,* ed. T. ASHE. Bohn's Standard Library. London, 1884.

CRAIG, HARDIN. "Shakespeare's Bad Poetry," in *Shakespeare Survey 1* (Cambridge, 1948), pp. 51–56.

————. *"The Shrew* and *A Shrew:* Possible Settlement of an Old Debate," in *Elizabethan Studies and Other Essays: In Honor of George F. Reynolds.* Univ. of Colorado Studies (Boulder, 1945), pp. 150–154.

CRAWFORD, CHARLES. "The Authorship of Arden of Feversham." *Jahrbuch der deutschen Shakespeare-Gesellschaft,* XXXIX (1903), 74–86; reprinted in *Collectanea,* 1st Ser. (Stratford-on-Avon, 1906), pp. 101–130.

————. "Belvedere, or The Garden of the Muses." *Englische Studien,* XLIII (1910–11), 198–228.

CROSS, GUSTAV. "The Authorship of 'Lust's Dominion.'" *Studies in Philology,* LV (1958), 39–61.

CRUICKSHANK, A. H. "Massinger and *The Two Noble Kinsmen."* Elizabethan Literary Society Lecture. Oxford, 1922.

————. *Philip Massinger.* Oxford, 1920.

DANKS, K. B. "'A Shrew' & 'The Shrew.'" *Notes and Queries,* CC (1955), 331–332.

DAVRIL, ROBERT. *Le Drame de John Ford.* Bibliothèque des Langues Modernes, 5. Paris, 1954.

DAY, CYRUS L. "Thomas Randolph and *The Drinking Academy."* *PMLA,* XLIII (1928), 800–809.

————. "Thomas Randolph's Part in the Authorship of *Hey for Honesty."* *PMLA,* XLI (1926), 325–334.

DEKKER, THOMAS. *Dramatic Works,* ed. FREDSON BOWERS. 4 vols. Cambridge, 1953–61.

DELIUS, NICOLAUS. "Die angebliche Shakespeare-Fletcher'sche Autorschaft des Drama's 'The Two Noble Kinsmen.'" *Jahrbuch der deutschen Shakespeare-Gesellschaft,* XIII (1878), 16–44.

————. "Fletcher's angebliche Betheiligung an Shakespeare's King Henry VIII." *Jahrbuch der deutschen Shakespeare-Gesellschaft,* XIV (1879), 180–206.

DOBELL, BERTRAM. "The Author of 'A Yorkshire Tragedy.'" *Notes and Queries,* 10th Ser., VI (1906), 41–43.

DODSLEY, ROBERT. *A Select Collection of Old English Plays,* ed. W. C. HAZLITT. 4th ed. 15 vols. London, 1874–76.

DUNKEL, W. D. "The Authorship of *Anything for a Quiet Life.*" *PMLA,* XLIII (1928), 793–799.

————. "The Authorship of *The Puritan.*" *PMLA,* XLV (1930), 804–808.

————. "The Authorship of *The Revenger's Tragedy.*" *PMLA,* XLVI (1931), 781–785.

————. "Did Not Rowley Merely Revise Middleton?" *PMLA,* XLVIII (1933), 799–805.

DUTHIE, G. I. *"The Taming of a Shrew* and *The Taming of the Shrew."* *Review of English Studies,* XIX (1943), 337–356.

EBERLE, GERALD J. "Dekker's Part in *The Familie of Love,"* in *Joseph Quincy Adams Memorial Studies,* ed. J. G. McMANAWAY *et al.* (Washington, D. C., 1948), pp. 723–738.

EDWARDS, PHILIP. "An Approach to the Problem of *Pericles."* *Shakespeare Survey 5* (Cambridge, 1952), pp. 25–49.

EKEBLAD, INGA-STINA. "An Approach to Tourneur's Imagery." *Modern Language Review,* LIV (1959), 489–498.

————. "A Note on 'The Revenger's Tragedy.'" *Notes and Queries,* CC (1955), 98–99.

————. "On the Authorship of *The Revenger's Tragedy."* *English Studies,* XLI (1960), 225–240.

ELIOT, T. S. "Cyril Tourneur," in *Selected Essays* (London, 1951), pp. 182–192.

————. "Thomas Middleton," in *Selected Essays* (London, 1951), pp. 161–170.

————. "Tourneur and 'The Revenger's Tragedy.'" *The Times Literary Supplement,* Jan. 1, 1931, p. 12.

ELLIS-FERMOR, UNA M. "The Imagery of 'The Revenger's Tragedie' and 'The Atheist's Tragedie.'" *Modern Language Review,* XXX (1935), 289–301.

————. *Shakespeare the Dramatist,* ed. K. MUIR. London, 1961.

————. *"Timon of Athens:* An Unfinished Play." *Review of English Studies,* XVIII (1942), 270–283.

EVERITT, E. B. *The Young Shakespeare: Studies in Documentary Evidence.* Copenhagen, 1954.

FARMER, RICHARD. *An Essay on the Learning of Shakespeare.* 3rd ed. London, 1789.

FARNHAM, WILLARD. "Colloquial Contractions in Beaumont, Fletcher, Massinger, and Shakespeare as a Test of Authorship." *PMLA,* XXXI (1916), 326–358.

FEUILLERAT, ALBERT. *The Composition of Shakespeare's Plays.* New Haven, 1953.

————. *John Lyly.* Cambridge, 1910.

FLEAY, F. G. *A Biographical Chronicle of the English Drama, 1559–1642.* 2 vols. London, 1891.

————. *A Chronicle History of the Life and Work of William Shakespeare.* London, 1886.

————. *A Chronicle History of the London Stage, 1559–1642.* London, 1890.

————. "A Fresh Confirmation of Mr Spedding's Division and Date of the Play of *Henry VIII,"* in *Transactions of the New Shakspere Society* (London, 1874), Appendix, p. 23*.

————. "Mr Hickson's Division of the *Two Noble Kinsmen,* Confirmed by Metrical Tests," in *Transactions of the New Shakspere Society* (London, 1874), pp. 61*–64*.

————. "On the Authorship of the *Taming of the Shrew,"* in *Transactions of the New Shakspere Society* (London, 1874), pp. 85–98.

————. "On the Authorship of *Timon of Athens,"* in *Transactions of the New Shakspere Society* (London, 1874), pp. 130–151.

————. "On Certain Plays of Shakspere of Which Portions Were Written at Different Periods of His Life," in *Transactions of the New Shakspere Society* (London, 1874), pp. 285–317.

————. "On Metrical Tests as Applied to Dramatic Poetry," in *Transactions of the New Shakspere Society* (London, 1874), pp. 1–15.

————. "On the Play of *Pericles*," in *Transactions of the New Shakspere Society* (London, 1874), pp. 195–209.

————. "On Two Plays of Shakspere's, the Versions of Which as We Have Them Are the Results of Alterations by Other Hands," in *Transactions of the New Shakspere Society* (London, 1874), pp. 339–366.

————. *Shakespeare Manual.* London, 1876.

————. " 'Sir Giles Goosecap.' " *The Athenæum,* June 9, 1883, p. 731.

FLETCHER, JOHN, *et al. The Honest Man's Fortune,* ed. J. GERRITSEN. Groningen, 1952.

————. *Rollo, Duke of Normandy,* ed. JOHN D. JUMP. Liverpool English Texts and Studies, 2. Liverpool, 1948.

FOAKES, R. A. "On the Authorship of 'The Revenger's Tragedy.' " *Modern Language Review,* XLVIII (1953), 130–134.

FOGEL, EPHIM G. "Salmons in Both, or Some Caveats for Canonical Scholars." *Bulletin of the New York Public Library,* LXIII (1959), 223–236, 292–308.

FORD, JOHN. *Dramatic Works,* ed. W. GIFFORD; rev. A. DYCE. 3 vols. London, 1869.

FREEMAN, ARTHUR. "The Authorship of *The Tell-Tale.*" *Journal of English and Germanic Philology,* LXII (1963), 288–292.

FURNIVALL, F. J. "Another Fresh Confirmation of Mr Spedding's Division and Date of the Play of *Henry VIII,*" in *Transactions of the New Shakspere Society* (London, 1874), Appendix, p. 24*.

————. "Discussion of Mr Fleay's *Macbeth* and *Julius Caesar* Paper," in *Transactions of the New Shakspere Society* (London, 1874), pp. 498–509.

————. "Mr Hickson's Division of *The Two Noble Kinsmen,* Confirmed by the Stopt-Line Test," in *Transactions of the New Shakspere Society* (London, 1874), Appendix, pp. 64*–65*.

GARNETT, RICHARD. "Ben Jonson's Probable Authorship of Scene 2, Act IV, of Fletcher's *Bloody Brother.*" *Modern Philology,* II (1905), 489–495.

GAUD, W. S. "The Authorship of Locrine." *Modern Philology,* I (1904), 409–422.

GAYLEY, C. M. *Beaumont the Dramatist.* London, 1914.

GOLDING, S. R. "The Authorship of 'Lust's Dominion.'" *Notes and Queries,* CLV (1928), 399–402.

——. "The Authorship of *The Maid's Metamorphosis.*" *Review of English Studies,* II (1926), 270–279.

——. "The Authorship of the 'Two Lamentable Tragedies.'" *Notes and Queries,* CLI (1926), 347–350.

——. "Robert Wilson and 'Sir Thomas More.'" *Notes and Queries,* CLIV (1928), 237–239.

GRAHAM, WALTER. "The *Cardenio-Double Falsehood* Problem." *Modern Philology,* XIV (1916), 269–280.

GRAY, HENRY DAVID. "'Appius and Virginia': by Webster and Heywood." *Studies in Philology,* XXIV (1927), 275–289.

——. "'A Cure for a Cuckold' by Heywood, Rowley and Webster." *Modern Language Review,* XXII (1927), 389–397.

——. "Greene as a Collaborator." *Modern Language Notes,* XXX (1915), 244–246.

——. "Heywood's *Pericles,* Revised by Shakespeare." *PMLA,* XL (1925), 507–529.

——. "Shakespeare's Share in Titus Andronicus." *Philological Quarterly,* V (1926), 166–172.

——. "*The Taming of a Shrew.*" *Philological Quarterly,* XX (1941), 325–333.

——. "*The Taming of a Shrew,*" in *Renaissance Studies in Honor of Hardin Craig,* ed. B. MAXWELL *et al.* (Palo Alto, 1941), pp. 131–141.

GREENE, ROBERT. *Dramatic Works,* ed. A. DYCE. 2 vols. London, 1831.

——. *Plays and Poems,* ed. J. CHURTON COLLINS. 2 vols. Oxford, 1905.

GREG, W. W. "Authorship Attribution in the Early Play-Lists, 1656–1671." *Edinburgh Bibliographical Society Transactions,* II (1938–45), 305–329.

——. "The Authorship of the Songs in Lyly's Plays." *Modern Language Review,* I (1906), 43–52.

———. *A Bibliography of the English Printed Drama to the Restoration.* 4 vols. London, 1939–51.

———. "The Handwritings of the Manuscript," in *Shakespeare's Hand in the Play of Sir Thomas More* (Cambridge, 1923), pp. 41–56.

———. Review of HAUGHTON, WILLIAM, *Englishmen for My Money,* ed. A. C. BAUGH. *Modern Language Review,* XIII (1918), 101.

———. Review of *The Queen,* ed. W. BANG. *Modern Language Review,* III (1908), 292.

———. Review of *Sidelights on Elizabethan Drama* by H. DUGDALE SYKES. *Modern Language Review,* XX (1925), 195–200.

———. Review of *Who Wrote "Titus Andronicus"?* by J. M. ROBERTSON. *Modern Language Review,* I (1906), 338.

GRIVELET, MICHEL. *Thomas Heywood et le drame domestique élizabethain.* Collection des "Études anglaises," 4. Paris, 1957.

HALLIWELL-PHILLIPPS, J. O. *A Dictionary of Old English Plays.* London, 1860.

HALSTEAD, W. L. "Collaboration on *The Patient Grissill.*" *Philological Quarterly,* XVIII (1939), 381–394.

HARBAGE, ALFRED. *Annals of English Drama,* rev. S. SCHOEN-BAUM. London, 1964.

———. "A Choice Ternary: Belated Issues of Elizabethan Plays." *Notes and Queries,* CLXXXIII (1942), 32–34.

———. "The Mystery of *Perkin Warbeck,*" in *Studies in English Renaissance Drama,* ed. O. CARGILL *et al.* (New York, 1959), pp. 125–141.

HARLOW, C. G. "A Source for Nashe's *Terrors of the Night,* and the Authorship of *1 Henry VI.*" *Studies in English Literature,* V (1965), 31–47, 269–281.

HART, ALFRED. *Shakespeare and the Homilies.* Melbourne, 1934.

HASTINGS, WILLIAM T. "The Hardboiled Shakspere." *Shakespeare Association Bulletin,* XVII (1942), 114–125.

HATCHER, O. L. "Fletcher's Habits of Dramatic Collaboration." *Anglia,* XXXIII (1910), 219–231.

———. *John Fletcher: A Study in Dramatic Method.* Chicago, 1905.

————. "The Sources and Authorship of *The Thracian Wonder*." *Modern Language Notes*, XXIII (1908), 16–20.

HAZLITT, W., the Elder. *Lectures Chiefly on the Dramatic Literature of the Age of Elizabeth*. London, 1820.

HAZLITT, W. CAREW. *A Manual for the Collector and Amateur of Old English Plays*. London, 1892.

HENSLOWE, PHILIP. *Diary*, ed. R. A. FOAKES and R. T. RICKERT. Cambridge, 1961.

————. *Diary*, ed. W. W. GREG. 2 vols. London, 1904–8.

HERBERT, SIR HENRY. *Dramatic Records*, ed. JOSEPH Q. ADAMS. New Haven, 1917.

HIBBARD, LAURA A. "The Authorship and Date of the *Fayre Maide of the Exchange*." *Modern Philology*, VII (1910), 383–394.

HICKSON, SAMUEL. "The Shares of Shakspere and Fletcher in *The Two Noble Kinsmen*," in *Transactions of the New Shakspere Society* (London, 1874), Appendix, pp. 25*–61*.

————. "Who Wrote Shakespeare's 'Henry VIII'?" *Notes and Queries*, II (1850), 198.

HILLEBRAND, H. N. "Sebastian Westcote, Dramatist and Master of the Children of Paul's." *Journal of English and Germanic Philology*, XIV (1915), 568–584.

HONIGMANN, E. A. J. "Shakespeare's 'Lost Source-Plays.'" *Modern Language Review*, XLIX (1954), 293–307.

HOSLEY, RICHARD. "Sources and Analogues of *The Taming of the Shrew*." *Huntington Library Quarterly*, XXVII (1963–64), 289–308.

HOUK, RAYMOND A. "The Evolution of *The Taming of the Shrew*." *PMLA*, LVII (1942), 1009–1038.

————. "The Integrity of Shakespeare's *The Taming of the Shrew*." *Journal of English and Germanic Philology*, XXXIX (1940), 222–229.

————. "Shakespeare's *Shrew* and Greene's *Orlando*." *PMLA*, LXII (1947), 657–671.

————. "Strata in *The Taming of the Shrew*." *Studies in Philology*, XXXIX (1942), 291–302.

HOWE, FRED ALLISON. "The Authorship of 'The Birth of Merlin,'" *Modern Philology*, IV (1906), 193–205.

HOY, CYRUS. "The Shares of Fletcher and His Collaborators in the Beaumont and Fletcher Canon." *Studies in Bibliography,* VIII (1956), 129–146; IX (1957), 143–162; XI (1958), 85–106; XII (1959), 91–116; XIII (1960), 77–108; XIV (1961), 45–67; XV (1962), 71–90.

INGRAM, JOHN K. "On the 'Weak Endings' of Shakspere, with Some Account of the History of the Verse-Tests in General," in *Transactions of the New Shakspere Society* (London, 1874), pp. 442–451.

JACKSON, MACD. P. "Affirmative Particles in 'Henry VIII.'" *Notes and Queries,* CCVII (1962), 372–374.

———. "Shakespeare and 'Edmund Ironside.'" *Notes and Queries,* CCVIII (1963), 331–332.

JACQUOT, JEAN. *George Chapman (1559–1634): sa vie, sa poésie, son théâtre, sa pensée.* Paris, 1951.

JENKINS, HAROLD. "Cyril Tourneur." *Review of English Studies,* XVII (1941), 21–36.

———. *The Life and Work of Henry Chettle.* London, 1934.

———. "A Supplement to Sir Walter Greg's Edition of *Sir Thomas More,*" in *Collections, Vol. VI* (Oxford: Malone Society, 1961 [1962]), pp. 177–192.

JOHNSON, SAMUEL. *Johnson on Shakespeare,* ed. W. RALEIGH. 5th impression. Oxford, 1925.

JONES, FREDERIC L. "Cyril Tourneur." *The Times Literary Supplement,* June 18, 1931, p. 487.

———. "An Experiment with Massinger's Verse." *PMLA,* XLVII (1932), 727–740.

———. "*The Trial of Chivalry,* a Chettle Play." *PMLA,* XLI (1926), 304–324.

JONES, RICHARD FOSTER. *Lewis Theobald.* New York, 1919.

JONES-DAVIES, M. T. *Un Peintre de la vie londonienne: Thomas Dekker, c. 1572–1632.* Collection des "Études anglaises," 6. Paris, 1958.

JONSON, BEN. *Works,* ed. W. GIFFORD. 9 vols. London, 1816.

———. *Works,* ed. C. H. HERFORD and P. and E. SIMPSON. 11 vols. Oxford, 1925–52.

———, *et al. Eastward Hoe,* ed. JULIA HAMLET HARRIS. Yale Studies in English, 73. New Haven, 1926.

KIRSCHBAUM, LEO. "The Authorship of *1 Henry VI*," *PMLA*, LXVII (1952), 809–822.

KITTREDGE, G. L. "Notes on Elizabethan Plays." *Journal of Germanic Philology*, II (1898–99), 7–13.

KOCHER, PAUL H. "Nashe's Authorship of the Prose Scenes in *Faustus*." *Modern Language Quarterly*, III (1942), 17–40.

KUHL, E. P. "The Authorship of *The Taming of the Shrew*." *PMLA*, XL (1925), 551–618.

KYD, THOMAS. *The Spanish Tragedy*, ed. P. EDWARDS. Revels Plays. London, 1959.

———. *Works*, ed. F. S. BOAS. Oxford, 1901.

LANGBAINE, GERARD, the Younger. *An Account of the English Dramatick Poets. Or, Some Observations and Remarks on the Lives and Writings, of All Those That Have Publish'd Either Comedies, Tragedies, Tragi-Comedies, Pastorals, Masques, Interludes, Farces, or Opera's in the English Tongue.* Oxford, 1691.

LARSEN, T. "The Canon of Peele's Works." *Modern Philology*, XXVI (1928), 191–199.

———. "The Growth of the Peele Canon." *The Library*, XI (1930), 300–311.

LAW, ROBERT A. "Further Notes on 'Two Lamentable Tragedies.'" *Notes and Queries*, CLIII (1927), 93–94.

———. "Holinshed and *Henry the Eighth*." *Texas Studies in English*, XXXVI (1957), 3–11.

———. "Yarington's 'Two Lamentable Tragedies.'" *Modern Language Review*, V (1910), 167–177.

LAWRENCE, W. J. "Dekker's Theatrical Allusiveness." *The Times Literary Supplement*, Jan. 30, 1937, p. 72; reprinted, with additions, in *Speeding up Shakespeare* (London, 1937), pp. 114–126.

———. "Massinger's Punctuation and What It Reveals." *The Criterion*, XI (1932), 214–221.

———. *Pre-Restoration Stage Studies*. Cambridge, Mass., 1927.

———. *Speeding up Shakespeare*. London, 1937.

———. *Those Nut-Cracking Elizabethans*. London, 1935.

LEE, JANE. "On the Authorship of the Second and Third Parts

of *Henry VI,* and Their Originals." *Transactions of the New Shakspere Society* (London, 1876), pp. 219–279.

LEECH, CLIFFORD. *The John Fletcher Plays.* London, 1962.

———. *John Ford and the Drama of His Time.* London, 1957.

———. Review of *Shakespeare as Collaborator* by K. MUIR. *Notes and Queries,* CCVI (1961), 156–157.

LILLO, GEORGE. *The Works of Mr. George Lillo; with Some Account of His Life.* 2 vols. London, 1775.

LITTLEDALE, HAROLD, ed. William Shakspere and John Fletcher, *The Two Noble Kinsmen.* Publications of the New Shakspere Society, Ser. II, No. 15, Pt. II. London, 1885.

LLOYD, BERTRAM. "The Authorship of *The Welsh Embassador.*" *Review of English Studies,* XXI (1945), 192–201.

LORD, GEORGE DE F. "Comments on the Canonical Caveat." *Bulletin of the New York Public Library,* LXIII (1959), 355–366.

LOUNSBURY, THOMAS R. *The First Editors of Shakespeare (Pope and Theobald).* London, 1906.

LYLY, JOHN. *Works,* ed. R. W. BOND. 3 vols. Oxford, 1902.

MACAULAY, GEORGE C. *Francis Beaumont.* London, 1883.

McMANAWAY, JAMES G. "Latin Title-Page Mottoes as a Clue to Dramatic Authorship." *The Library,* XXVI (1945), 28–36.

McNEIR, WALDO F. "Robert Greene and *John of Bordeaux.*" *PMLA,* LXIV (1949), 781–801.

MALONE, EDMOND. *A Dissertation on the Three Parts of King Henry VI.* London, 1787. [For *An Attempt to Ascertain the Order in Which the Plays Attributed to Shakespeare Were Written,* see Malone's edition of the *Plays and Poems* below, under Shakespeare, William.]

MARLOWE, CHRISTOPHER. *Doctor Faustus,* ed. JOHN D. JUMP. Revels Plays. London, 1962.

———. *Marlowe's "Doctor Faustus," 1604–1616. Parallel Texts,* ed. W. W. GREG. Oxford, 1950.

———. *Works,* ed. A. H. BULLEN. 3 vols. London, 1885.

———. *Works,* ed. A. DYCE. London, 1858.

MARSTON, JOHN. *Works,* ed. A. H. BULLEN. 3 vols. London, 1887.

MASSINGER, PHILIP. *Plays,* ed. W. GIFFORD. 2nd ed. 4 vols. London, 1813.

MAXWELL, BALDWIN. Review of *Sidelights on Shakespeare* by H. DUGDALE SYKES. *Modern Philology,* XXIII (1926), 365–372; reprinted, with revisions, as "Fletcher and *Henry the Eighth,*" in *Manly Anniversary Studies* (Chicago, 1928), pp. 104–112.

———. *Studies in Beaumont, Fletcher, and Massinger.* Chapel Hill, 1939.

———. *Studies in the Shakespeare Apocrypha.* New York, 1956.

MIDDLETON, THOMAS. *Works,* ed. A. H. BULLEN. 8 vols. London, 1885–86.

———. *Works,* ed. A. DYCE. 5 vols. London, 1840.

———, and ROWLEY, WILLIAM. *All's Lost by Lust* and *The Spanish Gypsy,* ed. EDGAR COIT MORRIS. Belles-Lettres Series. 2 vols. in 1. Boston, 1908.

———. *The Changeling,* ed. N. W. BAWCUTT. Revels Plays. London, 1958.

MILLER, HELENA F. "The Use of the Third Person Singular of *Have* and *Do* in the Works of Shakespeare and Massinger." *Philological Quarterly,* IX (1930), 373–378.

MINCOFF, MARCO. "The Authorship of the Revenger's Tragedy." *Studia Historico-Philologica Serdicensia,* II (1939), 1–87.

———. "The Authorship of *The Two Noble Kinsmen.*" *English Studies,* XXXIII (1952), 97–115.

———. "*Henry VIII* and Fletcher." *Shakespeare Quarterly,* XII (1961), 239–260.

MORRIS, EDGAR COIT. "On the Date and Composition of *The Old Law.*" *PMLA,* XVII (1902), 1–70.

MUIR, KENNETH. "Fifty Years of Shakespearian Criticism: 1900–1950," in *Shakespeare Survey 4* (Cambridge, 1951), pp. 1–25.

———. *Shakespeare as Collaborator.* London, 1960.

MUNRO, JOHN. "Biography," in *Frederick James Furnivall: A Volume of Personal Record.* Oxford, 1911.

MURRAY, PETER B. "The Authorship of *The Revenger's Trag-*

edy." *Papers of the Bibliographical Society of America,* LVI (1962), 195–218.

———. "The Collaboration of Dekker and Webster in 'Northward Ho' and 'Westward Ho.'" *Papers of the Bibliographical Society of America,* LVI (1962), 482–486.

———. *A Study of Cyril Tourneur.* Philadelphia, 1964.

NICOLSON, MARJORIE H. "The Authorship of *Henry the Eighth.*" *PMLA,* XXXVII (1922), 484–502.

NOSWORTHY, J. M. "Shakespeare and *Sir Thomas More.*" *Review of English Studies,* N.S., VI (1955), 12–25.

OLIPHANT, E. H. C. "The Authorship of *The Revenger's Tragedy.*" *Studies in Philology,* XXIII (1926), 157–168.

———. "'The Bloodie Banquet.' A Dekker-Middleton Play." *The Times Literary Supplement,* Dec. 17, 1925, p. 882.

———. "Collaboration in Elizabethan Drama: Mr. W. J. Lawrence's Theory." *Philological Quarterly,* VIII (1929), 1–10.

———. "How Not to Play the Game of Parallels." *Journal of English and Germanic Philology,* XXVIII (1929), 1–15.

———. "Marlowe's Hand in 'Arden of Feversham': A Problem for Critics." *New Criterion,* IV (1926), 76–93.

———. *The Plays of Beaumont and Fletcher: An Attempt to Determine Their Respective Shares and the Shares of Others.* New Haven, 1927.

———. "The Plays of Beaumont and Fletcher: Some Additional Notes." *Philological Quarterly,* IX (1930), 7–22.

———. "Problems of Authorship in Elizabethan Dramatic Literature." *Modern Philology,* VIII (1911), 411–459.

———. "Tourneur and Mr. T. S. Eliot." *Studies in Philology,* XXXII (1935), 546–552.

———. "Tourneur and 'The Revenger's Tragedy.'" *The Times Literary Supplement,* Dec. 18, 1930, p. 1087; Feb. 5, 1931, p. 99.

———. "The Works of Beaumont and Fletcher." *Englische Studien,* XIV (1890), 53–94; XV (1891), 321–360; XVI (1892), 180–200.

————, ed. *Shakespeare and His Fellow Dramatists.* 2 vols. New York, 1929.

OLIVER, H. J. *The Problem of John Ford.* Carlton, 1955.

ORAS, ANTS. " 'Extra Monosyllables' in *Henry VIII* and the Problem of Authorship." *Journal of English and Germanic Philology,* LII (1953), 198–213.

ORNSTEIN, ROBERT. *The Moral Vision of Jacobean Tragedy.* Madison, 1960.

PARROTT, T. M. "The Authorship of 'Sir Gyles Goosecappe.' " *Modern Philology,* IV (1906), 25–37.

————. "The Authorship of *Two Italian Gentlemen.*" *Modern Philology,* XIII (1915), 241–251.

————. "Marlowe, Beaumont, and *Julius Caesar.*" *Modern Language Notes,* XLIV (1929), 69–77.

————. "The Problem of Timon of Athens." Shakespeare Association Papers, 10. London, 1923.

————. "Shakespeare's Revision of 'Titus Andronicus.' " *Modern Language Review,* XIV (1919), 16–37.

————. "*The Taming of a Shrew*—A New Study of an Old Play." *Elizabethan Studies and Other Essays.* Univ. of Colorado Studies (Boulder, 1945), pp. 155–165.

PARTRIDGE, A. C. *Orthography in Shakespeare and Elizabethan Drama.* London, 1964.

————. *The Problem of Henry VIII Reopened.* Cambridge, 1949.

PEELE, GEORGE. *The Life and Minor Works of George Peele,* ed. DAVID H. HORNE. New Haven, 1952.

————. *Works,* ed. A. H. BULLEN. 2 vols. London, 1888.

————. *Works,* ed. A. DYCE. London, 1828–39.

PETER, JOHN. *Complaint and Satire in Early English Literature.* Oxford, 1956.

PIERCE, FREDERICK E. "The Collaboration of Dekker and Ford." *Anglia,* XXXVI (1912), 140–168, 389–412.

————. *The Collaboration of Webster and Dekker.* Yale Studies in English, 37. New Haven, 1909.

PITCHER, SEYMOUR. *The Case for Shakespeare's Authorship of The Famous Victories.* New York, 1961.

POLLARD, ALFRED W. "Elizabethan Spelling as a Literary and Bibliographical Clue." *The Library,* 4th Ser., IV (1923), 1–8.

———. ed. *Shakespeare's Hand in the Play of Sir Thomas More.* Cambridge, 1923.

PRICE, GEORGE R. "The Authorship and Manuscript of *The Old Law." Huntington Library Quarterly,* XVI (1953), 117–139.

———. "The Authorship and the Bibliography of *The Revenger's Tragedy." The Library,* 5th Ser., XV (1960), 262–277.

PRICE, HEREWARD T. "The Authorship of 'Titus Andronicus.' " *Journal of English and Germanic Philology,* XLII (1943), 55–81.

———. "Construction in Shakespeare." University of Michigan Contributions in Modern Philology, XVII (1951), 1–42.

———. "The First Quarto of Titus Andronicus," in *English Institute Essays 1947* (New York, 1948), pp. 137–168.

———. Review of *"The Contention" and Shakespeare's "2 Henry VI"* by C. T. PROUTY. *Modern Language Notes,* LXX (1955), 527–529.

PRIOR, MOODY E. "Imagery as a Test of Authorship." *Shakespeare Quarterly,* VI (1955), 381–386.

PROUTY, CHARLES T. *"The Contention" and Shakespeare's "2 Henry VI": A Comparative Study.* New Haven, 1954.

RANDOLPH, THOMAS. *The Drinking Academy,* ed. S. A. TANNENBAUM and HYDER E. ROLLINS. Cambridge, Mass., 1930.

RAVENSCROFT, EDWARD. *Titus Andronicus, or The Rape of Lavinia.* London, 1687.

REYBURN, MARJORIE L. "New Facts and Theories about the Parnassus Plays." *PMLA,* LXXIV (1959), 325–335.

RIBNER, IRVING. *Jacobean Tragedy: The Quest for Moral Order.* London, 1962.

ROBB, DEWAR M. "The Canon of William Rowley's Plays." *Modern Language Review,* XLV (1950), 129–141.

ROBERTS, C. W. "The Authorship of *Gammer Gurton's Needle." Philological Quarterly,* XIX (1940), 97–113.

ROBERTSON, JOHN M. *Did Shakespeare Write "Titus Andronicus"?* London, 1905.

————. *The Genuine in Shakespeare*. London, 1930.

————. *"Hamlet" Once More*. London, 1923.

————. *An Introduction to the Study of the Shakespeare Canon*. New York, 1924.

————. *Marlowe: A Conspectus*. London, 1931.

————. *The Problem of "Hamlet."* London, 1919.

————. *The Shakespeare Canon*. 5 vols. London, 1922–32.

————. *Shakespeare and Chapman*. London, 1917.

————. "Shakespearean Idolatry." *The Criterion*, IX (1930), 246–267.

————. *The State of Shakespeare Study*. London, 1931.

ROUTH, JAMES E., JR. "Thomas Kyd's Rime Schemes and the Authorship of *Soliman and Perseda* and of *The First Part of Jeronimo*." *Modern Language Notes*, XX (1905), 49–51.

SAMPLEY, ARTHUR M. "'Verbal Tests' for Peele's Plays." *Studies in Philology*, XXX (1933), 473–496.

SARGEAUNT, M. JOAN. *John Ford*. Oxford, 1935.

SCHELLING, FELIX E. *Elizabethan Drama, 1558–1642*. 2 vols. Boston and New York, 1908.

SCHOELL, F. L. *George Chapman as a Comic Writer*. Univ. of Paris thesis. Paris, 1911.

————. "A New Source of *Sir Gyles Goosecappe*." *Modern Philology*, XI (1914), 547–558.

SCHOENBAUM, S. *Middleton's Tragedies: A Critical Study*. New York, 1955.

————. "'The Revenger's Tragedy' and Middleton's Moral Outlook." *Notes and Queries*, CXCVI (1951), 8–10.

SCHÜCKING, L. L. "Shakespeare and *Sir Thomas More*." *Review of English Studies*, I (1925), 40–59.

————. *Zur Verfasserschaft der "Spanish Tragedy."* Bayerische Akademie der Wissenschaften. Philosophisch-historische Klasse, 4. Munich, 1963.

SENSABAUGH, G. F. "Another Play by John Ford." *Modern Language Quarterly*, III (1942), 595–601.

SEYMOUR, E. H. *Remarks Critical, Conjectural, and Explanatory, upon the Plays of Shakespeare*. 2 vols. London, 1805.

SHAKESPEARE, WILLIAM. *Hamlet,* ed. E. K. CHAMBERS. Warwick Shakespeare. London, 1894.

———. *1 Henry IV,* ed. A. R. HUMPHREYS. [New] Arden Shakespeare. London, 1960.

———. *1, 2,* and *3 Henry VI,* ed. ANDREW S. CAIRNCROSS. 3 vols. [New] Arden Shakespeare. London, 1957–64.

———. *1, 2,* and *3 Henry VI,* ed. J. DOVER WILSON. 3 vols. New Shakespeare. Cambridge, 1952.

———. *Henry VIII,* ed. R. A. FOAKES. [New] Arden Shakespeare. London, 1964.

———. *Henry VIII,* ed. J. C. MAXWELL. New Shakespeare. Cambridge, 1962.

———. *The Life of Tymon of Athens,* "As Written by W. Shakspere," ed. F. G. FLEAY, in *Transactions of the New Shakspere Society* (London, 1874), pp. 152–194.

———. *Mr. William Shakespeare His Comedies, Histories, and Tragedies,* ed. EDWARD CAPELL. 10 vols. London [1767–68].

———. *Pericles,* ed. F. D. HOENIGER. [New] Arden Shakespeare. London, 1963.

———. *Pericles,* ed. J. C. MAXWELL. New Shakespeare. Cambridge, 1956.

———. *The Plays and Poems of William Shakespeare,* ed. EDMOND MALONE. 10 vols. London, 1790. [Includes the *Attempt* and *Dissertation.*]

———. *The Plays of William Shakespeare,* ed. SAMUEL JOHNSON and GEORGE STEEVENS. 15 vols. London, 1793.

———. *The Strange and Worthy Accidents in the Birth and Life of Marina,* ed. F. G. FLEAY, in *Transactions of the New Shakspere Society* (London, 1874), pp. 211–241.

———. *Titus Andronicus,* ed. E. K. CHAMBERS. Red Letter Shakespeare. London, 1907.

———. *Titus Andronicus,* ed. J. C. MAXWELL. [New] Arden Shakespeare. London, 1953.

———. *Titus Andronicus,* ed. J. DOVER WILSON. New Shakespeare. Cambridge, 1948.

———. *The Works of Mr. William Shakespear,* ed. NICHOLAS ROWE. 6 vols. London, 1709.

————. *The Works of Shakespear,* ed. SIR THOMAS HANMER. 6 vols. Oxford, 1744.

————. *The Works of Shakespear,* ed. ALEXANDER POPE. 6 vols. London, 1725.

————. *The Works of Shakespear,* ed. ALEXANDER POPE and WILLIAM WARBURTON. 8 vols. London, 1747.

————. *The Works of Shakespeare,* ed. LEWIS THEOBALD. 7 vols. London, 1733.

————. *The Works of William Shakespeare,* ed. W. G. CLARK and W. A. WRIGHT. 9 vols. Cambridge and London, 1863–66.

SHERBO, ARTHUR. "A Reply to Professor Fogel." *Bulletin of the New York Public Library,* LXIII (1959), 367–371.

————. "The Uses and Abuses of Internal Evidence." *Bulletin of the New York Public Library,* LXIII (1959), 5–20.

SHERMAN, STUART P. "A New Play by John Ford." *Modern Language Notes,* XXIII (1908), 245–249.

SHIRLEY, JAMES. *Dramatic Works and Poems,* ed. W. GIFFORD and A. DYCE. 6 vols. London, 1833.

SHROEDER, JOHN W. *"The Taming of a Shrew* and *The Taming of the Shrew:* A Case Reopened." *Journal of English and Germanic Philology,* LVII (1958), 424–443.

SIMPSON, PERCY. "The Problem of Authorship of *Eastward Ho."* *PMLA,* LIX (1944), 715–725.

SIMPSON, RICHARD. "Are There Any Extant MSS. in Shakespeare's Handwriting?" *Notes and Queries,* VIII (1871), 1–3.

————. "On Some Plays Attributed to Shakspere," in *Transactions of the New Shakspere Society* (London, 1875), pp. 155–180.

————. Review of *Robert Greene's Leben und Schriften* by W. BERNHARDI. *The Academy,* V (1874), 310.

SISSON, C. J. *Lost Plays of Shakespeare's Age.* London, 1936.

SMITH, G. C. MOORE. "The Canon of Randolph's Dramatic Works." *Review of English Studies,* I (1925), 309–323.

SMITH, MARION BODWELL. *Marlowe's Imagery and the Marlowe Canon.* Philadelphia, 1940.

SPALDING, WILLIAM. "Dyce's *Beaumont and Fletcher"* (review-article). *Edinburgh Review,* LXXXVI (1847), 42–67.

————. *A Letter on Shakspere's Authorship of "The Two Noble Kinsmen"; and on the Characteristics of Shakspere's Style, and the Secret of his Supremacy.* Publications of the New Shakspere Society, Ser. VIII, No. 1. London, 1876.

————. "Recent Shakspearian Literature." *Edinburgh Review,* LXXI (1840), 446–493.

SPEDDING, JAMES. "On the Several Shares of Shakspere and Fletcher in the Play of *Henry VIII,*" in *Transactions of the New Shakspere Society* (London, 1874), Appendix, pp. 1*–18*.

————. "Shakespeare's Handwriting." *Notes and Queries,* X (1872), 227–228.

SPURGEON, CAROLINE F. E. "Imagery in the *Sir Thomas More* Fragment." *Review of English Studies,* VI (1930), 257–270.

————. *Shakespeare's Imagery and What It Tells Us.* Cambridge, 1935.

————. "Shakespeare's Iterative Imagery," in *Aspects of Shakespeare* (Oxford, 1933), pp. 255–286.

STOLL, E. E. *John Webster.* Boston, 1905.

SWART, J. "Shakespeare without Tears." *Neophilologus,* XXXVIII (1954), 221–224.

SYKES, H. DUGDALE. "The Authorship of the 'Witch of Edmonton.'" *Notes and Queries,* CLI (1926), 435–438, 453–457.

————. "Cyril Tourneur: 'The Revenger's Tragedy': 'The Second Maiden's Tragedy.'" *Notes and Queries,* 12 Ser., V (1919), 225–229.

————. Review of *The Plays of Beaumont and Fletcher* by E. H. C. OLIPHANT. *Review of English Studies,* IV (1928), 456–463.

————. "Robert Greene and 'George a Greene, the Pinner of Wakefield'" *Modern Language Review,* VII (1931), 129–136.

————. "Robert Greene and *George a Greene, the Pinner of Wakefield.*" *Modern Language Review,* VII (1931), 129–

————. *Sidelights on Elizabethan Drama.* Stratford-on-Avon, 1924.

————. *Sidelights on Shakespeare.* Stratford-on-Avon, 1919.

———. "Thomas Heywood's Authorship of "King Edward IV.' " *Notes and Queries,* CXLIX (1925), 183–184.

TANNENBAUM, S. A. *"The Booke of Sir Thomas Moore": A Bibliotic Study.* New York, 1927.

———. *Shakspere and "Sir Thomas Moore."* New York and London, 1929.

TEETGEN, ALEXANDER. *Shakespeare's "King Edward the Third," Absurdly Called, and Scandalously Treated as, a "Doubtful Play:" an Indignation Pamphlet. Together with an Essay on the Poetry of the Future.* London, 1875.

THOMAS, D. L. "Authorship of *Revenge for Honour." Modern Philology,* V (1908), 617–636.

THOMAS, SIDNEY. "A Note on *The Taming of the Shrew." Modern Language Notes,* LXIV (1949), 94–96.

THOMPSON, SIR EDWARD MAUNDE. "The Handwriting of the Three Pages Attributed to Shakespeare Compared with His Signatures," in *Shakespeare's Hand in the Play of Sir Thomas More* (Cambridge, 1923), pp. 57–112.

———. *Shakespeare's Handwriting.* Oxford, 1916.

THOMPSON, ELBERT N. S. "Elizabethan Dramatic Collaboration." *Englische Studien,* XL (1909), 30–46.

THORNDIKE, ASHLEY H. *The Influence of Beaumont and Fletcher on Shakspere.* Worcester, Mass., 1901.

TOURNEUR, CYRIL. *The Atheist's Tragedy,* ed. IRVING RIBNER. Revels Plays. London, 1964.

———. *Plays and Poems,* ed. J. CHURTON COLLINS. 2 vols. London, 1878.

———. *La Tragedie du vengeur,* ed. H. FLUCHÈRE. Collection bilingue des classiques étrangers. Paris, 1958.

———. *Works,* ed. ALLARDYCE NICOLL. London [1929?].

TURNER, CELESTE. *Anthony Mundy: An Elizabethan Man of Letters.* Berkeley, 1928.

UPTON, ALBERT W. "The Authorship of *The Woman Hater." Philological Quarterly,* IX (1930), 33–42.

WAGNER, B. M. "Cyril Tourneur." *The Times Literary Supplement,* April 23, 1931, p. 327.

———. "Robert Yarrington." *Modern Language Notes,* XLV (1930), 147–148.

WALDO, TOMMY RUTH, and HERBERT, T. W. "Musical Terms in *The Taming of the Shrew:* Evidence of Single Authorship." *Shakespeare Quarterly,* X (1959), 185–199.

WALLER, FREDERICK O. "Printer's Copy for *The Two Noble Kinsmen.*" *Studies in Bibliography,* XI (1958), 61–84.

WALLIS, LAWRENCE B. *Fletcher, Beaumont & Company: Entertainers to the Jacobean Gentry.* New York, 1947.

WALTER, J. H. "*Revenge for Honour:* Date, Authorship and Sources." *Review of English Studies,* XIII (1937), 425–437.

WEBSTER, JOHN. *Complete Works,* ed. F. L. LUCAS. 4 vols. London, 1927.

————. *Works,* ed. A. DYCE. 4 vols. London, 1830.

WELLS, WILLIAM. " 'Alphonsus, Emperor of Germany.' " *Notes and Queries,* CLXXIX (1940), 218–223, 236–240.

————. *The Authorship of Julius Caesar.* London, 1923.

————. "The Authorship of 'King Leir.' " *Notes and Queries,* CLXXVII (1939), 434–438.

————. " 'The Birth of Merlin.' " *Modern Language Review,* XVI (1921), 129–137.

————. " 'The Bloody Brother.' " *Notes and Queries,* CLIV (1928), 6–9.

————. "Thomas Kyd and the Chronicle-History." *Notes and Queries,* CLXXVIII (1940), 218–224, 238–243.

————. " 'Timon of Athens.' " *Notes and Queries,* VI (1920), 266–269.

WENDLANDT, WILHELM. "Shakespeare's *Timon von Athen.*" *Jahrbuch der deutschen Shakespeare-Gesellschaft,* XXIII (1888), 109–192.

WENTERSDORF, K. "The Authenticity of *The Taming of the Shrew.*" *Shakespeare Quarterly,* V (1954), 11–32.

WIGGIN, PAULINE. *An Inquiry into the Authorship of the Middleton-Rowley Plays.* Radcliffe College Monographs, 9. Cambridge, Mass., 1897.

WILSON, J. DOVER. "Bibliographical Links between the Three Pages and the Good Quartos," in *Shakespeare's Hand in the Play of Sir Thomas More* (Cambridge, 1923), pp. 113–131.

————. "The Elizabethan Shakespeare," in *Aspects of Shakespeare* (Oxford, 1933), pp. 202–226.

————. "Idolatry and Scepticism in Shakespearian Studies." *The Criterion,* IX (1930), 631–641.

————. "Malone and the Upstart Crow." *Shakespeare Survey 4* (Cambridge, 1951), pp. 56–68.

WRIGHT, ERNEST HUNTER. *The Authorship of Timon of Athens.* New York, 1910.

POSTSCRIPT

IN A LETTER which I received after this book had gone to press, Professor Foakes summed up the findings of his investigation into the authorship of *The Revenger's Tragedy* for his Revels Plays edition, which is shortly to be published. I am obliged to Professor Foakes for permission to quote from this personal communication. He writes:

The accumulation of evidence, bibliographical especially (i.e., G. R. Price's essay) is strong, but not conclusive for Middleton. There remain discrepancies between usages in Middleton and in *R.T.*—act headings, for example ('Incipit . . .' or 'Finis Actus . . .' in Middleton, including *A Trick,* but not in *R.T.*). All arguments based on similarities, etc., leave a final uncertainty; only external evidence could settle the matter. In the end there remains the conviction that *R.T.* differs from Middleton's known work in too many ways; and the fact that it was a King's Men's play, and Middleton had no known connection with them at the time. So all one can do is record 'the fact of uncertainty' (quoting Schoenbaum, *Bull. of the N.Y. Public Lib.,* 1961), but leave the balance tilted slightly in Tourneur's favour—lacking a better candidate.

Professor Foakes's latest reappraisal of the evidence has thus resulted in a verdict very similar to my own. I would differ from him only in questioning whether the balance is indeed tilted rather than level.

I have learned from Professor E. G. Fogel that the forthcoming *Evidence for Authorship: Essays on Problems of Attribution,* of which he is co-editor with Mr. David V. Erdman, will contain an Annotated Bibliography of Selected Readings, including a great many items on Elizabethan drama. The bulk of these concern the Shakespeare canon (*1, 2, and 3 Henry VI, Titus Andronicus, The Taming of the Shrew, Henry VIII;* plus the non-Folio plays *Edward III, Sir Thomas More, Pericles,* and *The Two Noble Kinsmen*); but a few of the other interesting authorship questions are represented. The bibliography should render the collection especially interesting to all students of Elizabethan dramatic authorship.

The publication has been announced of Paul Bertram's *Shakespeare and The Two Noble Kinsmen* (New Brunswick, 1965), in which, according to the publishers, it is demonstrated that the play "was probably Shakespeare's alone." I regret that the monograph was not yet available when I wrote Part Three of this study, where Bertram's view is mentioned (p. 136).

For a possible explanation of the misattribution of *The Coronation* to James Shirley on the title-page of the 1640 quarto, see T. J. King, "Shirley's *Coronation* and *Love Will Find Out the Way:* Erroneous Title-Pages," *Studies in Bibliography,* XVIII (1965), 265–269. The article appeared too late for appropriate notice on p. 152, where I discuss *The Coronation.*

This Postscript provides an opportunity, too good to let pass, to comment on a few pieces that escaped mention in my text. In "The Original of Sir John Falstaff—Believe It or Not," Baldwin Maxwell pursues to a *reductio ad absurdum* the attempt to identify a dramatist's personages with actual persons by the citation of parallels; the article, while not treating authorship attribution directly, parodies analogous abuses with mischievous effectiveness.[1] H. T. Price's "Towards a Scientific Method of Textual Criticism for the Elizabethan Drama" deals in large measure with tests (vocabulary, metrical, etc.) favored by ascriptional hypothesizers.[2] Price objects to the way in which "trivial and commonplace words" are brought forward as "absolute" proofs of authorship; he complains of premature generalizations based on insufficient data; he urges further investigation of Renaissance habits of imitation and plagiarism:

> The plays that go by the name of Beaumont and Fletcher are full of passages influenced by Shakespeare, which nobody attributes to Shakespeare. On the other hand, passages which appear to owe something to Massinger are usually given to Massinger. . . . No work on these two poets will be convincing until the attitude of each towards imitation has been carefully analysed. We may, I suggest, lay down the general rule that questions of authorship cannot be determined until the possibility of imitation has been thoroughly gone into and it has been made clear what sort of imitation we find in an author's undoubtedly genuine works. If a scholar wishes to rule out imitation, he must tell us why.[3]

In the course of an essay concerned largely with method, Price adduces additional vocabulary evidence for Shakespeare's authorship of *Titus Andronicus*. His sobering conclusion is that "this whole business of textual criticism needs a thorough shaking up." [4] Also, Lillian Herlands Hornstein's "Analysis of Imagery: A Critique of Literary Method" may be recommended for its effective exposure of some of the limitations of the Spurgeon school of image study, and especially of the dangers inherent

1. *Stud. in Phil.*, XXVII (1930), 230–232.
2. *Jour. of Eng. and Germ. Phil.*, XXXVI (1937), 151–167.
3. *Ibid.*, p. 155.
4. *Ibid.*, p. 167.

in drawing biographical inferences from statistical tabulations of figurative language.[5]

I should have cited in Part One Thomas Kenny's neglected *The Life and Genius of Shakespeare* (1864), much of which (pp. 245–367) is concerned with *1, 2,* and *3 Henry VI.* Kenny defends the authenticity of the entire trilogy, and in so doing provides an elaborate critique of Malone's *Dissertation.* He argues—and it is in this respect that Kenny's work is chiefly remarkable—that the *Contention* and *True Tragedy* are debased versions of *2* and *3 Henry VI* prepared for the printers by "a mere copyist." He thus diverges from the mainstream of Victorian authorship studies as represented, for example, by Jane Lee. Not surprisingly he was ignored and afterwards forgotten; Alexander arrived at his conclusions independently. But Kenny deserves credit for anticipating a major discovery of twentieth-century Shakespearean scholarship.

I am also sorry to have missed R. F. Hill's "The Composition of *Titus Andronicus," Shakespeare Survey 10* (1957), pp. 60–70. His purpose is "to establish by a full and impartial analysis of a group of Shakespeare's early plays what elements in the style of *Titus* are un-characteristic of his early manner" (p. 61). Hill's essay is refreshingly undogmatic in tone; he appreciates the methodological difficulties in the way of his quest. His conclusion— that the play, if entirely Shakespeare's, must have been written before 1590—is, needless to say, tentative.

The University of Nebraska Press has published a paperback edition of Edward A. Armstrong's *Shakespeare's Imagination* (Lincoln, 1963) with a new ap-

---

5. *PMLA,* LVII (1942), 638–653. The essay does not touch specifically upon authorship problems, although Professor Hornstein cites Marion Bodwell Smith's *Marlowe's Imagery and the Marlowe Canon.*

pendix on "Shakespearean Imagery in *The Two Noble Kinsmen*" (pp. 203–217). When applied to I,i, and V,i, the image-cluster test provides "definitive proof that Shakespeare wrote the scenes scrutinised, but peculiarities in style and imagery indicate that we are dealing with the poet's work when his creative imagination had passed its prime" (p. 204). The presence of "linkages" in other scenes indicates that Shakespeare's share in the play "may have been greater than is generally accepted" (p. 211). On the basis of the evidence he cites for I,i, and V,i—scenes attributed to Shakespeare by Hart, Muir, and others—Armstrong claims to have demonstrated the validity of his test. Like so many previous investigators, he adopts the vocabulary of confidence (*definitive, certain, vindicate,* etc.). I regret having to conclude on so positive a note.

INDEX

For the reader's convenience, plays are listed under title as well as author. In the author listings doubtful or mis-attributed works (preceded by *and*) follow those which are canonical; thus: Greene, Robert, *Orlando Furioso,* 67, 175; ———and *Arden of Feversham,* 86.

Evidence of authorship (*continued*)
and citations, 158–159; primary
importance of, 163–167; relation
to internal evidence, 159–162;
Revels Office-Book, 155–156; Stationers' Register, 154–155; title
pages, 151–153
Internal: cumulative effect of,
195–197; doubts of value of,
xviii–xix, 51; hypothetical nature
of, 218–219; limitations of, 149–
150; need for historical perspective, xvi–xvii; need for impartial
methodology, xvi–xvii, 115–116;
principles governing use of, 163–
183; relation to external evidence, 159–162. *See also* Tests of
authorship
Ewbank, Inga-Stina. *See* Ekeblad,
Inga-Stina

Fair Constance of Rome, 229
Fair Em, 50, 159, 175
Fair Maid of the Exchange, The,
6–7, 65, 183
Fair Maid of the Inn, The, 90, 92,
100, 131, 165, 172, 185
Fair Quarrel, A, 185–186, 191, 206
Fairy Knight, The, 139, 162
Faithful Friends, The, 230
Faithful Shepherd, The, 159
Faithful Shepherdess, The, 57, 95
False One, The, 104
Family of Love, The, 137, 190–191
Famous Victories of Henry V, The,
142, 167, 175, 176n
Fancies Chaste and Noble, The, 131
Faraday, Michael, 178
Farmer, Richard: *An Essay on the
Learning of Shakespeare,* 13–14,
22, 23
Farnham, Willard, 97
Faulkner, William, 168
Fedele, Il, 159
Fedele and Fortunio, 96, 98, 159–
161
Federalist Papers, The, 198
Feuillerat, Albert: *The Composi-*

tion of Shakespeare's Plays, 140–
142, 143; *John Lyly,* 74
Field, Nathan, 197; share in Beaumont and Fletcher plays, 130,
151; *The Knight of Malta,* 90–
91; ——and *Four Plays, or
Moral Representations, in One,*
90–91; and *The Honest Man's
Fortune,* 139
First Part of Jeronimo, The, 72
Fleay, F. G., 3–4, 5, 26, 37, 40–50,
52, 61, 66, 69, 88, 90, 100, 101,
104, 121, 147, 184, 227; achievement of, 49–50; on Beaumont and
Fletcher plays, 3–4, 42–43; compared with Boyle, 54–55; compared with Sykes, 89, 92; influence on E. K. Chambers, 118–
119; influence on Greg, 81, 83;
influence on Robertson, 108–109,
116; limitations of, 47–49; and
metrical tests, 3–4, 32–33, 41–42,
47–48; on *The Revenger's Tragedy,* 184, 203–204, 205; scientific
pretensions of, 40, 41–42; on
Shakespeare, 3, 43–46, 47–48
Fletcher, John, 74, 99, 138; *Henry
VIII,* xviii–xix, 4, 10n, 16, 22, 29,
33–38, 54, 55, 56, 90, 91, 96, 97,
119n, 120, 124, 128–130, 166, 167,
180, 188, 225; *The Two Noble
Kinsmen,* 4, 14, 16, 28, 29, 30–33,
51–53, 54, 55, 56, 57, 90, 96, 97,
99, 104, 125, 126, 127–128, 136,
166, 179, 188, 225; ——and *The
Queen,* 194, 201. *See also* Beaumont and Fletcher plays
Fluchère, Henri, 210
Foakes, R. A., on *Henry VIII,* xix,
37n, 129, 130; on Henslowe, 81;
on imagery, 124n; on *The Re-
venger's Tragedy,* 205n, 207n,
208, 218n
Fogel, E. G., 133n, 197, 199
Ford, John, 59, 60, 138, 139; *The
Broken Heart,* 131; *The Fancies
Chaste and Noble,* 131; *A Late
Murder of the Son upon the
Mother (Keep the Widow Wak-*

Pope, Alexander, xvi, 29, 179; *The Dunciad*, 11; ed. of Shakespeare, 9–11, 15, 16
Porter, Henry: *Hot Anger Soon Cold*, 225
Preston, Thomas: *Cambyses*, 73; and *Clyomon and Clamydes*, 73
Price, George R., 138; on *The Revenger's Tragedy*, 214, 215
Price, Hereward T., 134
Prior, Moody E., 133n, 168, 187n
Promos and Cassandra, 85
Prouty, Charles Tyler, 134
Puritan, The, 96, 138, 152, 182–183, 190

Quarterly Review, 59
Queen, The, or The Excellency of Her Sex, 78, 84, 90, 194, 197, 201, 218
Queen of Corinth, The, 91
Queen Elizabeth's Entertainment at Mitcham, 139

Raleigh, Walter, 28–29
Randolph, Thomas, 60, 97; *The Drinking Academy*, 100, 194–195, 197; *Hey for Honesty, Down with Knavery*, 96; *The Jealous Lovers*, 195; ——and *The Fairy Knight*, 139
Rare Triumphs of Love and Fortune, The, 87, 98
Ravenscroft, Edward, 7–9, 22; *Titus Andronicus, or The Rape of Lavinia*, 7–9
Repentance of Mary Magdalene, The, 157
Retrospective Review, The, 62
Return from Parnassus, The, 112. See also Parnassus plays
Revels Office-Book, 155–156
Revenge of Bussy D'Ambois, The, 157
Revenge for Honor, 65, 137, 164
Revenger's Tragedy, The, xix, 57, 86, 96, 100, 122, 138, 162, 172, 180, 186, 190, 199–218

Reyburn, Marjorie L., on *Parnassus* plays, 178
Reynolds, Sir Joshua, 17
Ribner, Irving, 203n, 212n, 213
1 Richard II, 87
Richard II, 17, 24
Richard III, 24, 28, 100, 167
Richard, Duke of York, The True Tragedy of. See The True Tragedy of Richard, Duke of York
Rickert, R. T., 81n
Ritson, Joseph, 24–25
Roaring Girl, The, 191, 206
Robb, Dewar M., on William Rowley canon, 138, 181
Roberts, C. W., 178n
Robertson, John Mackinnon, 27, 95n, 107–119, 121, 122, 140; and Fleay, 108–109; rejection of, 115–119; on *Titus Andronicus*, 112–114
Roderick, Richard, 33
Rogers, Richard, 6, 156, 157, 200
Rogers and Ley playlist, 6, 156, 157, 200
Rollins, Hyder, 100, 195
Rollo, Duke of Normandy, 139, 181, 197
Romeo and Juliet, 57, 115, 141
Routh, James E., Jr., 72
Rowe, Nicholas, ed. of Shakespeare, 9, 17
Rowley, Samuel, 92; *When You See Me You Know Me*, 176–177
Rowley, William, 43, 62, 137, 138, 151, 163n, 181, 197; *All's Lost by Lust*, 77, 157; *The Birth of Merlin*, 65, 95, 103; *The Changeling*, 49, 139, 164, 180, 185–186, 191; *A Cure for a Cuckold*, 87, 96; *A Fair Quarrel*, 185–186, 191, 206; *Fortune by Land and Sea*, 87; *Keep the Widow Waking (A Late Murder of the Son upon the Mother)*, 156, 229, 230; *The Maid in the Mill*, 156; *A Match at Midnight*, 87, 181; *The Old Law*, 43, 74, 138, 156, 162, 191,